ROUTLEDGE LIBRARY EDITIONS:
INDUSTRIAL ECONOMICS

Volume 1

COMPETITION AND INDUSTRIAL POLICY IN THE EUROPEAN COMMUNITY

COMPETITION AND INDUSTRIAL POLICY IN THE EUROPEAN COMMUNITY

DENNIS SWANN

LONDON AND NEW YORK

First published in 1983 by Methuen & Co. Ltd

This edition first published in 2018
by Routledge
2 Park Square, Milton Park, Abingdon, Oxon OX14 4RN

and by Routledge
711 Third Avenue, New York, NY 10017

Routledge is an imprint of the Taylor & Francis Group, an informa business

© 1983 Dennis Swann

All rights reserved. No part of this book may be reprinted or reproduced or utilised in any form or by any electronic, mechanical, or other means, now known or hereafter invented, including photocopying and recording, or in any information storage or retrieval system, without permission in writing from the publishers.

Trademark notice: Product or corporate names may be trademarks or registered trademarks, and are used only for identification and explanation without intent to infringe.

British Library Cataloguing in Publication Data
A catalogue record for this book is available from the British Library

ISBN: 978-1-138-30830-5 (Set)
ISBN: 978-1-351-21102-4 (Set) (ebk)
ISBN: 978-1-138-57220-1 (Volume 1) (hbk)
ISBN: 978-0-203-70216-1 (Volume 1) (ebk)

Publisher's Note
The publisher has gone to great lengths to ensure the quality of this reprint but points out that some imperfections in the original copies may be apparent.

Disclaimer
The publisher has made every effort to trace copyright holders and would welcome correspondence from those they have been unable to trace.

Competition and Industrial Policy in the European Community

DENNIS SWANN

METHUEN
LONDON AND NEW YORK

First published in 1983 by
Methuen & Co. Ltd
11 New Fetter Lane, London EC4P 4EE

Published in the USA by
Methuen & Co.
in association with Methuen, Inc.
733 Third Avenue, New York, NY 10017

© 1983 Dennis Swann

Typeset by Graphicraft Typesetters Limited,
Hong Kong
Printed in Great Britain at the
University Press, Cambridge

All rights reserved. No part of this book may
be reprinted or reproduced or utilized in any
form or by any electronic, mechanical or other
means, now known or hereafter invented,
including photocopying and recording, or in any
information storage or retrieval system, without
permission in writing from the publishers.

British Library Cataloguing in Publication Data

Swann, Dennis
Competition and industrial policy in the European
Community. – (Methuen's EEC series)
1. Competition – European Community countries
2. European Community countries – Commercial policy
I. Title
338.6'048'094   HD41

ISBN 0-416-32410-X
ISBN 0-416-32420-7 Pbk

Library of Congress Cataloging in Publication Data

Swann, Dennis.
  Competition and industrial policy in the European
Economic Community.

  (Methuen's EEC series)
  Bibliography: p.
  Includes index.
  1. Industry and state – European Economic Community
countries. 2. Competition – Government policy –
European Economic Community countries. 3. European
Economic Community. 4. European Coal and Steel Commun-
ity. I. Title. II. Series.
HD3616.E833S8 1983   338.6'048'094   83-13061
ISBN 0-416-32410-X
ISBN 0-416-32420-7 (pbk.)

Contents

	Abbreviations	vii
	General editor's preface	ix
	Author's preface	xi
1	**Definitions and distinctions**	1
	Competition policy and industrial policy defined	1
	ECSC and EEC – comparisons and contrasts	9
	Matters of procedure	16
2	**Tariffs, quotas and equivalent measures**	19
	Introduction	19
	Tariffs, quotas and equivalent measures	21
	Right of establishment and freedom to supply services	37
3	**Non-tariff barriers – the sta**[?]	43
	Introduction	43
	State aids (subsidies)	45
	Fiscal factors	58
	Technical standards	65
	Legal obligations	68
	Public purchasing	69
	State monopolies	71
	Administrative barriers	76
4	**Non-tariff barriers – cartels**	77
	Introduction	77
	EEC cartel rules and cases	81
	ECSC cartel rules and cases	101
5	**Non-tariff barriers – concentrations and other issues**	108
	Introduction	108
	The Rome Treaty	111

	The Paris Treaty	120
	Industrial and commercial property rights	128
	Public enterprises	131
6	**Industrial policy – the EEC**	**135**
	The search for a policy	135
	Industrial base	141
	Business integration	142
	Science and technology	149
	Winners and losers	154
7	**Industrial policy – the ECSC**	**162**
	Introduction	162
	Treaty powers	163
	The nature of the steel crisis	169
	The response – the Simonet Plan	171
	The response – the Davignon Plan, phase 1	171
	The response – the Davignon Plan, phase 2	175
8	**Concluding assessment**	**177**
	Industrial policy	177
	Competition policy	182
	Appendix	187
	Notes	192
	References	198
	Select bibliography	206
	Index	208

Abbreviations

ATIC	Association Technique de l'Importation Charbonnière
BCO	Business Co-operation Office
CAP	Common Agricultural Policy
CERD	European Research and Development Committee
CMLR	Common Market Law Reports
CML Rev	Common Market Law Review
CMPC	Common Market Patent Convention
COREPER	Committee of Permanent Representatives
COST	European Co-operation on Scientific and Technical Research
CREST	Scientific and Technical Research Committee
DG	Directorate General
EC	European Community(ies)
ECC	European Communities Commission
ECJ	European Court of Justice
ECSC	European Coal and Steel Community
EEC	European Economic Community
EECC	European Economic Community Commission
EFTA	European Free Trade Association
EMS	European Monetary System
EPC	European Patent Convention
EPD	European Parliament Debates
ERDA	European Research and Development Agency
EUA	European Unit of Account
Euratom	European Atomic Energy Community
FAST	Forecasting and Assessment in the Field of Science and Technology
GATT	General Agreement on Tariffs and Trade
GEORG	Gemeinschaftsorganisation Ruhrkohle GmbH

IMF	International Monetary Fund
IRC	Industrial Reorganization Corporation
IRI	Instituto per la Riconstruzione Industriale
JET	Joint European Torus
JNRC	Joint Nuclear Research Centre
JRC	Joint Research Centre
MFA	Multi-Fibre Arrangement
NCB	National Coal Board
NEB	National Enterprise Board
NICs	Newly Industrializing Countries
OECD	Organization for Economic Co-operation and Development
OEEC	Organization for European Economic Co-operation
OJ	Official Journal of the European Communities
PREST	Working Party for Scientific and Technical Research Policy
R & D	Research and Development
R D & D	Research, Development and Diffusion
REP	Regional Employment Premium
RDG	Regional Development Grant
SMEs	Small and Medium-Sized Enterprises
TES	Temporary Employment Subsidy
UA	Unit of Account
UNICE	Union des Industries de la Communauté Européenne
VAT	Value Added Tax

General editor's preface

The European Economic Community came into existence on 1 January 1958, having formally been established by the signature of the Treaty of Rome on 25 March 1957 and by its subsequent ratification by the governments of the original six member states. The Rome Treaty also established the European Atomic Energy Community (Euratom), while the European Coal and Steel Industry had been created in 1952 by the Treaty of Paris. These bodies, united since 1967 under a common Council and with a Common Commission and generally known as the EEC or the European Communities, are a powerful and complex force, affecting the lives of the citizens of all member states and the economies and policies of many non-member states.

Since 1958 many of the main policy objectives of the Rome (and the Paris) Treaty have been realized. There remain, however, policy areas where progress has been very slow and difficult, and on the whole it is these problems which draw attention and criticism. There is no doubt that the member states and sectoral interest groups of the enlarged and enlarging Community are still experiencing considerable difficulty in reaching an acceptable balance between national and Community interest, a situation which is not greatly assisted by the low level of general interest in the populace at large of the character, aims and procedures of the Community and its institutions.

The more widespread dissemination of information and opinion about the Community deserves higher priority than has hitherto been given. This series of books, in consequence, is designed to cater for the needs of both those with more specialist interests and those with a more general desire for ready access to fact and informed opinion. Each book is written by an expert on the particular subject, yet with a style and structure that will make it accessible to the non-specialist. The series is designed to facilitate the crossing of disciplinary boundaries and hence to encourage discussion and debate in a multi-disciplinary context (in the field of European Studies, for example) of one of the most powerful and dynamic communities in the world.

R. A. Butlin
Loughborough University of Technology

Author's preface

Competition policy is one of the most important features of EEC policy and also plays a major role in the ECSC. In the case of the EEC not only is it important but also it is one of the Brussels Commission's relative success stories. Unfortunately it is a subject which has been monopolized by legal scholars, and there is a dearth of books written with the student of economics, European studies, business studies, as well as the general reader, in mind. Scholars of the European Communities also seem to have been less than enthusiastic about trying to pull together all the various strands of EEC and ECSC industrial policy. Perhaps, in the case of the EEC, this is due to the fact that the ratio of aspiration to achievement is rather high. The neglect of the ECSC is however less understandable and also most regrettable and it is my hope that, in a small way, this book will help to remedy that deficiency.

I am most grateful to Dave Allen and Mike Fleming who have read and commented on the draft. I am of course solely responsible for all errors and omissions. I am greatly indebted to my secretary Brenda Moore who has with customary efficiency helped me to get to the editor on time. The staff of the Commission of the European Communities in London have been most helpful and I wish to record my thanks to them.

Dennis Swann
Loughborough University of Technology

1 Definitions and distinctions

Competition policy and industrial policy defined

As the title of this book indicates the focus of this study is the competition and industrial policies of the European Communities (EC). The title is however in need of some immediate amplification since it could be taken to imply that the book is directly concerned with *national* competition and industrial policies. This is not the intention. The book takes as its context attempts by member states to integrate their economies. The matters under discussion will therefore be the powers and policies arising from (a) the Paris Treaty of 1951, which find their expression in the European Coal and Steel Community (ECSC); and (b) the Rome Treaty of 1957, which similarly find their expression in the European Economic Community (EEC). We shall therefore be concentrating on policies evolved at Community level although inevitably we shall have to take account of the interaction between national and Community policies. Given that the Paris Treaty was merely concerned with coal and steel, while the Rome Treaty covers the rest of the economy (except certain nuclear matters[1]), inevitably there will be a bias towards EEC policies although the more *dirigiste* character of the Paris Treaty will mean that the space devoted to the ECSC will not fully reflect the minority position of coal and steel in the economy of the present-day Community.

It is equally important that we begin with some definitions since neither of the phrases 'competition policy' nor 'industrial policy' are entirely free from ambiguity. Competition policy is often thought of narrowly in terms of laws and executive organs concerned with restrictive business practices, monopolies, mergers and related phenomena. The antitrust dimension, to borrow a useful American term, is indeed an important ingredient of a policy designed to create and maintain competition. However in the context of economic integration, in which a major aspect is the elimination of barriers to trade between states, it is clearly imperative that other elements should be considered. The act of eliminating tariffs itself helps to open national markets to competition from producers located in other member states. However we have to recognize that there are a whole host of factors which can inhibit[2] competitive trade flows even if tariffs have been eliminated. This point was quite clearly understood by those who devised the detailed provisions of the founding treaties. Hans von der Groeben, who was the first Commissioner to be assigned the competition portfolio under the Rome Treaty, observed in 1961:

> It is ... beyond dispute ... and the authors of the Treaty were fully aware of this – that it would be useless to bring down trade barriers between Member States if the Governments or private industry were to remain free through economic and fiscal legislation, through subsidies or cartel-like restrictions on competition, virtually to undo the opening of the markets and to prevent, or at least unduly to delay the action needed to adapt them to the Common Market. (EPD 1961)

Some of these barriers – they are referred to as non-tariff barriers – consist of administrative complications which arise when goods cross frontiers.[3] Some of them arise from disparities between the indirect taxation systems of different member states. This type of problem pales into insignificance when compared with the effects of subsidies, referred to by von der Groeben, which distort competition and confer artificial competitive advantages; the effects of differing national laws and standards in respect of the design and composition of goods, which have the possibility of totally blocking trade flows;[4] the effect of buy-national policies adopted by governmental agencies and nationalized industries and recommended to the general public, and finally the discriminatory powers enjoyed by certain state monopolies. Within the Community context competition policy addresses itself to these problems as well as to the more familiar ones associated with antitrust activity.

It should however be added that the ECSC complicates matters further. While we might be willing to adopt the broader definition of competition policy we would nevertheless normally assume that, provided enterprises behaved in a genuinely competitive manner in the market, the way in which they made their competitive offers could be left to them. But in the case of the Paris Treaty rules have been laid down about the method of pricing – these relate to questions of price publicity and also prescribe the circumstances in which, and the degree to which, prices can be reduced below publicized levels.

As we can see there are no great difficulties to be encountered in attempting to arrive at a definition of the meaning of competition policy, even in the special circumstances of an economic integration exercise. When we come to industrial policy, matters are otherwise. It is true to say that academic economists still attend conferences in the hope that they might acquire a clearer view of what it really consists of and of course, and in fairness, what rationale if any lies behind it. There appear to be no overriding principles which enable us to produce a clear-cut agreement as to where to draw the line or, to put it another way, what to include and what to exclude. What we shall do therefore is to identify those ingredients about which there appears to be fairly general agreement.

Before we proceed to the identification of those ingredients we should note the somewhat obvious but unassailable point that industrial policy can be defined as the attitude of governments (and in our case international bodies) towards the industries for which they have some form of responsibility or which lie within their constituency. It would therefore be perfectly possible to describe *laisser faire* as being a form of industrial policy. Under such a system whether and how industries expanded or contracted would be left to market forces. If demand increased, profits would rise, existing firms would expand production and in due course new firms might enter the industry – supply would thus be augmented. If demand decreased, profits would fall, indeed losses might occur, existing firms would curtail output and some might exit from the industry – supply would decline. Thus individual industries would react to the shifting balance of demand and would redeploy resources accordingly. All this would be accomplished by the invisible hand of the price system. There would be no visible hand of state-interference nudging and steering industries this way and that. In matters of industrial structure the desire to profit maximize would induce firms to adapt to efficient scales of operation – scales which would also best ensure their survival. Equally matters of performance, such as Research and Development (R & D) spending, would be determined by market forces and the quest for profit.

If however we had phrased our earlier statement somewhat differently in terms of leaving the course of events to be determined by the free play of *competitive* market forces then the policy would have to be somewhat different. All the evidence suggests that, while it would not be true to say that if businessmen are left to themselves competition would totally disappear out of the window, there is no doubt that it would be significantly attenuated. Evidence suggests that businessmen do not like to compete but prefer to achieve at least an element of order as opposed to the hurly-burly of the competitive market place. It would therefore be necessary to have some form of antitrust policy in order to maintain competition. Antitrust policy is therefore properly to be viewed as a form of interventionism. It is also apparent that competition policy and industrial policy are not incompatible. Rather, competition policy may be regarded as an ingredient of industrial policy and indeed in terms of definitions the latter may be said to encompass the former. In most accounts of industrial policy commentators more or less automatically include a treatment of competition policy. The reader may therefore wonder why this book is not simply entitled 'Industrial Policy in the European Community'! The answer is that such a title would be misleading since whereas the competition dimension is well developed within the Community and thus will inevitably constitute a major part of our canvas, the non-competition element is relatively much less well developed, although the latter point is truer of the EEC than the ECSC.

Although we have recognized that industrial policy could be entirely passive, in practice it must be admitted that when economists talk about industrial policy they are usually referring to an active interventionist policy. Moreover they are not just referring to interventionism in the form of maintenance of competition but to other forms of intervention as well. What are these other forms of intervention?[5]

One relates to the active involvement of the state in the adjustment of particular industries to changes in the market and to other changes such as, for example, new technological opportunities. The objective may be to facilitate expansions as well as contractions of industrial output, capacity and employment. Perhaps we can begin with contractions since one of the major reasons for recent government interference has been the desire to assist in the adjustment of industries faced with the problem of competition from low wage Newly Industrializing Countries (NICs) as well as from more developed sources such as Japan.[6] These problems have since 1974 been overlaid by a recession of activity following the Oil Crisis. In the EC context textiles and steel are industries in such difficulties. It is however important to recognize that although difficulties may stem from competition from outside the Community, they may also stem from competition from within the grouping. A particular industry in one member state may succumb to competition from more efficient counterparts in other member states. The classic case of this was the experience of Belgian coal in the early days of the ECSC. The Belgian coal industry consisted of relatively inefficient pits operating in poor geological conditions. Although the demand for coal was declining in the face of cheap oil, the output and employment of the Belgian industry fell much more rapidly than that of its more efficient rivals in the Ruhr and elsewhere who, as a result of the creation of the ECSC, were able to penetrate Belgian domestic and export markets (McLachlan and Swann 1967, 44–50). Then again a decline of employment may proceed from the success of an industry in increasing labour productivity. For example, the clothing industry in the Community has experienced a substantial decline in employment in recent years. Some of this decline was due to NIC penetration but a major part of it in most member states during the 1970s was caused by increased productivity (De La Torre 1981, 124–48). Ironically one of the defensive reactions in such circumstances is to increase efficiency via even greater labour productivity but although this may help to stem the decline in output it only helps to accelerate the decline in employment.

The forms of intervention which are felt to be appropriate when declines of output and employment are being experienced are extremely diverse. However the following are not untypical: (a) measures including financial assistance to assist in the slimming down of capacity (this may be accomplished via mergers); (b) measures to facilitate the movement of resources into other industries; (c) measures to increase the efficiency and competitiveness of the remainder of the industry; (d) measures to facilitate or encourage a move up-market to more sophisticated goods and higher technologies where import competition may be less intense and the price factor less important. All this has on occasions been accompanied by protection. The latter has been viewed as a temporary phenomenon or as a device for slowing down the pace of (as opposed to preventing) import penetration. Either way the rationale put forward in defence has been that the industry would be afforded a breathing space within which to adjust. Typical examples of such protective policies have been, at the international level, the Multi-Fibre Arrangement which has set a limit to the growth of textile and clothing imports (although in practice it has not always been so generous); at the Community level, the negotiations between the EC Commission and third countries aimed at limiting exports of steel to the EC (this has been coupled with levies on artificially low-priced imports) and, on the national plane, various government to government and industry to industry arrangements designed to limit export efforts into certain markets – the latter are referred to as auto-limitation agreements.

Critics might object that this is an unduly flattering description of official intervention in industries in difficulties and that although some policies have contained a positive adjustment element, others have in practice consisted of 'lame-duck' rescues with too little or indeed no real rationalization element. Certainly in the UK selective intervention has not been motivated solely by the need to facilitate the process of contraction and competitive adjustment but has indeed been designed to keep firms in existence on the grounds that the unemployment consequences would be unacceptable and also that there were balance of payments or security advantages to be derived from keeping the firms in production.

Industrial policy also manifests itself in attempts to facilitate the expansion of firms or industries, notably when new products and technologies are emerging. The UK government's financial assistance through the agency of the National Enterprise Board (NEB) towards the development of microelectronics is a particularly good example. The taking of participatory stakes in individual firms was a key feature of the 1974–9 Labour government's industrial strategy and has also been a feature of French post-war policy (Hough 1979, 191). This sort of selective intervention is sometimes referred to as 'picking the winners'. Economists have sought to justify such interventions on a number of grounds. They have argued that inadequate information may result in private enterprises failing to identify opportunities for future development which may be more readily apparent to governments. This, it is alleged, is likely to be so in the case of new technology where the access of government to the results of basic research enables it better to forecast industrial applications. It is also asserted that state involvement is necessary because private enterprise is deterred by the risks involved. Not only are the outcomes uncertain but also some projects require large capital outlays and involve long gestation periods. There is however another school of thought which believes that businessmen are much more adept than civil servants at identifying the winners.

Again it has to be said that although picking winners may appear to be motivated by no more than a desire to speed up industrial reaction to new opportunities, in practice other motives are often at work. These include the desire to avoid the harmful consequences for employment (and the balance of payments) of failing to grasp significant new technological opportunities and the security advantage of having a domestic source of supply.

Policies for steering particular sectors have on occasions been generalized within the framework of national indicative plans. The French economy in the post-war period is the case *par excellence*. The function of the plan was to provide a forecast of the development of the economy over a five-year period. It should be emphasized that this was a growth rather than an adjustment exercise. The global plan was broken down by sector and industry and an attempt was made to reconcile the expansion of the various sectors and industries. Industrialists were involved in the formulation of targets. It was anticipated that this involvement would generate the view that the plan was feasible and that this in turn would induce firms and industries to conduct their investment activity on the basis of it. The plans were justified on the grounds that they gave rise to more favourable growth expectations and that these in turn produced more favourable growth performances. Although the phrase 'indicative planning' suggests an essentially voluntaristic exercise, it should be noted that the French government disposed of a large range of inducements and that these were deployed in line with the objectives of the plan.

In a developed economy context, picking winners often seems to mean sifting out promising new technologies. This conveniently leads us on to another aspect of industrial policy, namely the encouragement and support given to R & D activity. This may be selective, in which case it has much in common with the policy approach outlined above, although of course it may focus more on the earlier process of generating new discoveries (basic research and invention) as opposed to the later process of financing the development of marketable products and processes (innovation). On the other hand R & D policy may be general rather than selective, being designed to encourage and assist firms throughout the economy to devote more resources to R & D. Whatever the form, the policy may manifest itself in terms of R & D activity carried out by the government (possibly in co-operation with industry and the universities) or it may consist of the encouragement of industry-performed R & D by means of fiscal incentives, credits and grants, the promotion of co-operative research activities and government R & D contracts to industry.

At the European level it is quite apparent that Community organs have a clear power and obligation to discharge an R & D role in certain areas (e.g. Euratom, the European Atomic Energy Community). Beyond that however the development of a Community role depends on the identification of areas of common interest in which common programmes can eliminate wasteful duplications of effort and can pull together a level of financial support which may be beyond the means of individual states.

Industrial policy also consists of actively intervening to influence the structure of firms in particular industries. This often takes the form of policies designed to encourage mergers, although there is no reason why in principle it should not consist of policies designed to facilitate divestitures. Legislation with the latter intention in mind has been proposed for the US (Swann 1979, 312). Typical examples of policies following the selective merger path are the creation of the Industrial Reorganization Corporation (IRC) in the UK in 1966 by the 1964–9 Labour government. The IRC had a number of functions but the one for which it is especially remembered is that of acting as a merger broker. The object in facilitating mergers was not the achievement of greater size as such but the establishment of units which could compete successfully on world markets (Howe 1978, 220–330). A policy of encouraging mergers has also been a conspicuous aspect of French industrial policy (Hough 1979, 197–8) and did in fact lead to the creation of the Industrial Development Institute in 1970 in imitation of the UK's IRC.

Within the Community context the adaptation of industrial structures mainly takes the form of facilitating cross-frontier mergers and other cross-frontier joint arrangements and, on a wider plane, takes in the whole question of enterprises being able to organize their activities (e.g. relations between parents and subsidiaries) on a truly European scale. Mergers may at the best of times be difficult to consummate but in the Community context they encounter additional difficulties stemming from differences between and discriminations in the company laws and fiscal systems of the various states as well as from the possibly inhibiting effects of national industrial strategies, national competition policies and fears of foreign domination.

While on the topic of the size of firms we should note that governments have also elaborated policies of assistance for small and medium-sized firms. These policies are designed to strengthen their financial position, to encourage technological innovation, to improve management knowledge and practices and to alleviate certain handicaps.

The above account pretty well encapsulates the main ingredients of industrial policy although some would also include matters such as the promotion of greater managerial efficiency. This in turn tends to lead to an extension of the definition to include the promotion of manpower efficiency generally.

ECSC and EEC – comparisons and contrasts

The communities have two substantial points in common – one economic and one political. We shall consider these comparisons first.

In economic terms both communities are exercises in economic integration – details of the arrangements are discussed in Chapter 2. Economic integration can give rise to economic benefits and may be embarked upon purely in order to take advantage of them. What are these benefits?

The removal of tariffs and quotas (and factors which have an equivalent effect to tariffs and quotas) *as between the participating states* may lead to a better allocation of resources. Tariffs, etc. protect inefficient industries. When, for example, they are removed by integrated state A we may expect its inefficient industries to contract, being replaced by cheaper imports from more efficient industries in the other integrated states. This is pure trade creation and it resolves itself into a production effect (in this case a production gain) and also a consumption effect (in this case a consumption again). If *all* traded goods gave rise to such pure trade creation then the tariff disarmament would be unquestionably beneficial (although it would not follow that such a regional free trade arrangement was the only way of obtaining such a benefit).

However another effect can arise which pulls in the opposite direction. This is referred to as trade diversion. The integration arrangement may be accompanied by the retention of tariff and similar protection against third countries. The EEC took this form but the Paris Treaty left the participating states with substantial discretion in the matter of external protection and so the degree and form of such protection was less predictable – see Chapter 2. Let us assume that protection is retained *vis-à-vis* third countries. It may be that prior to the integration exercise those countries were the cheapest source of supply for integrated state A. Consequently supplies were drawn from them. The act of integration, however, gives rise to discrimination in that countries who are potential suppliers of the goods in question, who are party to the integration exercise, will now no longer face a protective barrier while the third country suppliers will continue to be subject to it. These other integrated states are less efficient than the third country suppliers but, because their goods will no longer be subject to tariffs, they may be able to undercut the third countries when selling in integrated state A. If they do undercut then trade will be diverted from the more efficient third countries to the less efficient sources of supply within the integrated area. This trade diversion loss will, however, be accompanied by some mitigating trade creation gain (production and consumption effects) arising from the fact that the tariff has been lowered.

The welfare consequences of the union depend on a balancing of the foregoing effects. For example, if the gains from goods subject to pure trade creation are accompanied by, but outweigh, *net* losses from goods subject to trade diversion then, on balance, the integration exercise can be said to lead to an improvement in economic welfare. Empirical evidence on the size of trade creation and trade diversion effects in the context of the EEC has certainly pointed in the direction of a welfare gain on balance although the benefit has been very modest indeed. The benefit is also a once-for-all affair. Prior to the exercise a particular allocation of resources exists and the countries involved enjoy an associated level of economic welfare. After the exercise is completed the allocation of resources changes and the countries in question move to a new and higher level of welfare. But the increase in the welfare level occurs only once.

It is possible to envisage other sources of welfare gain. These can arise from a fuller enjoyment of the economies of large-scale production and distribution. Prior to the integration exercise firms may be constrained, in terms of output, by the limited size of the national market and by the fact that they are kept out of other national markets by tariffs, etc. If these latter barriers are removed, an enlarged market becomes available and sub-optimal firms can then expand and thus become more efficient. Essentially this too is a once-for-all effect. Initially firms are sub-optimal. They then become optimal or move nearer to the optimum. This increase in the level of efficiency arises only once.

These essentially static-type benefits may be accompanied by a dynamic benefit. The integration exercise seems likely to affect industrial structures and to make them potentially more competitive. If, for example, there is a monopoly situation in each national market then when, say, six states integrate their economies the enlarged market is inevitably oligopolistic. If the national markets were originally oligopolistic then the enlarged market is structurally more competitive since the number of competitors is greater and the degree of concentration is lower. If such changes of structure intensify the degree of competition, and if the latter forces firms to, for example, devote proportionately more of their resources to R & D, and if more intensive R & D efforts give rise to a more rapid rate of innovation, then we may expect a *sustained* increase in the rate of growth.

Economic aspirations of these kinds no doubt lay behind the integration exercises. On some points we can be quite certain that this was so. Thus those who were involved in drawing up the *actes préparatoires* of the Rome Treaty were aware that in some industries economies of scale were such as to be only compatible with a monopoly at the national level. The attraction of the integration process was that consumers could continue to enjoy the benefits of large-scale production but also have the benefit of competition between erstwhile monopolies. Thus the Spaak Report points out that:

> This fusion of markets will open up vast outlets for the employment of the most modern techniques. There are some types of production calling for such huge resources or for machinery with such a large output that they are no longer within the capability of a single market. But above all, in many branches of industry, the national markets offer the chance of attaining optimum dimensions only to enterprises having a de facto monopoly. The strength of a vast market lies in the fact that it reconciles mass production with the absence of monopoly. (Spaak 1956, 13–14)

However if we consult the Paris and Rome Treaties we look in vain for specific reasons as to why economic benefits will accrue. The texts are devoid of references to technicalities such as trade creation, trade diversion, scale economies and structure, conduct and performance relationships. That does not mean that the treaties do not explicitly entertain expectations of economic benefits. The preamble to the Paris Treaty lays much emphasis on political aspirations but the signatories also see the need for establishing 'common bases for economic development' which will be the means of 'expanding their basic production, to raise the standard of living' as well as being a way to further the work of peace. Moreover Article 2, where the objectives of the ECSC are explicitly laid out, calls for a community which will 'progressively bring about conditions which will themselves ensure the most rational distribution of production at the highest level of productivity, whilst safeguarding the continuity of employment and taking care not to provoke fundamental and persistent disturbances in the economies of the Member States'. In the Rome Treaty preamble economic aspirations are more apparent than in the Paris Treaty counterpart. The signatories resolve 'to ensure economic and social progress', affirm as an essential objective 'the constant improvement of the living and working conditions of their peoples' and indicate an anxiety to unify their economies and 'ensure their harmonious development'. In Article 2, where the major tasks of the Community are identified, it is declared that the creation of a common market and the harmonization of economic policy are to be the means of promoting throughout the community 'a harmonious development of economic activities, a continuous and balanced expansion, an increase in stability, an accelerated raising of the standard of living' and also closer relations between states. Clearly, and hardly surprisingly, in both cases economic integration was embarked upon because of the economic benefits which were expected to derive from it.

However in explaining why the member states have ventured upon these integration exercises, mere economic factors will not suffice. Political considerations have also been a compelling force. Both the ECSC and the EEC were reflections of a desire for greater political unity in Europe, a desire which became manifest within a few years of the ending of the Second World War. In the case of the ECSC however, besides the general desire for unity there was a specific problem – namely could German industry be allowed to expand and if so under what conditions? This problem arose acutely in connection with coal and steel. In 1950 Germany was asking to be allowed to increase her steel production from 11 to 14 million tons per annum and this gave rise to considerable fears notably on the part of the French. The response, the Schuman Plan, was a French initiative. The idea was that French and German coal and steel production should be placed under a joint high authority. The actual ownership of the productive resources would not be affected, rather the emphasis was laid upon the idea that the output of these two industries (basic materials of a war effort) should be equally accessible to both partners (and indeed to any others who should care to participate). In the words of Robert Schuman, the French foreign minister, 'war between France and

Germany becomes not only unthinkable but in actual fact impossible' (Schuman 1950, 49).

By the time the Rome Treaty was being discussed the political situation had changed. The Schuman Plan had envisaged the idea of a European federation but subsequent attempts in this direction in the shape of the European Defence Community and the European Political Community had ultimately failed. The desire for political unity was however still strong but it was recognized that it would have to be approached more gradually. Integration on the economic plane, this time on a much broader front, would progressively create the necessary conditions for a spill-over on to the political plane. It has to be said that events have not validated this theory although there are promising signs of growing collaboration on foreign and defence policy issues.

Up to a point the *method* of economic integration envisaged in both the Paris and Rome Treaties was similar. Integration would proceed on the basis of competitive trade. The removal of tariff and non-tariff barriers would stimulate a growth of intra-Community trade and thus the member states would become increasingly interdependent. (This has happened – intra-Community trade has grown more rapidly than member countries' trade with the rest of the world (Hallett 1981, 17–19). The pattern of production in any member state – i.e. whether individual industries expanded or contracted – would depend on competitive strength. It would have been possible to conceive of an integration process quite different in character which was based on a central planning system. Decisions as to where goods were to be produced could have been determined by a central Community planning organization and likewise the quantity of goods entering into trade, their destinations and prices could have been decided at the centre. This however was never a serious option under either the ECSC or the EEC. Rather the Schuman declaration envisaged a competitive system and expected that as a result conditions would be progressively created which would automatically ensure 'the most effective rationalization of production on the basis of the highest level of productivity' (Schuman 1950, 50). A significant role for competition is envisaged in Article 3(g) of the Paris Treaty which anticipates an orderly expansion and modernization of production and an improvement of quality 'with no protection against competing industries that is not justified by improper action on their part or in their favour'. As for the Rome Treaty its colours were clearly nailed to the mast in Article 3. That article lays down the main objectives of the EEC and Article 3(a) requires the creation of free trade between the partners while, most significantly, Article 3(f) calls for the establishment of a system ensuring that competition in the common market is not distorted.

We should not however press this economic equivalence too far. Those who first conceived the idea of a coal and steel community did so against a background of considerable uncertainty and some anxiety. The coal and steel industries were to be launched on to the high seas of international free competition and this was bound to be something of a novel experience given that the past had been characterized by tariff protection and certainly in the case of steel by international cartelization. Because of this the founding fathers of the ECSC did not opt for a simple competitive solution. The competition stemming from tariff disarmament and from the attack on non-tariff barriers (subsidies were prohibited and cartels, market-dominating enterprises and mergers were to be controlled) was to be hedged around by certain safeguards. First, and undoubtedly reflecting the influence of Jean Monnet, whose French indicative planning system we have already discussed, a somewhat similar system was to operate in respect of the two industries. Forecasts of future demand were to be undertaken and on the basis of them the High Authority was to render opinions on investment projects in order to avoid excesses or shortages of capacity which would destabilize the market. Excessive investment might, for example, provoke cut-throat competition and dumping and might in turn provoke a call for cartelization and protection. These were possible reactions which Monnet greatly feared (Monnet 1950, 51–6). Since the High Authority was to be empowered to borrow on the international capital market and lend on to the Community industries a further source of official influence was evident. Secondly, the process of making competitive offers in the market-place was to be subject to certain rules – these were referred to earlier. Thirdly, the High Authority was to be empowered to intervene directly in the market for coal and steel. It would be able to introduce quotas on production or to impose maximum or minimum prices. In all these ways the Paris Treaty was relatively speaking a significantly *dirigiste* document.

By contrast when the Rome Treaty came to be drafted conditions were such as to give less ground for anxiety. The atmosphere was one of buoyancy and expansion. Less efficient industries might not necessarily expect to decline absolutely but perhaps to enjoy a less favourable growth than their more efficient rivals in other member states. Also the experience of the ECSC did not suggest that international competition would generate insuperable problems. The approach of the Rome Treaty was significantly different. As we have seen the central objective was the removal of tariff barriers coupled with an attack on the non-tariff variety in order to create conditions of undistorted competition. The more *dirigiste* mixture dispensed in respect of coal and steel within the ECSC was not extended to industry generally within the EEC. The Rome Treaty with its flavour of free trade and competition owes much to the economics of Adam Smith. Competition is well entrenched within it. Powers of intervention are conspicuous by their absence – the phrase industrial policy does not appear in the treaty. Under Article 235 it would have been possible to add such a general power, but no such power has in fact been taken. It should be added that limited programmes of action were agreed in 1973/4 but we shall also see that these have been largely honoured in the breach rather than the observance.

This is perhaps as good a point as any to draw the reader's attention to the fact that the Rome Treaty, which needless to say still exerts a major controlling influence on Community policy-making, reflects the economic circumstances which prevailed at the time that it was being drafted. This fact highlights a major difficulty in policy-making based on treaties. Having been drafted and ratified they are difficult to change. Yet circumstances change. Expansion and buoyancy have been replaced by recession, unemployment, excess capacity and a need to adjust to sources of competition unforeseen in the 1950s.

There is one other major point of contrast between the Paris and Rome Treaties which we must note. As we have seen both treaties are overwhelmingly concerned to create and maintain a free flow of trade across frontiers and powers are conferred upon the Brussels Commission (which now administers both treaties) to that end. The powers conferred under the Paris Treaty apply without restriction. That is to say they apply to goods sold to domestic users as well as to those sold to consumers in other member states. For example, a price-fixing agreement affecting the sale of steel falls due for consideration under Article 65 of the Paris Treaty irrespective of whether the steel is sold domestically or is exported to another member state. By contrast powers conferred under the Rome Treaty are often more limited in scope. The object of the exercise is the integration of economies and the restrictions on competitive trade which are really of major concern are those which affect inter-state trade. Thus on the basis of this more restricted view not all restrictive practices are prohibited under Article 85 but only those which, among other things, affect inter-state trade. Equally not all state aids are prohibited, rather Article 92 seeks to single out those which affect the unity of the market. It follows that in respect of, for example, antitrust policy there are both Community and domestic laws and enforcement agencies. They co-exist but do not have to follow similar principles because they address different problems.

Matters of procedure

Since in this book we shall be concerned with policy, it is appropriate that we address ourselves if briefly to the process whereby policy decisions are made. Here we shall note further contrasts.

Originally there were three executives – a High Authority for the ECSC and a Commission each for the EEC and Euratom. As we noted earlier these executives were subsequently fused and there is now one EC Commission. However although the executives have been fused, the treaties remain separate and there are some procedural distinctions which we need to note. Since we will be mainly focusing on the EEC and ECSC it will be the procedural differences between the Rome and Paris Treaties which will be of immediate relevance.

The base of policy is the treaties although in some cases details were left to be fleshed out later and it should be added that it has been possible through the agency of summit meetings of Heads of State and of Government[7] to open up new lines of policy not originally envisaged by the founding fathers. In the case of the EEC the detailed laws and decisions which derive their authority from the Rome Treaty (and extensions of it) stem from the activity of the Council of Ministers. It is the law-maker. The EC Commission *when acting in this context* has a somewhat subordinate role. It feeds the Council of Ministers with the draft decisions, draft regulations, draft directives, etc., which are necessary in order to achieve the objectives set out in the treaty. If they are acceptable to the Council it places its *imprimatur* upon them and they then become the law of the EEC.

Under the Rome Treaty a decision is binding in its entirety upon those to whom it is addressed, whether it be a member state, a legal person (e.g. a company) or a natural person (i.e. an individual). We shall, for example, encounter a decision when we come to look at the arrangements which have been made regarding the right of establishment and the freedom to supply services. It has been necessary in this connection to harmonize the training and entry qualifications for certain professions, and committees have been established to oversee the process. They have been established by decision. Much more important in the context of this book are the activities of the Council of Ministers in making regulations and adopting directives.

Under the Rome Treaty regulations have general applicability and are directly binding on nationals. There is no need to introduce further laws to give effect to them – they themselves are laws. For example, in 1962 the Council made a regulation in connection with Articles 85 and 86. The latter are concerned with restrictive business practices and the abuse of market-dominating positions which involve a restriction of competition and affect inter-state trade. In order to apply those articles the EC Commission was given enforcement powers under the regulation. When a case has been launched the enterprises involved are legally obliged by virtue of that regulation to supply the Commission with the information which it requires and failure to comply can lead to financial penalties.

By contrast a directive, under the Rome Treaty, is addressed to governments. It is directly binding as to the results to be attained but leaves the member states free as to the form and method by which they are achieved. In practice a directive will normally require member states to introduce appropriate changes in their domestic legislations. Later, for example, we shall be discussing the reasons why member states have had to harmonize their national laws concerning design and composition of goods. Community standards have been substituted for the varying national standards.

Under the Rome Treaty a decision is not purely an instrument of the Council of Ministers. The EC Commission acts as a policeman and is empowered to prohibit acts and practices contrary to the treaty. It can prohibit the anti-competitive practices and abuses of enterprises. Equally it can prohibit competition-distorting aids given by states. When it does so it issues a decision to that effect and, as we noted, such a decision is directly binding on the individual, the enterprise or the state to which it is addressed. It is of course possible for the individual, the enterprise or the state to appeal against the decision to the European Court of Justice (ECJ). Its judgement is final. It should also be mentioned that there are sanctions in cases of non-compliance. In the case of individuals or enterprises who refuse to terminate an anti-competitive practice or abuse, fines can be inflicted. In the case of a state which refuses to terminate an aid the EC Commission can take the offending state to the Court of Justice for a final determination. There are no financial sanctions against states and they have been known to prevaricate for a while before coming into line. In passing we should note that the Court is also approached by member state courts who require a preliminary ruling on the interpretation of treaty articles.

The intention of those who drafted the Paris Treaty was that the High Authority should have considerable powers of initiative. Indeed the Council of Ministers, which was added to the institutional structure devised by Schuman and Monnet, was something of an afterthought. This significant role for the old High Authority – *now vested in the EC Commission* – is reflected in its powers to act by means of decisions and recommendations. Here we must be careful to note some terminological differences.

A decision is binding in its entirety. It may be specific (e.g. addressed to an enterprise) or it may be general. If it is specific it parallels the Rome Treaty decision which as we saw is an instrument of both the Council and Commission. If it is general it is similar to the Rome Treaty Council of Ministers regulation.

A recommendation on the other hand is binding as to the aims to be pursued but leaves the choice of appropriate method for achieving them to those to whom the recommendation is addressed. Here there is a clear parallel with the Rome Treaty Council of Ministers' directive.

Before we leap to the conclusion that the old High Authority was all-supreme by comparison with the old EEC Commission, it should be noted that when, for example, ECSC decisions are taken, in certain cases consultation is called for with the Consultative Committee and the Council of Ministers and in respect of the latter in quite a number of cases qualified majorities or even unanimity in Council is needed.

The Court of Justice also plays a role in relation to ECSC powers – indeed the present Court is a carry-over from the Paris Treaty. Member states and enterprises (and also associations of enterprises) can appeal against decisions and recommendations of the EC Commission made under the powers of the coal and steel treaty. Interestingly in the same context the Council of Ministers can appeal to the Court against the actions of the Commission.

2 Tariffs, quotas and equivalent measures

Introduction

This chapter and the subsequent one are concerned with barriers that impede the process of integration and which have their origin in the activities of the *state*. Quite clearly such inhibiting factors include tariffs, quotas, and so on, but account must be taken of a variety of non-tariff barriers which also owe their existence to state involvement in the economy – see Chapter 3. Chapters 4 and 5 will be concerned with other non-tariff barriers which for the most part will be *private* in origin. In the previous chapter we noted that in varying degrees it was envisaged that economic integration under the Paris and Rome Treaties was to be accomplished through the agency of competitive trade. The growth of interpenetration and interdependence required that the *internal* barriers should be removed. However since we are concerned with the competition policies of the two Communities it is necessary that we also address ourselves to the question of the degree of *external* protection. The latter is quite crucial since the degree of competition within the integrated area depends not merely on the ease with which industries and firms in each member state can sell in the markets of other member states but is also governed by the extent to which the integrated market can be penetrated from without. Indeed there are some industries, such as clothing and textiles, where it is quite clear that the main competitive threat is external rather than internal. It would also be quite legitimate to extend our analysis of competition policy to include a discussion of the rules which govern rivalry between Community firms in third country markets. In practice this is not a major concern of either the Paris or the Rome Treaty although some Community policy decisions do relate directly to it and others are indirectly relevant.[1]

Since our analysis must take place within the framework of the economic integration process it is appropriate that at the outset we should identify the different forms that integration can take. The least demanding form is the free trade area where the contracting parties agree to remove barriers to trade within the area but leave each party free to determine the level of protection to be applied to imports emanating from without. Next comes the customs union which parallels the free trade area in so far as it involves free trade within the bloc but differs from it in that it requires the contracting parties to apply a common level of external tariff protection. The level of the external tariff may not be the same for all goods but for any particular class of good each state is required to apply the same rate of tariff. A common market involves the addition to the customs union of conditions which provide for the free movement of factors of production. Complete economic unions are common markets which also entail a complete unification of monetary and fiscal policy. These matters would be controlled by a central authority so that the member states would become regions of the union.

Since we are at this point concerned with competition policy it is the arrangements in respect of internal and external protection which are of immediate relevance, i.e. in the case of the EEC the customs union element. It is however easy to slip into the assumption that the only form of protection is that relating to goods. But of course the integrating states will also seek to sell each other services and therefore barriers which impede such sales must also be considered. While it is obvious that the free movement of factors (such as capital and labour) is outside our immediate terms of reference, the free movement of entrepreneurial skills is a different matter. The alternative to competing by selling goods or services across frontiers is to establish a firm on another national territory and to compete on the spot.[2] Indeed competing on the spot may be the only feasible system. We shall therefore consider what is referred to in EEC parlance as the freedom to supply services and the right of establishment at the end of this chapter. It will be appropriate to do so because quite often the factors which inhibit such freedom derive directly or indirectly from the state.

We shall not of course concern ourselves in this book with matters of unification in the fields of monetary and fiscal policy. While not denying a connection between the macro and micro factors it is nevertheless necessary to limit the discussion to the immediately relevant issues.

Tariffs, quotas and equivalent measures

INTERNAL ARRANGEMENTS – EEC

From what has gone before it is apparent that as far as the trade in goods is concerned the Rome Treaty provides for the establishment of a customs union. Article 3 of the Treaty, which lays down the main objectives of the EEC, calls in section (a) for the elimination of customs duties and quantitative restrictions on trade and for the removal of all measures having equivalent effect. Section (b) looks to the establishment of a common customs tariff and a common commercial policy towards third countries. Article 9 specifically reiterates the customs union requirements of the removal of internal protection and the creation of a common level of protection against the rest of the world. We shall treat these items in that order.

Articles 12 to 17 relate specifically to the elimination of customs duties on trade between the member states. A twelve-year transition period (from 1 January 1958 when the Treaty came into operation) was envisaged by the original Six and it was anticipated that internal tariff disarmament would be accomplished within that period. Tariff reductions were in fact carried out in a series of steps – see Table 2.1 – and total elimination was achieved ahead of schedule, on 1 July 1968 rather than 31 December 1969.

It is necessary to remind the reader that, following Articles 3(a) and 9, member states are required to eliminate charges which have an 'equivalent effect' to import (or export) duties. For example, Italy was in the habit of levying what it called a statistical levy on imports and exports. The Commission endeavoured to persuade the Italian government that this levy was equivalent to a customs duty and should be abolished. The Italian government refused and the matter was referred to the Court of Justice which upheld the Commission's action (ECJ 24/68).

As we have seen it was also recognized as important that quantitative restrictions on trade between the member states should be eliminated. Clearly high on the list were quotas. Article 30 calls for the elimination of import quotas and Article 34 requires the abolition of the export variety. Quotas on imports were to be eliminated by the end of the transition period – export quotas were to be terminated within a shorter time-span. In practice quota disarmament gave rise to no difficulty since by the time of the signing of the Rome Treaty such

Table 2.1 Internal tariff reductions of the EEC (per cent)

	1.1.59	1.7.60	Acceleration of* 1.1.61	1.1.62	Acceleration of 1.7.62	1.7.63	1.1.65	1.1.66	1.7.67	1.7.68
Individual reductions made on 1 January 1957 level	10	10	10	10	10	10	10	10	5	15
Cumulative reduction	10	20	30	40	50	60	70	80	85	100

Source: ECC (1968), 34
Note: * Acceleration is a reduction made ahead of schedule

quantitative restrictions were no longer the hindrance to trade that they had been in the period immediately following the Second World War – a fact which was due to measures of liberalization evolved within the framework of the International Monetary Fund (IMF), the General Agreement on Tariffs and Trade (GATT) and, above all, the Organization for European Economic Co-operation (OEEC) (McLachlan and Swann 1967, 20).

When the UK, Ireland and Denmark joined the Community on 1 January 1973 they were allowed a five-year period within which to dismantle all the above mentioned forms of protection and Greece, which became a full member on 1 January 1981, was given a similar period within which to adapt.

It is essential to appreciate that when Article 3(a) refers to the elimination of protection it applies not merely to quantitative restrictions but also to all other measures having 'equivalent effect' to quantitative restrictions. Not surprisingly therefore when Articles 30 and 34 call respectively for the abolition of import and export quotas they also require the elimination of measures having equivalent effect. What then are these equivalent measures?

In the *Dassonville* case the Court of Justice declared that 'All trading rules enacted by member-States which are capable of hindering, directly or indirectly, actually or potentially, intra-Community trade are to be considered as measures having an effect equivalent to quantitative restrictions' (ECJ 8/74). This then provides a broad scope for policing action by the EC Commission although it does not specify the actual kinds of rules and practices which would violate Articles 30 and 34. For actual examples we have to look at specific cases.

In *Dassonville* the issue was certificates relating to the origin of goods. Scotch whisky, which had originally been sold to France, was then indirectly imported into Belgium. However Belgian law made it an offence to sell spirits bearing a designation of origin adopted by the Belgian government unless the spirits were accompanied by an official document certifying their right to such a designation. In other words the Belgian government recognized certain descriptions of origin and if goods bore a claim to such an origin then documents had to be produced to prove that the goods had come from where it was claimed they had come from. Unfortunately the Belgian importer, having obtained the whisky from French importers, did not possess the necessary documentation. Proceedings were taken against the importer, by name Dassonville, by the Belgian Public Prosecutor. Not surprisingly two companies, Fourcroy and Breuval, who were the official distributors of the whiskies in question in Belgium (and imported direct from the UK) joined in against Dassonville. The matter was then referred to the Court of Justice for guidance by the Belgian court since the possibility existed that the strict enforcement of the Belgian law would be a breach of Article 30. The Court of Justice noted that while it was in principle relatively easy for the direct importer to obtain the necessary formal documentation, indirect importers such as Dassonville would find it difficult to obtain such documents. The Court therefore decided that if a member state required a certificate of authority which was less easily obtainable by indirect importers (such as Dassonville) than by direct importers (such as Fourcroy and Breuval) then that would constitute a measure having an equivalent effect to a quantitative restriction as referred to in Article 30 and would thus be prohibited. The Court has always been anxious to protect parallel imports[3] of the Dassonville kind and thus to avoid compartmentalization of the common market. This theme will arise later notably in connection with the *Grundig-Consten* case (see Chapter 4) and subsequent decisions and judgements.

There was an interesting sequel to the *Dassonville* case. The EC Commission was unhappy with the response of the Belgian government to the ruling. It therefore brought an enforcement action which unfortunately for the Commission was dismissed. The Court recognized (in its *Scotch Whisky* judgement, ECJ 2/78) that Belgium had liberalized its system although the EC Commission had proposed a sealing and labelling arrangement which it regarded as even more liberal in terms of its effect on indirect imports. Although the Court felt that the reformed Belgian arrangements did not breach Article 30 it added a rider to the effect that indirect imports should not be 'placed at a disadvantage in relation to direct imports, save in so far as it appears reasonable and strictly necessary to ensure the authenticity of those products'. It would appear that some disadvantage may be permissible but the degree of it must be the minimum which is necessary to achieve the legitimate objective of the national law. A test of reasonableness was therefore introduced.

An even clearer example was provided by the now famous *Cassis de Dijon* case (ECJ 120/78). Cassis de Dijon is a French liqueur manufactured from blackcurrants. The German company Rewe-Zentral AG sought to import the French liqueur and requested an authorization from the West German Federal Monopoly Administration for Spirits.

The latter informed Rewe that West German law forbade the sale of liqueurs with less than 32 per cent alcohol content although for liqueurs of the Cassis type a minimum of 25 per cent was allowed. Since Cassis had an alcohol content of only 15–20 per cent it could not be imported. Rewe contested the matter in the German courts and the matter was referred to the Court of Justice. The Court declared that the West German law in question was in these specific circumstances an equivalent measure of the kind prohibited under Article 30 of the Rome Treaty.

Another example of an equivalent measure is provided by national price control systems which allow a measure of profit but fix the price on the basis of the cost of national products alone. By not allowing for the supplementary costs and charges inherent in importation this method of pricing produces a situation in which imported products are no longer profitable.

It would therefore appear from all that has gone before that member states must abolish tariffs, quantitative restrictions (such as quotas) and all measures having the equivalent effect of both tariffs and quantitative restrictions. The question which then arises is – is this duty absolute? In other words are there any grounds upon which a member state could apply protection? Quite clearly a restoration of protection could undermine the whole concept of a customs union and membership of the EEC implies an acceptance of that arrangement. However there are two possible loopholes.

First, Article 109, which falls under the heading of Conjunctural Policy, allows a member state to take protective measures in the case of a sudden crisis in its balance of payments. No limit is set on the kind of protective measures which could be imposed and so it would appear that a restoration of, for example, tariffs would be possible. However before we conclude that member states who found common market competition too hot for their industries could reimpose protection, we should take account of the following points. Article 109 enjoins that any protective measures must cause the least disturbance to the functioning of the common market and must not be wider in scope than is strictly necessary in order to remedy the sudden difficulty. Altogether more important is the point that a member state having applied such protection is not free to retain it. The Council of Ministers has the power, certain procedural requirements having been met, to amend or indeed to abolish such protection. In practice if a member state encountered balance of payments problems it would be expected to pursue courses other than protectionism and facilities exist to enable it to do so. In the first place credit arrangements exist within the Community under the European Monetary System (EMS), as well as externally via the IMF, which would enable the member state to finance the deficit while other policy measures were being introduced which would eventually rectify the problem. The state could deflate demand, thus reducing imports and forcing goods into the export market, and in the longer term deflation would help to restore international price competitiveness. Even membership of the EMS 'super-snake' does not preclude devaluations of the exchange rate and this would be another possible avenue to a restoration of competitiveness. Domestic interest rates could also be raised and this could induce a helpful inflow of foreign currencies. If the balance of payments deficit was at least in part associated with capital movements, and if those capital movements disturbed the functioning of the capital market in the member state, then protective measures relating to capital movements could be introduced. This is provided for in Article 73. The upshot of all of this is that while restoration of tariff and other protection is possible *de jure de facto* it is not normally a serious option.

Secondly, we have to take account of Article 36. It provides grounds upon which member states may continue to apply quantitative restrictions and measures having equivalent effect – this exception does not however allow the retention of tariffs. The derogations of Article 36 apply to restrictions on imports and exports

> justified on grounds of public morality, public policy or public security; the protection of health and life of humans, animals or plants; the protection of national treasures possessing artistic, historic or archaeological value; or the protection of industrial or commercial property.

The Article goes on to require that prohibitions or restrictions so justified shall not be a device for operating arbitrary discrimination. In addition member states must not try to pass off what are in effect attempts to block trade by specious references to the objectives listed in Article 36.

The concepts of public morality, public policy and public security[4] are not easy to define. Differences of national interpretation are almost inevitable. As a result a common Community definition is difficult to envisage and differences of application as between member states are inevitable. The Court of Justice has therefore been prepared to allow a margin for national discretion. The provision relating to the protection of public morality would legitimately enable one member state, for example, to ban from its territory pornographic material which another member state was prepared to allow to be published.[5] Equally the protection of the health of humans would legitimize the enactment of laws and regulations which had the effect of preventing the importation of what member states regarded as dangerous drugs or what they deemed to be foodstuffs containing dangerous additives, etc. Similarly the provision relating to animals would appear to uphold the right of states to lay down humanitarian regulations or even bans regarding the transport of animals while the need to prevent the spread of diseases such as rabies would properly allow for controls, conceivably even bans, to be placed on the import of pets. A control on the loss of national treasures is clearly possible although it is important to recognize that items are likely to lose their claim to special protection once they have been put on the market or have become a source of revenue to the government when being allowed to leave the country. As Lasok observes, 'It seems, therefore, that only rare objects of national piety or historical sentiment being *extra commercio* would be exempt from the freedom of movement' (1980, 74). The protection of industrial or commercial property[6] relates to patents, trade marks, copyrights, and so on, which confer on the owners thereof, or their licensees, a monopoly within the territory of the authority granting the patent, trade mark or copyright. The problem here is that this monopoly, which Article 36 seeks to protect, conflicts with the concept of goods being free to move between markets[7] and this raises the question of whether, for example, a good produced under a patent taken out in country A can enter the market of country B where the same patentee or his licensee has apparently got a monopoly of supply. We shall come back to this point in Chapter 4.

When we refer to the example of states laying down standards with regard to drugs, foodstuffs, etc., we recognize that Article 36 provides a basis for legitimizing such activity although it is equally obvious that to the extent that member states adopt different standards trade is likely to be inhibited or indeed totally prevented. In order to circumvent this type of problem the Rome Treaty also provides under Article 100 for the possibility of national standards being harmonized. We shall return to this point in Chapter 3 when discussing technical and non-technical standards as non-tariff barriers. At the same time

Cassis de Dijon will be analysed further since it and related cases have an important bearing on the harmonization issue.

Before we leave Articles 30 to 36 it is interesting to note that when in 1978 the Commission addressed a communication to the European Parliament, the Council of Ministers and the member states on the subject of safeguarding the freedom of trade within the Community it observed:

> The free movement of goods, a prime objective of the Treaty of Rome and function of the Common Market, has been and continues to be the subject of an ever increasing number of restrictive measures of all types taken by national public authorities to favour one or another national industrial sector or to restrain imports coming from other Member States. (ECC 1978a, 1)

It went on to note that it was investigating 400 dossiers on hindrances to the free movement of goods: in many cases these inhibitions were violations of Articles 30 to 36.

During 1981 the UK car market provided an extremely interesting example of such a hindrance. It related to the import of cars from the continent and gave rise to a vigorous press campaign, some ministerial embarrassment and the exchange of angry words between Brussels and London. The press drew attention to the marked differences in the price of cars on the continent as compared with the UK – the British consumer paid more for cars than any of his EEC counterparts. Basic prices in the rest of the EEC, net of tax, were in some cases as much as 50 per cent cheaper. There was therefore a considerable temptation to purchase models on the continent and then to import them into the UK. However certain obstacles stood in the way of such parallel imports and it was alleged that the existence of those obstacles was the result of an amalgam of vested interests. The official motor distributors were keen to protect their profit margins and the UK government was not anxious to see prices falling and, as a result, the subsidy bill to a major car producer rising.

At the centre of the problem were the national 'type approval' regulations which detail the British safety and technical standards to which cars allowed on British roads must conform. Interestingly the UK government had delegated the issue of certificates of conformity to the official car distributors. Not surprisingly individuals, and commercial importers outside the official dealer network, encountered some problems in obtaining these certificates. *The Economist* (1981a, 47–8) pointed out that since one of the technical safety checks involved crashing a car into a concrete wall, it was not worth the bother to apply! Perhaps more significant was the fact that those who were empowered to issue the certificates were refusing to issue them or were asking extremely high prices for the service.

There was however a loophole in the system. Individuals could import 'personal cars' provided that they had used the car abroad. The conditions attached were reasonably accommodating and had been designed to assist businessmen, servicemen and diplomats returning from abroad. Such personal imports did not require a type approval certificate. During 1981 it was reported (*Motor* 1981, 6) that the Society of Motor Manufacturers and Traders had approached the Department of Trade about the growth of personal imports and were pressing the UK government to tighten up the conditions by requiring that cars should have been used abroad for six months.

The press campaign and pressure from the EC Commission were ultimately effective. The UK government decided that the conditions governing personal imports should not be tightened up and it also proposed that official distributors should give rival importers the necessary certificates automatically without charge or fuss. It was also reported that the EC Commission intended to require that the price of any particular model, net of tax, should not vary from country to country by more than 12 per cent. If implemented the effect of this rule and the freeing of parallel imports was expected to reduce the price of cars in the UK by as much as 30 per cent.

The change in machinery introduced by the UK government did not however mark the end of the story. Car manufacturers and dealers appear to have done their best to frustrate the growing tide of cheap parallel imports, many of which were emanating from dealers in Brussels. The supply of right-hand-drive cars on the continent began to dry up. Ford refused to supply but the Brussels Commission ordered it to resume sales. Other car producers were also involved – in September 1982 it was reported that a British businessman had complained to the Commission because BMW had suddenly escalated the price of its right-hand-drive cars sold in Belgium. In the UK a car dealer who imported cut-price Metros had his credit and discount facilities withdrawn by a BL distributor – the Office of Fair Trading pounced on this particular practice. Rumours were also circulating that warranty services would not be available for such imports although this would appear to be in contravention of Community law. Clearly parallel imports are not popular in all quarters and sometimes encounter vigorous opposition.

We have seen that, subject to certain very limited exceptions, the free movement of goods is a cardinal principle of the Rome Treaty. The other cardinal principle is that there must be no discrimination on grounds of nationality. This principle of non-discrimination, to be found in Article 7, provides a reinforcing general authority for the attack on a wide range of barriers to trade. The attack on discrimination is reiterated in other treaty articles dealing with specific aspects of the economy.

INTERNAL ARRANGEMENTS - ECSC

Article 4 of the Paris Treaty prohibits import (and export) duties or charges having equivalent effect. It equally proscribes quantitative restrictions on the movement of products. The treaty entered into force on 25 July 1952 and after a six-month preparatory period free movement of coal, iron ore and scrap came into existence - that is on 10 February 1953. The problem of abolishing duties hardly arose since with one exception there were no such duties on these products. The exception was Italy which imposed a 15 per cent duty on coke and this was allowed to continue on a degressive basis, being finally eliminated at the expiration of the five-year transition period[8] - i.e. on 10 February 1958. Imports of these products were also generally free from quantitative restriction.

In the case of iron and steel products completely free movement was required by 1 May 1953. Here the situation was different. All the Community countries had imposed duties on iron and steel imports - see Table 2.2. In practice the French and German duties were in suspension and so in their case the practical effect was to prevent the French and German rates ever being applied to intra-Community trade at a later date. As in the case of Italian coke imports, Italian import duties on iron and steel were phased out progressively over the transition period. Quantitative restrictions were also removed from steel exports within the Community and quantitative import restrictions, which were important in the case of France, were also abolished.

A separate regime existed for special steels. These were not integrated into the common market until 1 August 1954 and again Italy was allowed the benefit of a progressive reduction over the transition period.

Table 2.2 Iron and steel import duties of the Six in 1952 (per cent)

	Pig-iron	Crude and semi-finished steel	Hot-finished steel products	Finished steel products
Benelux	0–1	1–2	1–6	6–8
France	5	7–10	10–18	10–22
West Germany	12	15–18	15–25	15–28
Italy	11–20	11–15	15–20	15–23

Source: Menderhausen (1953), 2–17

The High Authority, which was originally charged with the task of implementing the treaty, had to deal with a series of equivalent measures which had a protective effect. For example, the Italian government charged an 'administrative duty' of 0.5 per cent on imports of ECSC products and the Belgian government made the issue of licences for the import of coal from the Ruhr the subject of certain transport regulations. These and other obstacles were removed as a result of efforts by the High Authority.

The Convention on the Transitional Provisions which was annexed to the Paris Treaty provided an adaptation mechanism which was not repeated in the case of the Rome Treaty. In order to assist the less efficient coal industries of Belgium and Italy an equalization levy was introduced during the transition period. This was imposed on the output of those countries whose costs of production were below the weighted Community average. In effect this meant that Germany and the Netherlands subsidized Belgium and Italy. Although some rationalization of the latter two industries was achieved it did not prove sufficient for them to compete on equal terms with other coal producers in the Community and outside. These industries were put under severe pressure during the recession of 1958/9. As a result in 1959 the Belgian government requested that special action should be taken under Article 37. This enables the High Authority (now the EC Commission) to intervene when a member state is experiencing 'fundamental and persistent disturbances in its economy'. The result was High Authority Decision 46/59 (OJ 1959) which isolated the Belgian coal market. Restrictions were placed on imports of coal from other member states and from third countries. It should be added that as a *quid pro quo* exports of Belgian coal to other member states were also controlled. Belgian coal was reintegrated into the Community as from 1 January 1963 (ECC 1977a, 83).

No account of the provisions relating to the free movement of ECSC goods would be complete without reference to the question of non-discrimination. Under Article 4 of the Paris Treaty discrimination generally, and particularly in matters of pricing and transport, is declared to be incompatible with the common market for coal and steel. Articles 60 to 64 deal with this ban on discrimination in matters of pricing and Article 70 returns to the theme in the context of transport. Both these aspects will be dealt with later in Chapter 7 when we shall consider the pricing rules for ECSC products. It should however be noted that, because the Paris Treaty has authority over all sales of coal and steel products and does not merely focus on the interstate trade aspect, the ban on discrimination is general and does not merely single out that which is grounded on nationality. In other words discrimination by a French producer against a French consumer is as much against the Paris Treaty as is discrimination by a French producer against a German consumer.

EXTERNAL ARRANGEMENTS - EEC

In the case of the trade in goods the EEC is, as we have seen, based upon a customs union. Article 3(b) therefore requires the establishment of a common customs tariff (what is often referred to as the common external tariff). The reader will recollect that Article 3(b) also calls for the creation of a common commercial policy towards third countries. The common commercial policy is highly relevant to our discussion of the common external tariff because, as we might expect, the level of the tariff is one of the key variables in the Community's commercial stance towards the rest of the world.

Following Article 18 the original common external tariff was calculated on the basis of an unweighted average of the import duties of the four customs territories (Germany, France, Italy and the Benelux Economic Union) on 1 January 1957.[9] There were however a series of lists of commodities in respect of which rates of duty other than those based on the simple averaging rule were to apply. Taking the structure of imports into the Community in 1958 as a base it appears that the unweighted average incidence of the original common external tariff was 7.6 per cent while the weighted average was 9.1 per cent. However these figures conceal considerable variations. Whereas the average incidence for raw materials was 0.1 per cent, that for capital goods was 12.5 per cent and in the case of industrial products 17.3 per cent.

The Community subsequently participated in international tariff negotiations within the GATT which reduced the level of the external tariff. The Dillon Round (1960–1) led to a cut of 7–8 per cent while the Kennedy Round (1964–7) resulted in a further fall of 35–40 per cent. More recently the EEC was involved in the somewhat protracted Tokyo Round (1973–9). This will lead to a reduction of about a third over an eight-year period which began in 1980. The Community was satisfied that this cut would still preserve a reasonable degree of protection for its producers.

Although Article 23 merely envisaged that the Six would align their import tariffs on the common level by not later than the end of the transitional period, in fact the alignment was completed by 1 July 1968 – see Table 2.3. Under the terms of the accession treaties, new members were given five-year periods within which to bring their tariffs into line.

Table 2.3 The creation of the common external tariff (per cent)

	Acceleration of		Acceleration of		
	1.1.61	1.1.62	1.7.63	1.1.66	1.7.68
Industrial products					
adjustment	30		30		40
cumulative adjustment	30		60		100
Agricultural products					
adjustment		30		30	40
cumulative adjustment		30		60	100

Source: ECC (1968), 34

The common commercial policy is primarily governed by the provisions of Articles 110 to 116. Article 111 required that during the transition period the founding states should co-ordinate their trade relations with third countries so as to pave the way for a common commercial policy. Such a policy would, according to Article 113, be based

> on uniform principles, particularly in regard to changes in tariff rates, the conclusion of tariff and trade agreements, the achievement

of uniformity in measures of liberalization, export policy and measures to protect trade such as those to be taken in case of dumping or subsidies.

The post-transition period uniformity of trade policy, envisaged by Article 113, was to be accomplished in two ways. First, common rules were to be laid down for trade with the rest of the world, with separate arrangements for Communist (state trading) countries, while trade agreements already entered into with third countries were to be modified in the light of common rules and were eventually to become a Community responsibility. (Member states who joined later were also required to come into line.) Secondly, when new trade agreements were negotiated they would be Community rather than member state arrangements.

From all this it should be apparent that member states cease to be free to determine unilaterally the level of tariff and quota protection *vis-à-vis* third countries. If a member state finds that its industry, or a part of it, is being undermined by competition from outside the Community, it is not empowered to impose protection. Any protective action must be taken by the Community or must be taken on the basis of authority provided by the Community. Equally if changes in the level of the common external tariff are to be negotiated (as for example in the Tokyo Round), or if quotas are to be negotiated with respect to imports (as was the case in the Multifibre Arrangements) then in the light of Article 113 the Council of Ministers will lay down the guidelines and the actual bargaining will be conducted by the EC Commission. When the negotiations are concluded they will be adopted by the Council on a qualified majority basis and are then binding on member states.

One of the generally accepted grounds for taking protective action is that a foreign competitor is indulging in dumping. It should at this point be emphasized that under international rules the concept of dumping does not apply to trade flows within a unified market such as the EEC. Reflecting this there are no anti-dumping rules relating to intra-Community trade in the post-transition period. If unfair competition is alleged within the EEC the only remedies that are available are those that can arise under Articles 85, 86 and 92. The former two articles might enable a case to be mounted against a cartel or a dominant firm which was able to discriminate between markets – high prices in one part of the common market financing artificially low prices in another. The latter article could be applicable in circumstances where a member state was providing aid of some kind which had the effect of subsidizing exports or disadvantaging imports. However anti-dumping powers do exist in respect of unfair competition emanating from *third country suppliers* when selling within the Community. The current provisions are contained in Regulation 926/79 (OJ 1979a).[10] Following hearings, remedial action, such as the imposition of anti-dumping duties, can be taken when the export price to the Community is less than the 'normal' value of the like product and the dumping 'causes or threatens to cause material injury to an established Community industry or materially retards the setting-up of an industry whose early establishment in the Community is envisaged'. The regulation provides for a variety of methods of demonstrating that the export price is less than the 'normal' value. Indeed it prescribes no less than eight different reference prices which, according to the circumstances, may be utilized to determine the 'normal' value. The most obvious one is the domestic price in the country of origin. However this may not be an appropriate bench-mark. Such is the case when goods are produced on the basis of near or total monopoly conditions in a state trading country. In this circumstance a number of alternatives are available such as the sale price of the product in a free market third country economy, the constructed value in a third country or the price payable for a like product in the EEC. In the *Herbicides from Romania* case (OJ 1979b) the US market price for the products was chosen as the 'normal' value. The US price, although subject to adjustment, was also used as the bench-mark in the *Lithium Hydroxide from USA and USSR case* (OJ 1980a). In the *Sodium Carbonate from the USSR* action (OJ 1980b) the Russian export price was compared with the market value of the same product in Austria.

It is most important to emphasize that the damage sustained refers to the entire EEC production of like products. Normally damage suffered by a national segment of a Community industry will not provide sufficient grounds to launch an action. Equally it should be noted that the EC Commission, not member states, is empowered to implement Regulation 926/79. Once again we see that member states alone do not have the power to protect themselves.

While it is true that anti-dumping measures can normally only be applied where a *Community* industry is damaged, we should not conclude that protective action is not permitted in cases where *national* industries suffer serious injury. Regulations have been introduced which enable quotas to be applied to imports *from third countries* (OJ 1979c) and *from state trading nations* (OJ 1979d). Where the imports so increase as to threaten the national industry the Commission acting *ex officio*, or at the request of the affected state, can authorize the application of quota restrictions. A member state can itself take *emergency* protective action but this can be revoked by the Commission. It is interesting to note that other member states can appeal against such protective action. Thus in 1979 the UK successfully requested Commission permission to restrict the inflow of polyamide yarn for carpets. West Germany appealed to the Council of Ministers against the action but the Council upheld the Commission's action (OJ 1980c). Yet again we see that member states are not free to impose unilaterally permanent protection.

EXTERNAL ARRANGEMENTS – ECSC

In its original conception the ECSC was not formally based upon a customs union. Article 71 of the Paris Treaty makes it quite clear that subject to certain exceptions the powers of the member states in matters of commercial policy shall not be affected by the treaty. Article 72 reflects this difference of emphasis as compared with the Rome Treaty. It merely provides for the possibility that the Council of Ministers on the basis of unanimity *may* fix maximum and minimum rates of duty as between which the member states are free to fix their own rates. In earlier days, certainly in the case of steel, import duty levels varied but more recently a unified tariff has been applied. In the case of coal the tariff level is zero except for West Germany which applies an import duty. Article 74 enables the Commission to recommend to member states the application of any protective measures and this obviously includes quotas. This power is applicable when dumping is taking place, when foreign suppliers are able to offer low quotations because they operate under conditions of competition different from those of the Community or when imports increase at such a fast rate that they cause or threaten to cause injury to a Community industry. This third condition only justifies the introduction of *quotas* when, under Article 58, a state of manifest crisis is declared in the Community industry. We shall discuss the manifest crisis concept in Chapter 7. In practice in the application of quotas, notably in the case of coal, member states have tended to insist on their freedom to act individually and co-ordinated policies have repeatedly failed to materialize.

In 1977 an anti-dumping Recommendation (under Article 74(3)) was issued by the EC Commission in respect of ECSC products (OJ 1977a). It indicated that normally defensive action would be undertaken by the Commission although it also allowed for national measures to be taken when no Community interest was involved. In the light of the difficulties faced by the steel industry, partly as a result of the competition from cheap imports from third countries, the dumping mechanism was subsequently revised. A 'fast-track' system was introduced at the beginning of 1978. Whereas normally anti-dumping procedures involved hearings at which the accused can make their case, the Commission devised a much speedier remedial system. Basic prices were published which were based on the lowest normal costs in the supply country or countries where there were normal conditions of competition. Any difference between the published basic price and the actual delivered price led to the immediate levying of a provisional countervailing duty. This temporary arrangement was designed to induce third country suppliers to accept discipline in respect of their sales efforts in the Community market. It was a prelude to the conclusion of bilateral agreements on prices and quantities between the EC Commission and individual third countries. More will be said about this in the context of ECSC Industrial Policy in Chapter 7. It should also be noted that in 1979 a new anti-dumping Recommendation was adopted (OJ 1979e) which as far as possible paralleled that simultaneously introduced in respect of EEC products (see above).

Right of establishment and freedom to supply services

Earlier it was indicated that we should return to these aspects of the Rome Treaty. (There are no equivalent provisions in the Paris Treaty.) Articles 52 to 58 require the removal of restrictions on the ability of self-employed individuals and enterprises established in one member state to set up permanent operations – factories, branches, offices – in other member states. This is what is meant by the right of establishment. Equally, just as by virtue of tariff and quota disarmament the self-employed and enterprises in one state are free to supply goods in other member states, it was also recognized in Articles 59 to 66 that they should be free to supply services across frontiers. Hence the concept of the freedom to supply services.

At the outset we must take account of two important cases which were heard before the Court of Justice – the *Reyners* case (ECJ 2/74) and the *Van Binsbergen* case (ECJ 33/74). The upshot of these cases was as follows. Since the end of the transition period (i.e. since 1 January 1970) according to *Reyners* and *Van Binsbergen* respectively the right of establishment (specifically provided by Article 52) and the freedom to supply services (specifically provided by Articles 59 and 60) can be invoked in the courts and all discrimination *on grounds of nationality* is automatically prohibited. The implication of all this will perhaps be clearer when we note that as early as 1961 the Council of Ministers adopted two general programmes, one for the abolition of restrictions affecting the right of establishment (OJ 1962a) and one on the removal of restrictions on the freedom to supply services (OJ 1962b). In these it established priorities for action and thereafter patiently proceeded to produce separate directives for many areas of trade and industry (e.g. wholesale and retail trade, the food and beverage industry, mining and quarrying) and for some professions (e.g. doctors). As a result a significant amount of liberalizing legislation was enacted. However it would appear that some of this activity was really redundant since in the light of *Reyners* and *Van Binsbergen* this basic right and this basic freedom are self-executing. That is to say after 1 January 1970 they were automatically enjoyed and no legislative activity at Community level was needed in order that national discriminations should be removed so that advantage could be taken of them.

However it would not be true to say that there has been no need for legislative activity of any kind on the part of the Council of Ministers. If we consider, for example, the position of many of the professions in earlier years, despite what the Rome Treaty might say and how the Court might interpret it, the right and the freedom would not have been sufficient to enable a professional person to travel to another state and supply a service or to set up in business in another state and proceed to practise his or her profession. The reason for this was that member states have laid down the qualifications which various professional persons must possess before they can practise. Unfortunately the qualifications possessed by a professional person may not be recognized in another member state. Moreover the cases which we have discussed recognized the right of states to enact such protective legislation – as we have already emphasized what those cases have outlawed is discrimination on grounds of nationality. In order for professional persons to be able to practise anywhere in the Community legislative activity is needed which leads to a recognition by states of each other's professional qualifications, provides for training to be harmonized, and so on. Generalizing on this topic is difficult since the details vary from case to case. What we shall therefore do is to consider two cases – insurance and doctors.

In the case of insurance the general programmes indicated that the order of priority should be re-insurance, non-life insurance and then life assurance and this sequence has been followed in practice. We shall consider the position in respect of non-life insurance which is concerned with fire and accidents and includes big risks such as the insuring of jumbo jets. In 1973 the Council adopted a directive on the right of establishment (OJ 1973a). It required the abolition of restrictions which prevented companies, etc., from establishing themselves in a host country under the same conditions and with the same rights as those enjoyed by the nationals of that country. For example, Ireland had previously required insurance companies to be registered under the Irish Companies Acts and, more to the point, stipulated that two-thirds of the shares had to be owned by Irish citizens and that the majority of the directors (other than the full-time managing director) had to be of Irish nationality. In the light of *Reyners* national discriminations of this kind would appear to be automatically contrary to the treaty and not surprisingly thereafter a number of draft directives which were addressed to this kind of problem in other areas were dropped.

Altogether more important was the directive on the co-ordination of laws relating to the taking up and pursuit of the business of non-life insurance (OJ 1973b). This was necessary because in order to protect their citizenry the member states require insurance companies to be licensed and a condition of holding a licence is that companies meet certain standards in terms of technical reserves, solvency margins, etc. These differed between states and therefore the possibility existed that a company wishing to set up a branch in another member state could be debarred from doing so if the conditions demanded by the host government were more stringent than those demanded by the government of the country in which the company had its head-quarters. The directive delineates the kinds of insurance and companies covered. It requires that the taking up of the business of non-life insurance should be subject to official authorization by each member state. This applies to an undertaking which has its head office in a member state and also to branches of enterprises which have head offices in other member states. Uniform procedural requirements are laid down, such as the need to submit a scheme of operations, and most important of all, uniform standards are specified in respect of technical reserves and margins of solvency.

Although the 1973 directives dealt satisfactorily with the right of establishment, they did not tackle the problem of freedom to supply services. In other words obstacles still existed when, for example, an insurance company *located in the UK* wished to insure a risk in West Germany. The problem here is that member states with, among other things, consumer protection in mind tend to intervene in the matter of the terms and conditions of insurance contracts. Clearly were a UK company's branch in West Germany to insure the West German risk then the West German authorities would be able to exercise control since West German law would apply. However in the case of the insurance being effected by the UK company direct then it is possible to envisage that the contract might be governed by UK law, West German law or indeed the law of a third country. Such a choice was indeed suggested by the EC Commission in its original draft directive (OJ 1976a). This met with some opposition in the European Parliament and the draft was subsequently amended (ECC 1978b) so as to require contracts to be governed by the law of the country in which the risk was situated. However in respect of certain risks the amended draft allowed for an important derogation whereby the parties could choose the law which should apply. The practical effect of this was that in the case of large commercial risks, where those insured could be expected to be able to take care of themselves, the choice of law principle was to operate. In respect of the insurance of those risks where the insured were likely to be less expert the domestic law requirement was to operate.

Unfortunately this amended proposal has not yet found favour, and freedom to supply services does not yet obtain. Much of this has been due to West German opposition. The West Germans subject insurance contracts to relatively close legal control and are aware that countries such as the UK leave these matters more to self-regulation by the insurance companies. The West Germans have been opposed to allowing some insurance business to be conducted under what they would no doubt regard as laxer systems. The UK on the other hand has taken the position that the amended draft deals adequately with the need for consumer protection. For example, airlines are quite capable in a choice of law situation of insisting that the necessary protective terms be included in contracts. The more vulnerable would continue to be protected by domestic provisions. There have been other complications. For example, France is the only country which levies tax on insurance contracts. It has insisted on being able to continue to do so. This would require a company to have a representative in the taxing country in order to be responsible for assessment and payment of tax. This would hit smaller insurance companies.

In the case of doctors the main problem was one which we have already identified, namely differing professional qualifications and training. Because of the poor progress in the medical field Commissioner Ralf Dahrendorf, before he left Brussels, decided to hold a unique common market meeting. This occurred in 1973 when the Commission invited ninety-nine doctors to a public hearing to discuss the central problem of the mutual recognition of medical qualifications and the training which lies behind them. The doctors who attended were members of the Standing Committee of Doctors of the Common Market, and of Universities, and there were observers present from other professional bodies and from governments. Draft directives had been published in 1969 indicating the solution envisaged by the Commission but much criticism had been levelled at them. The public hearing was judged to have been a success and certainly substantial progress was subsequently made in 1975 when two directives and two decisions were adopted by the Council. The object of the directives was to make the right of establishment and the freedom to provide services a reality in the case of doctors. One directive (OJ 1975a) provided for the mutual recognition of diplomas, certificates and other evidence of formal qualifications in medicine. The specific diplomas, etc., were listed in the directive. Provisions were also laid down which are designed to meet the requirements of a host state when proof of good character or good repute is called for. Clearly requirements such as compulsory registration with a professional organization (i.e. the General Medical Council in the UK) could be an obstacle to the freedom to supply services. The directive therefore exempts nationals from other member states from that requirement but subjects them to the domestic rules of professional conduct in the state where the service is being supplied. The second directive (OJ 1975b) in effect recognized that some greater degree of harmonization in the length and content of medical training – in terms of what is a minimum acceptable standard – was desirable. It therefore laid down such requirements and provides for their subsequent introduction. One of the decisions established an Advisory Committee on Medical Training to assist in the introduction of comparably demanding standards of medical training as between the member states (OJ 1975c). The other decision set up a Committee of Senior Officials in Public Health whose job it is to assist in dealing with difficulties arising in the implementation of the two directives (OJ 1975d).

3 Non-tariff barriers – the state

Introduction

In June 1981 the EC Commission addressed a Communication to the Council of Ministers on the state of the internal market (ECC 1981a). What it had to say was far from flattering. It observed:

> The customs union, the implementation of which is intended to ensure the internal market, is proving to be increasingly inadequate for the achievement of this aim. The substance of what has been achieved is instead being jeopardized and undermined by the fact that old barriers have survived for too long and new barriers have been created.

It went on to draw attention to protectionist measures connected with technical standards, taxes, state aids and public purchasing. The imperfections of the customs union were further emphasized by a number of reports which pointed to marked differences in the price of particular goods in the various member state markets. A study by the Bureau Européen des Unions de Consommateurs showed marked disparities in the basic price, net of tax, of cars. The data, shown in Table 3.1, indicated that the UK was not the odd man out. The Italian price for the Fiat 132 2000 was 42 per cent of the UK price but the French was 72 per cent and the Irish 91 per cent. A study undertaken for the EC Commission by a group of Belgian economists revealed marked disparities in the price of electrical appliances and hi-fi and video products. The average price of 100 selected electrical goods in October/November 1978 ranged from nearly 40 per cent above the UK level in the case of Denmark to just over 16 per cent below the UK level in the case of Italy. In September 1981 *The Economist* (1981b) carried out its own snap survey of car, butter and pen prices and produced some interesting disparities. For example, the price of a

Table 3.1 Comparison of basic prices (net of tax) of cars in EC as percentage of highest price (1981)

Make and Model	DK	LUX	B	NL	GER	F	IRL	UK
Alfasud Super 1350	49	71	70	63	71	76	85	100
Audi 80 GLE	54	55	59	60	63	62	64	100
BMW 320	52	71	72	69	72	79	87	100
Citroën GSA Club	53	73	73	70	77	83	81	100
Citroën CX 2400 Pallas	49	56	64	66	65	62	85	100
Fiat 127 Sport	52	71	70	69	72	83	84	100
Fiat 132 2000	46	70	70	64	71	72	91	100
Ford Escort 1.3 L	54	66	69	65	70	73		100
Ford Granada 2.3 GL		54	57	57	58	66	69	100
Honda Prelude	63	67	67	64	75	73		100
Jaguar XJ6 4.2 Auto	67	62	66	62	71	73	86	100
Lada 1200 Estate		64	63	76	87	80		100
Mazda 323 GT 1.5	60	62	66	64	68			100
Mercedes 230E	69	66	67	72	63	75		100
Mini City 1000		58	60	62	64	68	99	100
Mini Metro HLE			65	64	69	70	76	100
Opel Kadett 1.3 SR	55	62	62	65	67	72		100
Peugeot 305 GLS	48	74	76	74	74		86	100
Renault 5 GTL		68	68	67	70	75	82	100
Renault 20 TS		66	66	64	67	68	89	100
Rover 3500	46	55	54	59		61		100
Talbot Horizon 1.3 GL	53	56	58		60	69	68	100
VW Polo L	50	71	66	69	72	71		100
VW Golf 1.5 GLS Auto	59	64	64	67	67	72	76	100
Volvo 343	60	72	75	68	82	80	84	100
Average	55	65	66	66	70	72	82	100

Source: Bureau Européen des Unions de Consommateurs (1981)

Parker 25 pen ranged from well below £3 in Belgium, Italy and Luxembourg to about £4 in Denmark and France. *The Economist* (1981c) also drew attention to the widespread habit of buying pesticides on the continent. Farmers making day trips to France and Germany were finding that they could make average savings of 25 per cent.

Such price differences are partly the result of factors of the kind discussed in Chapter 2 and partly the result of non-tariff barriers and in this chapter and the subsequent two we shall consider what the Rome and Paris Treaties have to say on the non-tariff barrier problem and how they seek to deal with it.

State aids (subsidies)

State aids or subsidies can obviously distort competition by giving an unfair advantage to domestic producers when they export to other member state markets or seek to compete against imports coming from Community producers located in other member states. Article 92(1) of the Rome Treaty declares incompatible with the common market state aids which (a) distort, or threaten to distort, competition by favouring certain enterprises or the production of certain goods; (b) in so far as trade between member states is affected. (Obviously aids with purely local effects are excluded – we noted this point in Chapter 1.) With this as its general posture the Rome Treaty then explicitly recognizes two categories of exception. One consists of a series of aids which are definitely excepted from the general ban (Article 92(2)). The other consists of a series of aids which *may* according to circumstances be excepted (Article 92(3)).

The definitely excepted category consists of aids of a social character granted to individuals. Aid granted to children in the form of free school milk presumably falls in this class. The aid has, however, to be given without reference to where the goods come from. Discriminatory treatment whereby British milk was subsidized but other EEC milk was not would not normally be acceptable. Aids may also be given to alleviate hardship caused by natural disasters (or other exceptional occurrences) and to areas in West Germany bordering on the German Democratic Republic which have been disadvantaged by that geographical division.

We come now to the second category. Clearly although there is no separate title in the Rome Treaty relating to regional policy, those who drafted it were aware of pronounced differences of standards of living within the EEC and of the existence of a regional problem. They could also hardly fail to recognize the possibility that in certain circumstances these problems might be aggravated by the creation of the EEC. Moreover given that the preamble to the treaty affirmed the desirability of achieving a 'harmonious development by reducing the differences existing between the various regions and the backwardness of the less favoured regions', a continued role for regional aids was therefore inevitable. Reflecting this Article 92(3)(a) provides for the possibility that aid to promote the development of areas where the standard of living is abnormally low or where there is serious unemployment *may* be declared compatible with the common market. Clearly a blanket exception could not be given since regional aids might be excessive and thus become not a means of offsetting or overcoming certain locational disadvantages but a source of unfair competitive advantage.

Article 93(2)(b) also provides for the possible compatibility of aids granted to promote the execution of an important project of common European interest or to remedy a serious disturbance in the economy of a member state. The former has included the construction of a road tunnel under the Alps and a hydro-electric scheme in Luxembourg providing energy for France and Germany. The projected Channel Tunnel could fall into this category. Some legal commentators have observed that the remedying of a serious disturbance is akin to the natural disasters provision discussed above but this seems to be based on a misreading of the provision. The serious disturbance has to occur in the economy and it seems clear that it refers to matters such as general recessions or deficits in the balance of payments although it could also refer to financial difficulties being experienced by industries or firms which play a proportionately important role in the economy of a member state. If a very sizeable firm or a major industry collapsed significant unemployment and economic disruption would ensue. This is undoubtedly one reason why the EC Commission chose not to contest the aid made available to British Leyland and Chrysler by the UK government (ECC 1976a, 85).

The idea that aids may in certain circumstances be declared compatible with the common market also applies in the case of assistance which facilitates 'the development of certain economic activities', i.e. industries. Here in Article 92(3)(c) there is an express provision that the aid must not affect trading conditions to an extent contrary to the common interest. In short what are called sectoral aids may also be capable of exemption. Article 92(3)(c), with the same express proviso, envisages the possible exemption of aid for the development of certain economic areas. There thus appears to be an overlap with Article 92(3)(a) but it is critically important to appreciate that the latter refers to areas with serious difficulties and presumably because of this the express proviso about the effect on trading conditions and the common interest is absent.

Article 93 imposes upon the EC Commission the task of keeping under constant review all systems of aid. Since the member states may grant aids only within the terms of the Rome Treaty it follows that they must inform the EC Commission of plans to grant aids or to alter them[1] and must equally abide by the Commission's recommendations in connection therewith. If the EC Commission finds that an aid is not compatible with the treaty it has the power to issue a Decision requiring the state to amend it suitably or to abolish it.[2] If the state does not comply the EC Commission will initiate an enforcement action under Article 169 with the ultimate possibility that the matter will be referred to the Court of Justice. Member states may themselves initiate enforcement actions before the Court (Article 170) but since states are not normally given to suing each other the tendency is for the enforcement role to be discharged by the Commission.

Next we turn to the status of the different forms of aid. In respect of export aid the EC Commission has taken a very categorical stance. Such aid cannot benefit from any exception whatsoever (ECC 1978c, 170-1) and the Commission has constantly been on the attack. Typical was its action in 1976 in asking member states to confirm that they did not directly or indirectly make funds available to reduce the cost of export credit in respect of sales to other member states. Most states confirmed that they did not but France and the UK admitted that they granted aid and subsequently took steps to terminate the practice (ECC 1978c, 171; ECC 1979a, 153-4). The Commission had a protracted dispute with the Netherlands, the Dutch government seeking to escape from any obligation by arguing that it was the Dutch Central Bank and not it which was responsible. However the Commission argued that it always regarded credit facilities given by member state central banks as state aids. A threat of an action before the Court of Justice immediately brought the Dutch government into line (ECC 1980a, 117-18).

Regional aid schemes have indeed posed a very considerable control problem for the Commission. The basic difficulty was that the various regions of the Community began to compete with each other to attract foot-loose investment capital. Regional aid schemes became more costly as a result of competitive outbidding and this process of bidding up did not appreciably increase the flow of investment. Rather it tended to give rise to reciprocal neutralization with unjustified profits for the beneficiary enterprise. Also aids tended no longer to correspond to the relative seriousness of the situation. In some cases the aid schemes in operation were such that it was difficult to estimate just how generous they were.

The EC Commission eventually succeeded in bringing the situation under some control. In 1971 the Commission submitted a Communication to the Council of Ministers laying down principles which should govern regional aid giving (ECC 1971a, 37). This was accepted by Council. The Communication had a twofold aspect. It laid down certain general requirements and it prescribed specific aid ceilings. Aids should be transparent. Opaque aids should be progressively rendered transparent or, if that was not possible, they should be dropped. Aids should be regionally specific. They should not normally cover whole national territories but should apply to the problem regions therein and their intensity should be adjusted to the seriousness of the specific problem. In the Community's 'central' regions the ceiling was to be 20 per cent of the investment in net grant equivalence, i.e. the net grant remaining to the beneficiary after deduction of profits tax. The peripheral regions were not regulated in terms of a ceiling. When the UK became a member its aid giving in its 'central' regions was subjected to the 20 per cent rule. Almost immediately this provoked a clash because the Commission proposed to classify some of the Development Areas and Special Development Areas as central! For a while this led to those two types of areas being left unclassified. In 1975 a new ceiling system was introduced which also took in the peripheral regions (ECC 1976a, 69). In the case of Greenland, Iceland, the Mezzogiorno and Northern Ireland the ceiling was fixed at 35 per cent: there were, however, certain additional conditions and qualifications. In the French regions eligible for industrial development grants, in certain areas in Italy (other than the Mezzogiorno) and in the assisted areas in Great Britain (but not the Intermediate Areas) the aid ceiling was to be 30 per cent. The reader will note that the Community had quietly accepted the British position. In West Berlin, in the areas bordering East Germany and in certain assisted areas in Denmark an aid limit of 25 per cent was prescribed. In all other regions the ceiling was to be 20 per cent, but it was desirable that this should be reduced as quickly as possible. In the case of the UK this latter category included all areas outside the British assisted areas and Northern Ireland. Intermediate areas were of course in the 20 per cent category.

It is important to emphasize that these are aid *ceilings*. It does not follow that, for example, a member state can automatically make a grant of 20 per cent in a particular part of a 'central' region. Rather the EC Commission will exercise supervision and will ultimately be able to decide whether that particular area can be scheduled as one entitled to receive regional aid. Equally the Commission will appraise the socioeconomic conditions in the area and determine what degree of aid (up to 20 per cent) is acceptable.

The EC Commission has sought to influence not only the level of aid but also the type of aid instrument which can be applied. UK experience in this matter has been particularly revealing. From the beginning the Commission did not like the Regional Employment Premium (REP) which was a continuing *per capita* weekly labour subsidy payable to manufacturers located in the Development Areas (MacLennan 1979, 245-71). It was never specifically banned and this may be because initially it was planned to run for only a seven-year experimental period - it was due to expire in September 1974. Moreover the Conservative Party indicated that they disliked this device, which had been introduced by Labour, and that if they got back into office they would get rid of it. The EC Commission thus had reason to hope that eventually the problem would go away. In practice it ultimately did although not as quickly as might have been expected. It was indeed prolonged until 1977 although retained in Northern Ireland. Action against the REP was also inhibited by the renegotiation of the UK terms of entry to the EC - the need to retain effective control of regional policy was one of the main planks of Labour's renegotiation position.

The REP was unacceptable to the EC Commission because it broke all the rules. It was not measurable according to the Commission's formula. In essence the latter transmutes aids into a proportion of the investment involved but the REP would give different results as capital: labour intensities varied. The formula assumes an act of investment: the REP required none. The Commission is opposed to continuing subsidies, particularly of an indiscriminate kind: it envisages an initial act of assistance after which the project should be able to survive. The decision to drop REP may have owed something to Community pressure although the ostensible reason according to Chancellor Healey was that there were doubts as to whether the REP was any longer fulfilling its task of attracting employment to the regions and that a more selective approach was preferred.

In 1978 the Commission adopted new regional aid rules (OJ 1979f). Bowing to Italian and UK pressure to the effect that the old system (of

1971 and 1975) was biased in favour of capital intensive projects, the new rules added an alternative criterion of units of account per job created per new investment. This allowed a wider range of aids to be measured. However, it did not save the REP type because the Commission continued to insist that the concept of *new* investment be retained.

The main instrument of UK regional policy has been the Regional Development Grant (RDG) which is of course a percentage subsidy given in relation to capital expenditure on buildings, machinery and plant in the Development Areas.[3] Interestingly this too has attracted adverse criticism from the EC Commission. As we have noted the Commission favours a once-for-all capital subsidy with the expectation that thereafter the assisted investment will generate sufficient funds to facilitate its replacement without further assistance. However in the eyes of the EC Commission the UK RDG involves an element of continuing operating subsidy in that a grant is made available not only partly to finance the original purchase of, for example, a machine but also when the machine, having depreciated, is replaced. The second purchase may generate no new jobs and thus the system merely gives rise to a continuing subsidization of the operating costs of a given employment structure. The system favours certain firms and thus distorts competition in intra-Community trade without making any compensatory contribution to regional development. Following protracted discussions

> The United Kingdom agreed to amend the RDG by 1984 at the latest so as to eliminate its element of operating aid and make it compatible with the rules of the common market. The British government undertook that investment in capital equipment made by an existing firm for the purpose of keeping it in business or maintaining its level of business without affecting any basic change would no longer qualify for assistance. (ECC 1981b, 122)

Sectoral aid (i.e. aid to individual firms or industries) is another main area of Commission supervisory activity. The Commission has not felt the necessity to define its attitude to aid in every specific industrial sector. Only in the case of industries which have been encountering structural problems *across the Community* has it felt the need to take a specific stance. It has, for example, done so in respect of textiles and clothing, man-made fibres and shipbuilding. We shall not deal with these approaches at this point but reserve discussion until Chapter 6 when these industries will be examined in the context of industrial policy. The Commission has however indicated its general philosophical approach to sectoral aids. It did so in 1972 in its *First Report on Competition Policy* (ECC 1972, 129-32). Its position at that point in time was strict. Aids should be selective, that is to say thay should only be given to enterprises which were likely to become viable in due course. Aids should not be designed merely to prop up enterprises but to enable them to readapt. In other words the aid should eliminate excess capacity and redirect investment and R & D spending into more promising lines of activity. Mere bailings out with no plan of adaptation were not acceptable. It also followed from all this that aids should be degressive over time. They should also be transparent – a word much favoured by the EC Commission. That is to say aids should be capable of evaluation in terms of the amounts involved, their true incidence and their effectiveness. If there was a choice of aid method, the one having the least effect on intra-Community competition should be selected.

Subsequently the economic position in the Community changed. The recession which began in the second half of 1974, and the growing competition from NICs and Japan, has compelled a reappraisal. The meeting of Heads of State and Government in Copenhagen in 1978 noted the need to restore the competitiveness of industries in distress. Clearly state aids have a role to play here and given the more difficult general economic climate the length of time before a turn-round could be achieved was likely to be greater. Some element of keeping firms afloat while they tackled their problems was bound to be necessary. There followed a dialogue between the Council and the Commission after which the Commission issued a new statement of general principles (ECC 1979a, 122-7). While this reiterates some of the ideas of 1972 it is notable for a softening of tone notably in respect of the need for a breathing space before longer-term solutions can be worked out. Although long-term viability must be the aim, resources can be used to cushion enterprises in the interim and thus avoid sudden and severe economic and social shocks. The new guidelines also explicitly recognize the role of state aid in speeding up the response of the private enterprise system to new investment and technological opportunities (the picking the winners referred to in Chapter 1) and the adaptation of industries which need to contract and redeploy resources (which we also discussed in Chapter 1).

More recent actions by the EC Commission also indicate its

intention to control the activities of bodies such as the National Enterprise Board (NEB). The Commission was concerned about the latter because it feared that the NEB would be able to obtain capital from the UK Treasury at concessionary rates and would be able to pass this advantage on in its industrial interventions. This would give UK firms an artificial advantage as compared with firms in other parts of the Community which had to pay commercial rates of interest. The Commission was also aware that some of the NEB funding was made available on a Public Dividend Capital basis. Here there was no fixed interest commitment on the part of the NEB. Given that the NEB was required to operate on a commercial basis the Commission framed the following system of surveillance. As regards routine operations, where the NEB operated on its own initiative, it would be sufficient if the UK government rendered an annual report on the Board's operations. But when the NEB was required by the Secretary of State for Industry to intervene, and where therefore the government might be tempted to use its powers to adjust the NEB's financial duties, it was necessary for the specific intervention to be notified in advance (ECC 1978a, 162-5). The return of the Thatcher Conservative government, with a different economic philosophy, has meant that the activities of the Board have been significantly curtailed.

It is by no means easy to draw out any watertight philosophy from the Commission's specific interventions in areas other than those such as textiles and shipbuilding. The reason for this is that the main sources of information are the by no means detailed reports of negotiations with states which often stop short of more fully argued decisions and court judgements. The Commission's willingness not to intervene against aids for British Leyland indicates a preparedness to give a fair, if not indeed a generous, crack of the whip to attempts to restructure and bring back to viability an ailing firm. Here the Commission can be seen to be allowing aids as a means of facilitating adjustment in the face of the need for contraction and resource redeployment. Equally the Commission has, in its willingness to allow aid to be given to the UK microelectronics industry, been prepared to allow the state to speed up the response of private industry to new technological developments. It should however be noted that the EC Commission did compel a reduction in the scale of the latter (ECC 1979a, 145-6).

General aid schemes have long been a cause of considerable anxiety to the EC Commission. These, as their title clearly indicates, have no designated specific objective and can be applied on an individual, sectoral or regional basis as the national need arises. The attitude of the Commission has been that as they stand they are incompatible with the Rome Treaty. They ought to be transformed into regional and sectoral aids which address particular problems. They would then be capable of assessment under the specific provisions of the Treaty. This was the longer-term objective. Meanwhile the Commission should be kept informed.

In the early days the scale of the problem was apparently not such as to cause overwhelming concern. However, as we have just noted, during the second half of 1974 the Community economy began to enter a period of depression. The upshot of this was an intensified application of existing general aid schemes and the introduction of economic recovery measures of limited duration. Although the Commission could have raised objections, it seems to have recognized that the exceptional economic and social situation confronting the member states justified the adoption of exceptional measures. In so doing it drew attention, prudently perhaps, to Article 92(3)(b) which allows aids to be granted which are designed 'to remedy a serious disturbance in the economy of a Member State' (ECC 1976a, 93). The Commission however required that the established practice whereby it was notified about general aid schemes should also apply in the case of economic recovery measures and it continued to discharge a policing role.

A little more needs to be said about the notification system. More recently the EC Commission appears to have become reconciled to the fact that member states find it advantageous to have general aid powers at their immediate disposal. The hope that they would be progressively phased out seems to have receded, perhaps permanently. The Commission does not therefore raise objections to the taking of general powers but it emphasizes that the fact that it raises no objection to the taking of those powers does not imply a favourable pre-judgement of individual (firm), sectoral (industry-wide) or regional applications. The Commission has laid down detailed notification thresholds (ECC 1980a, 111). A good illustration of its approach to individual applications is provided by the *Philip Morris* case.

Under section 6 of the Dutch Act of 1978 on the promotion and guidance of investment the Dutch government can pay an additional subsidy for larger schemes where the investment exceeds 30 million florins. The actual amount paid depends upon the number of jobs created and may amount to 4 per cent of the investment in question.

This is additional to any regional grant which may be payable. When the scheme was at the bill stage the Commission pointed out that the additional subsidy element was a general aid since it related to no specific industrial or regional objectives. Because of this the Commission indicated that it could not declare that the subsidy scheme was compatible with Article 92 (3)(a), (b) or (c) and that it would have to vet individual applications on their merits and that in turn would require that they should be notified in advance.

Later in 1978 the Dutch government decided to grant a subsidy to Philip Morris, the Dutch subsidiary of a multinational tobacco manufacturer. The proposed aid amounted to 6.2 million florins (3.7 million European Units of Account (EUA)), being 3.8 per cent of the investment involved. In addition regional aid amounting to 10 million florins (3.7 million EUA) would also be payable. This assistance was in connection with the closure of the Philip Morris factory at Eindhoven and the concentration of production at its Bergen-op-Zoom plant. The result was to be a 40 per cent increase in Morris's Dutch cigarette production capacity and a 13 per cent increase in cigarette production capacity in the Netherlands. The project was such as to require advance notification and the Dutch government duly complied. In turn the Commission considered the aid under the various sections of Article 92(3). Sections (a) and (c) offered the possibility of a regional development justification. However the project was already entitled to regional aid (and the Commission did not object to that) but there was nothing special about the Bergen-op-Zoom area which justified the general aid being piled on top of the regional aid (the standard of living was not abnormally low nor was unemployment serious). In any case the Dutch government did not seek to justify the general aid on regional grounds. The Commission was left with three possibilities. It could consider the aid under section (b) but on examination it did not see the concentration and expansion at Bergen-op-Zoom as being a project of European importance nor could it see it as being necessary to remedy a serious disturbance in the Dutch economy since the latter, in terms of unemployment, was relatively well placed in the Community. The third and final possibility was that under section (c) the aid might be required 'to facilitate the development of certain economic activities'. However the economic conditions in the cigarette industry were not such that prices and profits *unaided* were inadequate to call forth an adequate supply. In sum the Commission could find no justification under the treaty for the subsidy and so decided (OJ

1979g). This was appealed against by Philip Morris (not the Dutch government) but the Court of Justice supported the Commission in its original Decision (ECJ 730/79).

The Commission has also had to contend with various aids to employment. It has tended to favour schemes which create new jobs as opposed to those which maintain existing ones. It is possible to detect a certain softness of approach in this area which undoubtedly is a reflection of current economic difficulties faced by all states. Certainly the UK scheme for employment subsidies for young workers, introduced in 1975, was acceptable to the Commission as apparently has the more recent youth opportunities scheme. However the Temporary Employment Subsidy (TES) met a much different fate. The continued prolongation of the arrangement gave rise to protests from other member states, not least because the bulk of the assistance was concentrated on the textile, clothing and footwear industries. When in January 1978 the UK proposed to continue to operate the scheme in the fiscal year 1978/9 the EC Commission intervened and compelled it to curtail the budget drastically and the degree to which firms and certain industries could benefit (ECC 1979a, 161-3). In 1979 the TES was finally dropped.

Before we turn to the Paris Treaty we should note that there are other aspects of state aid policy with which we have not dealt. The Commission is currently very interested in state aid to *public* enterprises – we shall discuss this in Chapter 5. It should also be noted that the transport section of the Rome Treaty contains provisions relating to aids and the reader's attention is directed to Articles 77 and 80. Aids are also permitted in agriculture – see Article 42. The Commission has for a long time been trying to harmonize the aids given to farmers – these constitute an extremely important part of farm income and can distort the working of the Common Agricultural Policy (CAP).

Article 4 of the Paris Treaty takes a firm stance on state aids and subsidies. They are, in any form whatsoever, incompatible with the treaty. Article 67 complements this by providing the authority for the EC Commission to take action against aids. It applies to all actions by states which have appreciable effects on the conditions of competition in the coal and steel industries – this obviously includes state aids. If aid granted by member state A has a harmful effect on the coal or steel industry in member state B then the EC Commission can authorize the government of member state B to grant aid to its industry. If this was the end of the matter it would imply that control merely amounted to allowing member state B to give aids to counter the effect of aids given by member state A. However this is not the case since Article 67 enables the EC Commission to make recommendations to member state A with a view to remedying the harmful effects.

The sweeping provision of Article 4 did not preclude the introduction of substantial subsidies. The first problem arose in the coal sector. At the time of drafting the Paris Treaty coal was the predominant source of energy supply in the Community. The coal industry was responsible for about three-quarters of the Community's primary energy supplies, oil contributing a mere 10 per cent. The competitive position of coal was strong and one of the major problems was curbing the market power of the coal cartels. However following the Suez Crisis the market position changed fundamentally. Progressively in the late 1950s and much of the 1960s the price of Community coal rose while the price of imported crude oil (and indeed imported US coal) fell. The competitive position of coal declined and coal output and employment fell. By the beginning of the 1970s oil was the predominant source of energy and coal had shrunk to a minority status – indeed the position was almost the reverse of that existing prior to the Paris Treaty.

The difficulties of the coal industry prompted member states, acting unilaterally, to subsidize their mines in order to cushion them from the impact of the new market realities. These subsidies were technically in breach of Article 4. It would have been possible to approach the problem via the introduction of a common energy policy. The old High Authority attempted to get such a policy off the ground. However it failed, partly because neither the Paris Treaty nor the two Rome Treaties called for such a policy, partly because of the difficulty arising from the fact that the various sources of energy were covered by three distinct and separate treaties but above all because of a lack of political will. Energy was abundant and becoming cheaper by the day – there was no overwhelming compulsion to act. Nevertheless these necessary subsidies had to be regularized. This was accomplished by the Protocol of Agreement of 1964 on energy problems. It set out some broad objectives of energy policy but in terms of practical relevance its most important contribution was that it recognized the need for support measures which would enable the industry to rationalize and adapt to the new market conditions. The High Authority was given the task of co-ordinating the aids in order to prevent competition from being distorted. A Decision was issued in 1965 (OJ

1965a) authorizing a system of *national* subsidies subject to prior approval by the High Authority. Article 95 provides a power which enabled the Community itself to institute subsidies which would otherwise have been banned by Article 4. The power to grant subsidies has been renewed from time to time and has continued even since the oil crisis. In defence of the latter it has been argued that the special circumstances in, and burdens laid upon, the coal industry continue to make aids necessary even though its competitive position has radically improved.

Subsidies for coal were followed by subsidies for coking coal and coke for the steel industry. These arose from the Protocol of Agreement of 1967 on coking coal and coke for the Community iron and steel industry. This was followed by the Decision of 1967 (OJ 1967a) laying down a system of subsidies – again this action was regularized by resort to Article 95. The impetus for this particular initiative was the difficulties arising from the import of cheap American coal. Because there is no *common* external tariff or *common* commercial policy under the Paris Treaty, member states are free to protect their coal industries, or alternatively to import coal at world prices. To the extent that member states tended to import American coal two effects were apparent. One was that countries such as the Netherlands and Italy which had sited their steel plants on the coast were in a good position to take advantage of these cheap supplies. On the other hand, West German iron and steel enterprises were highly dependent on the higher-priced domestic supplies. This distorted conditions of competition within the Community iron and steel market. The other effect was that cheap imported coal contributed towards a further erosion of the position of Community coal producers. The High Authority therefore proposed a subsidy for Community coking coal and coke. It was argued in justification that if no subsidy were given intra-Community imports would dry up as industry switched to imported supplies, and that the subsidy would help to buttress the domestic industry. Opposition was encountered from the French but eventually the Council of Ministers was able to agree to a subsidy system. Where coking coal and furnace coal produced in a particular member state was delivered to the steel industry of that state, the subsidies would be paid by the member state government concerned. For coking coal and coke entering into intra-Community trade the subsidies (which were to be limited in size) were to be financed from two sources. The producing country had to meet 40 per cent of the cost; the other 60 per cent was borne by a common fund. The Six contributed to the latter as follows: France 28 per cent, West Germany 28 per cent, Italy 14 per cent, Belgium 11 per cent, the Netherlands 10 per cent and Luxembourg 9 per cent. The ceiling for subsidies on intra-Community trade was initially to be 22 million Units of Account (UA). The power to grant subsidies has been renewed from time to time.

Not surprisingly the difficulties encountered by the steel industry since 1974, which gave rise to rescue operations under the titles of the Simonet and Davignon Plans, also forced member state governments to grant subsidies to their steel producing enterprises. The measures adopted to control these aids and to phase them out will be dealt with in detail in Chapter 7 when we come to review ECSC Industrial Policy.

Fiscal factors

In so far as non-tariff barriers can arise from fiscal factors it is the indirect rather than the direct tax which is responsible. In other words it was the turnover and excise tax systems of the various member states which were in need of modification.

It is not immediately obvious why indirect taxes of the turnover variety should give rise to a non-tariff barrier problem. The full import of that remark must, however, wait upon a discussion of two other issues. The first is the nature of turnover taxes as they existed within the Six at the time when the Rome Treaty was being drafted. The second is the traditional treatment of indirect taxes on goods entering into international trade.

Within the general category of turnover tax the Six operated two main kinds – the cascade and the value added systems. (The latter was of course adopted by the UK in place of purchase tax and selective employment tax partly in anticipation of British membership of the Community.) The French had opted for the Value Added Tax (VAT) but the rest of the Community applied cascade systems.

The cascade tax was a multi-stage tax in that it was levied at each stage of the productive process. In practice it covered a broad range of products. It was therefore unlike the old British purchase tax, which was a single-stage tax levied at the wholesale stage, covering a relatively narrow range of goods. Cascade taxes were levied on the gross value of output at each stage in the chain of production. The important point to note is the cumulative nature of the system: tax is applied at each stage upon the whole selling value including tax. If the product is used in further production, the selling price of the resulting product upon which tax is charged will be inflated by tax paid at the previous stage. Under the cascade system the cost of producing a given item excluding tax (that is, the value added) will be the same whether produced by a vertically integrated firm or by a vertical series of independent enterprises, but the tax paid on the product of the latter will be greater than that levied on the former.

The basic feature of VAT is that it is paid at each stage in the process of production upon the value added at each point in the productive chain. The final price of the product, in the absence of turnover tax, is equal to the sum of the values added at each point. Because of this fact it makes no difference whether the tax is collected at several points or as a single payment on the final product. The tax collected will be the same in either case – the tax is therefore neutral as between production which is carried out in a vertically integrated firm and production which is carried out by several separate firms with tax levied at the intermediate stages.

We turn now to the treatment of indirect taxes in international trade. (In practice we will assume that the trade takes place between members of a customs union.) Here we have to distinguish between the origin and destination principles. The origin principle can be explained as follows. Let us suppose that good X is manufactured in Country I and Country I applies a general turnover tax which amounts to 10 per cent on the cost of producing a good. If good X is exported to Country II it retains the 10 per cent tax and is thus delivered to consumers in Country II with the tax applied. Suppose that Country II applies a 20 per cent tax to good X which it produces itself then, other things being equal, good X coming from Country I has an artificial competitive advantage. Indeed if producers of X in Countries I and II are equally efficient then producers in Country II will find their sales falling as they are undersold by Country I producers.

In the case of the destination principle, however, good X produced in Country I will when exported have the 10 per cent tax remitted. It would thus be exported to Country II free of the tax and Country II would apply to it its own tax at the 20 per cent rate. In other words the exported good bears the tax of the country of destination and not of origin.

The importance of the remark made earlier is now clear. In the case of the destination principle, *and this is the principle normally applied in international trade*, good X produced in Country I and good X produced in Country II are treated equally, in terms of the tax levied on them, when sold in Country II. *Differences in tax rates do not therefore lead to distortions of competition between the two countries.* Why then does Article 99 of the Rome Treaty indicate a concern to harmonize the indirect tax systems of the member states?

In a large measure as far as turnover taxes are concerned the answer lies in a consideration of the problems encountered in remitting such taxes on exports when a cascade system is operating. Specifically the problem is that it is extremely difficult to know with any accuracy just how much tax is incorporated in the price of the good and therefore how much should be remitted. Too much may deliberately be remitted in which case an artificial export aid, and probably a concealed one at that, will operate. In this case we have a non-tariff barrier which *distorts* competition and which would indeed be a direct breach of Article 96 of the Rome Treaty which requires that

> Where products are exported to the territory of any Member State, any repayment of internal taxation shall not exceed the internal taxation imposed on them whether directly or indirectly.

There were however a number of other points which compelled action. Some were directly related to the non-tariff barrier problem – others were more broadly concerned with efficiency and the preservation of competition. From what has gone before it is evident that the cascade system gives an artificial incentive to vertical integration. This has several disadvantageous effects. First, it may be more efficient to specialize in one stage of a productive process, but the tax discourages this. There may, of course, be no advantage as between vertically integrated and non-vertically integrated firms from the point of view of productive efficiency. But the vertically integrated firm enjoys an artificial competitive advantage. Secondly, although from the view of maintaining competition it is usual to regard horizontal concentrations as the main problem, there are reasons for fearing the vertical variety. A firm which is integrated backwards can control supplies of raw materials and semi-finished products to competitors and force them out of business or force them to conform to its wishes. However, this problem arises only if firms at an earlier stage in the production process are concentrated horizontally, and this is not inevitable since the tax does not bias industrial structures in this way. But it could be argued that by integrating vertically an enterprise could acquire financial resources which would enable it to concentrate horizontally. Such resources would enable it to endure the price wars which might be necessary to discipline non-vertically integrated firms. Thirdly, there are reasons for believing that vertical integration in industry tends to impede cross-frontier competition. This argument is based on the proposition that in the absence of such integration firms at any stage of production have the alternative of buying the products of the previous stage either from domestic enterprises or from foreign firms. In effect an import gap exists. With vertical integration this possibility does not exist.

It should also be noted that while the destination principle eliminates any distortion of competition arising from different national rates of turnover tax, it does none the less give rise to a fiscal frontier. That is to say goods which pass over frontiers are subjected to a special taxation process which does not apply to goods sold within a state. Not only is there a psychological difference, in the sense that the market is thus not truly common, but also there are administrative procedures and expenses which materially discriminate against exports.

As we have already noted Article 99 of the Rome Treaty required the Commission to consider how the indirect tax systems of the member states could be harmonized in the interests of the common market. From what has gone before obviously the VAT was superior to the cascade system in that it is much easier to calculate the tax which has to be remitted on exports. The possibility of deliberate distortions is thus reduced. Also there is no incentive to vertical integration. It is not therefore entirely surprising that the Six should have decided in favour of the VAT as the form of turnover tax which all should adopt. In 1967 two Directives were adopted to this end (OJ 1967b; 1967c). Member states were to shift over to the VAT by 1 January 1970 but time extensions had to be granted to Italy and Belgium. The three new members posed no great problem since Ireland and Denmark had already gone over to this system before membership and as we noted earlier the UK had taken a decision to do so in 1971 although she did not actually introduce the system until April 1973. Greece has also operated a turnover tax of the value added type although it will require modification. The Third, Fourth and Fifth Directives were merely concerned with extensions of the original time limit. The Sixth Directive (OJ 1977b) was however important since apart from reiterating the conditions for zero rating, it prescribes the goods and services which are exempt from VAT and lays down detailed rules for the application of the tax.

It should however be noted that so far the Community has only agreed on the form of the tax. It has *not* agreed on a harmonized rate or set of rates. Actual rates differ considerably as can be seen from Table 3.2. Because of this the destination principle, and the fiscal frontier, still exist. Ultimately it is hoped that national rates will be harmonized. The Community could then shift to the origin system and the fiscal frontier would disappear.

Table 3.2 VAT rates in the EEC 1 July 1979 (per cent)

	Zero	Reduced	Standard	Intermediate	Increased
Belgium	—	6.0	16.0	—	25.0
Denmark	—	—	20.25	—	—
France	—	7.0	17.6	—	33.3
Germany	—	—	13.0	—	—
Ireland	0	10.0	20.0	—	—
Italy	—	1.0, 3.0, 6.0, 9.0 and 12.0	14.0	18.0	35.0
Luxembourg	—	5.0 and 2.0	10.0	—	—
Netherlands	—	4.0	18.0	—	—
UK	0	—	15.0	—	—

Source: ECC (1980b), 24–5

Excise duties have not posed the same kind of problems as the turnover tax. Distortions in connection with excessive remissions on export have not been a problem. An incentive to vertical integration does not arise. But the application of the destination principle does give rise to the fiscal frontier and here there is a parallel with the VAT while it remains unharmonized as to rates. Apart from the latter, which would disappear if national rates were harmonized and the origin system was adopted, it is not immediately apparent what non-tariff barriers arise under the present largely unharmonized excise arrangements.

However the EC Commission has observed some problems. For example, excise duties on mineral oils vary both in respect of the rates applied and the exemptions allowed therefrom. Here we are referring to the differences in the rates (for particular products) *as between states*. In so far as this product is an input in the production of other goods and services a distortion of competition is created through the differential effect on costs of production. On the other hand differences in the rate of excise duty on final products such as cigarettes, wine and spirits do not distort competition since the destination system places imports and home products on an equal footing. Ignoring the fiscal frontier, the situation in respect of mineral oils does not therefore provide a general case for harmonizing the rates of excise duty applied by the various member states to particular products since in most cases the destination principle comes to the rescue.

However there is also the problem of the differences in excise rates *as between products* in each member state and this the destination principle does not solve. The Commission can point to cases of unfair competition which arise from this factor. A good example was provided in the case of the *Commission* v. *Denmark*. Here Article 95 was at issue. The first part of the article requires that member state A must not apply an indirect tax on a particular product of member state B which is higher than the tax which member state A applies on the same product when produced domestically. However the article goes on to enjoin member state A not to apply an indirect tax on a particular product of member state B where the effect is to afford *indirect protection to other products* produced by member state A. The former would have applied if Denmark had imposed a higher excise duty to imported aquavit (or schnapps) than to domestically produced supplies thereof. However this it did not do but what it did do was to apply a higher excise duty on other spirits than on aquavit. Moreover a large part of domestic spirit consumption derived from domestically produced aquavit. There was no significant domestic production of other spirits (whisky, vodka, cognac, gin and rum) but about a quarter of Danish spirit consumption consisted of such products some of which were imported from other member states. In short Denmark applied a lower rate of excise duty on the consumption of spirits which it largely produced itself but imposed a higher excise on spirits which were more or less exclusively imported. This was regarded by the EC Commission as an offence under the second part of Article 95 and in that decision the Court of Justice concurred (ECJ 171/78). Similar issues were at stake in *Commission* v. *France* (ECJ 168/78), *Commission* v. *Italy* (ECJ 169/78) and *Commission* v. *UK* (ECJ 170/78). In the latter the EC Commission drew attention to the lower excise applied to beer than to wine. One of the problems which arose was how the incidence of duty was to be calculated. The Commission based its comparison on alcoholic content by unit of volume where a marked element of discrimination existed. However against that it was argued that the comparison ought to be on the basis of the volume of beverages normally offered to consumers. That would have entailed a comparison between, say, a pint of beer and a glass of wine. On that basis the tax burden was indeed almost identical. Because of this difficulty the case before the Court of Justice was not resolved. The Commission and the UK government were ordered to re-examine the issues and to report back, after which the Court undertook to render a final judgement. In 1981 the Commission duly reported and in July 1983 the Court finally found in favour of the Commission.

Clearly the kind of problems which have arisen with mineral oils and beverages would not exist if excises were harmonized as between products and as between states.[4] For this to happen it will be necessary to agree on the products which are to be subject to excise duty – at present there are wide variations between states. The EC Commission would like to see the tax confined to tobacco, beer, alcohol, wine and mineral oils with an agreement that member states should not thereafter extend the coverage. It will also be necessary to agree on common structures – these too vary with some taxes taking a lump sum or specific form and others being based on an *ad valorem* or percentage system. The actual rates would have to be harmonized or brought nearer together. As yet little progress has been made in this area. As early as 1972 a programme of harmonization was proposed by the Commission but little has been achieved. The only notable step has been a series of directives on tobacco products which envisage the ultimate harmonization of rates. The concrete element of these directives has been concerned with the tax structure for cigarettes. The Community system will be part specific and part *ad valorem*.

Turnover taxes are not explicitly referred to in the Paris Treaty. The only taxes to which it alludes are those which are equivalent to import or export duties and they are prohibited under Article 4. Quite early on however a dispute broke out between the Germans and the French on the proper treatment to be accorded to turnover taxes. The French supported the destination principle, the Germans the origin principle. The High Authority therefore set up a committee of economists to analyse the matter so that an appropriate solution might be devised. While there are some who would consider this a dangerous proceeding with the possibility that a diversity of opinions would result, in fact a very useful analysis of the tax problem of partial integration emerged. The committee recommended that the destination principle should be retained and the High Authority accepted the advice.

Technical standards

Member states interfere on a very considerable scale in establishing standards. These are laid down for a variety of reasons of which a desire to protect the public against physical harm and deception are high on the list. In the case of drugs and proprietary medicines the need for government surveillance and control is obvious. The experience with Thalidomide leaves no doubt on that score. In the UK, for example, under the Medicines Act 1968 a licence is required before products can be marketed. The licensing body is the Department of Health and Social Security which has a number of committees to assist it including the Committee on Safety of Medicines. In the case of foods, standards have to be set in relation to both contaminants and additives. The former are such things as lead and mercury which tend to find their way into food but must not exceed certain levels. Additives consist of preservatives, antioxidants, colouring agents, flavourings, sweeteners, emulsifiers and stabilizers. Again standards have been established which lay down the kind of substances which are permitted additives and prescribe in what quantity they can be incorporated in foods. Certain substances are banned, for example the sweetening agent cyclamate. Consumer durables, such as electrical equipment and cars, can also give rise to injury and so national legislation prescribes safety standards, the relevant UK legislation being the Consumer Safety Act of 1978.

Where the consumer is not likely to be harmed he may be deceived. For this reason there are rules on labelling designed to indicate to the consumer what certain designations, for example of textiles, really mean. Standards are also laid down about the quality of key ingredients incorporated in certain products, e.g. fruit in jam.

The laying down of standards or standardization is also an important factor in the manufacturing sphere. Standard specifications for products and components, from the size of screws upwards, greatly facilitate manufacturing efficiency.

The desirability of such standards is not in question but to the extent that they differ significantly between states they do undoubtedly constitute a non-tariff barrier (and may be deliberately exploited to that end). Either they mean that goods cannot be exported with a consequent loss of competition across frontiers, or if they are exported they have to be adapted to the rules of each national market. Either way the economies of large-scale production, in the form of longer runs of a standardized product, are sacrificed. There are also other benefits which are lost.[5]

A solution to the problem is to harmonize standards. This was recognized by those who drafted the Rome Treaty, the relevant article being Article 100 which enables the Council of Ministers, *acting unanimously* on a proposal from the EC Commission, to issue *directives* for the approximation (read 'harmonization') of provisions laid down by law, regulation or administrative action in the member states which directly affect the creation and functioning of the common market.

Harmonization measures fall into either the 'total' or 'optional' category. Total harmonization requires that all products covered by the directive must conform to the standards set out in the directive. In such a case national standards have to be abolished and the Community standard substituted. Such total harmonization is usually adopted when consumer safety is involved (e.g. cosmetics) although this approach was also adopted in the case of textile labelling which was purely informational. Optional harmonization permits the parallel existence of Community and national rules. Manufacturers who produce in accordance with the Community standard acquire access to all national markets while those who continue to apply only national standards have access only to their home market.

In passing it should be noted that the standards that are specified as appropriate for products marketed in the EEC are usually consistent with internationally accepted standards. In certain cases the standards conform to those issued by the International Standards Organization but in addition there are a variety of European bodies whose work also provides a basis for EEC norms (Dennis 1981, 20).

By 1980 the Council of Ministers had adopted 136 directives relating to industrial products and over fifty concerned with foodstuffs. Within the industrial category major progress has been made in the fields of motor vehicles, metrology (measuring instruments), cosmetics, solvents (and other dangerous substances) and electrical equipment. About forty directives have been adopted in respect of motor vehicles (dual circuit breaking systems, safety glass, etc.) and in addition over a dozen have been introduced to deal with tractors. The EC

Commission can now boast that in the case of cars its achievements represent a higher degree of harmonization than exists between the states of the USA. Directives have been introduced which govern the composition, labelling and packaging of beauty products. In respect of composition a list of 'positive' constituents has been drawn up. Their use is permitted while 'negative' constituents are banned. In the case of foodstuffs, directives govern their labelling (e.g. durability, additives used), packaging (restriction on the use of PVC), presentation, advertising and composition. Additives have been subject to provisions specifying maximum levels.

Although significant progress has been made major problems do exist. First, the harmonization process is extremely time-consuming by virtue of, among other things, the degree of consultation which is necessary. The EC Commission estimates that at least 300 directives are necessary in the industrial field alone so that a lot yet remains to be achieved. Secondly, there is the problem of obsolescence as a result of the onward march of technical progress. The Community has therefore been forced to adopt a speedier process for amendments to standards or what in Brussels are called adaptations to technical progress. Thirdly, under Article 100 the Community's harmonization powers can only be used where legislation, regulations or administrative measures exist within member states. Standards institutions operating on behalf of industry under private law and standards fixed by companies for their subcontractors do not fall within the ambit of Article 100 harmonization.

Earlier, in Chapter 2, it was indicated that we would return to the *Cassis de Dijon* case. The reason for this is that *Cassis de Dijon* and related cases have profound implications for harmonization. They suggest that the burden of harmonization may not be as great as was originally thought. At one stage the EC Commission came forward with a variety of harmonization measures covering products such as beer, bread, toys, and so on. However the ruling in *Cassis de Dijon* would appear beneficially to sound the death knell for such activities and to inject an additional safeguard, if one is needed, for national individuality. The point is that in its ruling the Court of Justice observed that any product legally made and sold in one member state must in principle be admitted to the market of any other member state. Even if national rules apply without distinction to domestic and imported goods, member states may create barriers to imports only where these are necessary to satisfy 'mandatory requirements' such as public health, fair trading, consumer protection, etc. Moreover any such rule must be the 'essential guarantee' of the interest the protection of which is recognized as justified.

All this sounds rather complicated! What does it mean in practical terms? If we examine the pleading in *Cassis de Dijon* we find that the German government defended the minimum alcoholic content rule on the grounds of the protection of the consumer. But the Court of Justice observed that such an end could equally well be served by merely requiring suppliers to indicate on the label the actual alcoholic contents. If that rule was adopted the legitimate national desire to protect the consumer would be satisfied and *Cassis*-type liqueurs could be imported. The actual rule employed was not *essential* to guarantee the protection of the consumer.

From all this we should not conclude that harmonization is now redundant. Certainly a lot of national differences will not be essential in the *Cassis de Dijon* sense and in such cases goods having been legitimately sold in one member state market will have to be admitted to others – a point which the Commission has made in a Communication to member states (OJ 1980d). However we recollect that Article 36 does indentify certain interests which do enable member states to restrict imports and where these national rules are the essential guarantee of those interests then harmonization must remain the only way forward.

The harmonization of technical standards which has been a topic of much debate and some acrimony in the EEC, has been a totally uncontroversial aspect of ECSC activity. Euronorms are harmonized technical specifications for steel products. They are drawn up and published under the aegis of the EC Commission and are adopted by the Co-ordinating Committee on Nomenclature for Iron and Steel Products, on which each member state is represented.

Finally the reader should note that the subject of harmonization of technical standards has been an ingredient of industrial policy and more will be said on the topic in Chapter 6.

Legal obligations

Since at least 1972 the EEC has been developing a policy on consumer protection. Apart from the harmonization, to which we have just referred, the EC Commission has tabled draft directives on matters such as unit pricing, door-step selling and product liability. These are not matters of central concern to this book except the latter.

Product liability refers to the liability of a producer towards a consumer who is injured or killed when using or in some way consuming his product. National laws on this matter vary. Some, as for example that of the UK, require the injured party to prove negligence on the part of the manufacturer.[6] On the other hand some laws adopt a 'strict liability' approach whereby a producer is automatically liable for goods which lead to death or material injury. No proof of fault or negligence is necessary. These laws may also make manufacturers bear the development risk. In other words the producer is still liable even if at the time the good was produced it was from a scientific point of view regarded as harmless – i.e. the subsequent harm was unknowable. Thus if a strict liability approach, with the development risk falling on the producer, had been operative in the UK when the Thalidomide tragedy occurred, there would have been an automatic case for compensation even though at the time when it was marketed the drug was, in the light of the existing scientific knowledge, thought to be harmless.

Manufacturers can insure against claims but obviously the cost of the insurance will vary according to the posture of the law. Laws, such as that of the UK, tend to make it difficult to establish a claim because proving negligence is extremely difficult. Insurance costs will be modest whereas they will be heavier when strict liability prevails. The EC Commission, noting that the laws of the member states vary, has drawn the conclusion that insurance costs will also vary and that this distorts competition. It also argues that the decision whether or not to sell in a market may be influenced by the kind of claims which may arise there. The Commission has therefore proposed that national laws be harmonized. It has also sought to kill two birds with one stone by espousing a measure which would improve the position of many consumers. To these ends it proposed in 1976 that national laws should be modified so as to provide for strict liability with the development risk falling on producers (OJ 1976b). The draft directive is still under discussion.

Public purchasing

The public sector – that is to say central and local government and nationalized bodies – is a major spender in the economic systems of

Western economies. Such public spending does not always take place in a non-discriminatory way. Rather than accepting the cheapest and/or best offers, the institutions of the public sector often adopt 'buy national' attitudes. The motives are various, but include balance of payments considerations, the desire to build up particular industries (for example computers), prevention of unemployment and sheer prestige.

This discriminatory behaviour is contrary to Articles 7, 30 and 34 of the Rome Treaty. It is also a breach of Directive 70/50/EEC (OJ 1970a) which prohibits measures, imposed by law, regulation or administrative practice, which prevent the supply of imported products from other member states, which grant domestic products a preference or which make the supply of imported products more difficult or costly than domestic products.

The EEC Commission recognized the seriousness of this problem early on and in 1960 indicated that it had already begun to analyse it. The initial focus was on public works contracting; however, it is apparent that substantial problems were encountered and progress was extremely slow. Work was also begun on public procurement contracts. Draft directives were subsequently submitted to the Council of Ministers in respect of both these topics. The Council first took action in respect of public works contracting. In 1971 it issued three directives. The first (OJ 1971a) swept away all obstacles to the freedom to supply services, the second (OJ 1971b) drew up common rules for the awarding of contracts and the third (OJ 1971c) established an advisory committee on the subject of public works contracting. The second directive relates to contracts of 1 million UA or more but leaves those relating to energy and water for separate treatment. As a result of this directive contractors throughout the Community are guaranteed free and effective competition on all major public works contracts offered by member states. Contractors are informed of pending contracts through the Community's *Official Journal*. Competent authorities are obliged to accept tenders from all qualified contractors in the Community and are required to award contracts on purely economic and non-discriminatory grounds. All discrimination of a purely technical nature was to be eliminated. A complaints procedure has been established. In 1976 the Council followed up with a directive on public procurement – it was officially described as a directive co-ordinating procedures for the award of public supply contracts (OJ 1977c). As a result central, regional and local authorities in seeking to award public supply contracts in excess of 200,000 EUA must publish a notice in the *Official Journal*, giving potential tenderers all the information needed to make an offer. In considering tenders the contract-awarding authority must treat all offers equally - i.e. there must be no discrimination between home and foreign bids. Because of differences of legal status the purchases of transport, telecommunications, water, gas and electricity authorities were not included. The settlement of complaints will be dealt with by the body which discharges that role in respect of public works contracts. It has been given the title of Advisory Committee for Public Contracts.

Despite all this legislative activity the EC Commission has recently had to take action to deal with discriminatory purchasing behaviour on the part of member states. In 1981 it instituted cases against France (OJ 1981a) and Ireland (OJ 1981b). Both were accused of encouraging and promoting the purchase of domestic goods in preference to imported ones - a breach of Article 30 of the Rome Treaty and of the obligations set out in Directive 70/50/EEC.

As we have seen discrimination is banned under the Paris Treaty. Such activity in connection with public purchasing does not however seem to have been a major problem. Public purchasing, like the harmonization of technical standards, has been an element of industrial policy and the reader's attention is also drawn to Chapter 6.

State monopolies

At this point we shall deal with state monopolies *of a commercial character* - a phenomenon singled out for attention by Article 37 of the Rome Treaty. At the outset our basic question must be - how do we identify such monopolies? Are they, for example, to be equated with nationalized industries?

The rulings of the Court of Justice throw some light on this question. Equally, the phenomena to which the EC Commission has addressed itself also give us a clue. In the *Italy* v. *Giuseppi Sacchi* case (ECJ 155/73) the Court made it clear that Article 37 covers only state monopolies of *goods* - the Court decided this on the basis that Article 37 is located in that part of the treaty which relates to restrictions on the free movement of goods. In the *Flaminio Costa* v. *ENEL* case (ECJ 6/64) the Court considered that the nationalization of the electricity industry in Italy and the marketing of electrical power by the state was not 'commercial'. The Court decided that 'to come within the terms of the prohibition of this article, national monopolies and bodies must on the one hand have as objects transactions in commercial products capable of competition and exchanges between Member States; and on the other hand play a leading part in such exchanges'. These two points seem automatically to exclude nationalized industries engaged in transport, gas, electricity, water and broadcasting. The EC Commission for its part has directed its attention at a limited number of state monopolies. In the case of France they were concerned with alcohol, manufactured tobacco, explosives and gunpowder, matches, potash, basic slag and aspects of the petroleum industry. In Germany the sole example was afforded by alcohol. In Italy there was a substantial list including manufactured tobacco, cigarette papers, lighters, flints, matches, salt and saccharin. Some of these goods have an inelastic demand which makes them ideal for manipulation with a view to state revenue raising.

Arrangements have varied from monopoly to monopoly but recurring elements have been either exclusive powers in relation to manufacturing or a monopoly of the purchase (and thus resale) of private output, together with a control over the various aspects of the marketing mix which has extended to wholesaling and, in the case of consumer goods, retailing. In the case of the French manufactured tobacco monopoly retailers have been licensed, only nationals have been admitted to the trade. French retailers have in fact been classed as public servants. State monopolies have also enjoyed exclusive powers in relation to imports and exports – the former being a critically important element in the overall scheme of control.

These monopolies have restricted trade flows in a variety of ways. Let the EC Commission speak for itself:

> To give but a few examples, mention should be made of the clear refusal to import, of quantitative restrictions of imports, of the imposition of more onerous marketing conditions for imported products than those applied to national products, or of conditions which are discriminating against the advertising of foreign products or against information [as] to imported products as far as retailers are concerned. (ECC 1972, 148–9)

This is a very brief catalogue and for details of the rich variety of actual restrictions and discriminations the reader is referred to the EC Commission's annual *Reports on Competition Policy*. Here he will be able to observe a long-drawn-out war of attrition, perhaps an elaborate game of cat and mouse is a more apt description, in which the EC Commission has secured what it thought were satisfactory arrangements only to discover yet further layers of restriction and discrimination!

Article 37 does not require the abolition of these monopolies – a point which was reiterated by the Court in the *Pubblico Ministero* v. *Manghera* case (ECJ 59/75). Rather it requires that during the transition period (both for the Six and new members) they should be *adjusted* so as to eliminate *discrimination* regarding the conditions under which goods are procured and marketed between nationals of the member states. Member states are also required to refrain from subsequently introducing new measures which involve such discrimination. (The reader should also consult Article 90 – it too has implications for state monopolies. This matter is discussed in Chapter 5 when we review policy towards public enterprises.)

The task of the EC Commission was significantly eased by virtue of the fact that a number of monopolies were totally abolished and others were reformed in various ways. As a result, although not without some pressure on the part of the EC Commission, explosives, gunpowder, potash, slag and matches in France and salt, cigarette papers, lighters, flints and saccharin in Italy ceased to be matters of major concern. The hard-core problems were alcohol, manufactured tobacco and petroleum in France, alcohol in Germany and manufactured tobacco and matches in Italy.

One of the main themes of the Commission's attack was the need to eliminate the monopoly control over imports, thus hopefully opening up national markets to supplies from other member states. As early as 1970 it secured the agreement of the Italian and French governments to the removal by 1976 of such monopolies in respect of manufactured tobacco. In this it was supported by the Court of Justice in the *Manghera* case which maintained that such exclusive rights to import were a discrimination of the kind which is prohibited by Article 37. The Commission therefore had a general authority to support it and in due course member states fell into line. Germany and France terminated their exclusive import rights in respect of alcohol, France and Italy did likewise in the case of imported manufactured tobacco while Italy had earlier made this adjustment in its arrangements for matches. The French government's system of authorization in relation to the import of petroleum was also significantly liberalized in 1979 (ECC 1980a, 128–30).

As we have seen in this area of policy matters are rarely as simple as they seem. Two other problems have been encountered by the Commission. First, even if exclusive import rights are eliminated it is still possible for a state monopoly to protect the sale of domestic products by imposing levies on imported products, by imposing higher taxes on imported than on domestic products or by granting domestic producers tax concessions or exemptions which are not extended to imports. Equally the protective element can be achieved by subsidizing the production and sale of domestic products. The Court of Justice dealt with problems of this kind in a clutch of cases including *Rewe Zentrale des Lebensmittel - Grosshandels eGmbH* v. *Hauptzollamt Laudau/Pfalz* (ECJ 45/75), *HZA Göttingen* v. *Miritz* (ECJ 91/75) and *Hansen GmbH* v. *Hauptzollamt Flensburg* (ECJ 91/78).

Miritz is a classic case of protective action. Following a Recommendation by the EC Commission the West German government decided to modify its alcohol monopoly. It opened up its frontiers to imports but in the case in question (which related to citrus peel distillates) it applied a variable levy for the purpose of offsetting the difference between the selling price of the product in the exporting state and the higher price paid by the national monopoly to domestic producers of the corresponding product. The matter was referred by a West German court to the Court of Justice for a preliminary ruling and the latter declared against the practice on the basis of Article 37. *Rewe* was a somewhat complicated case. It too was concerned with the West German alcohol monopoly and again involved a request for a preliminary ruling. The product under consideration was imported Italian Vermouth and the issue was the tax treatment accorded to the imported product as compared with domestic competitors. The tax consisted of a straight excise element together with a component which related to the cost of operating the monopoly. However although tax was levied on both domestic and imported products the actual mode of operation led to discrimination against imports by virtue of differences in the size of the monopoly cost element. The Court observed:

> There is, in fact, no discrimination within the meaning of Article 37 where the imported product is subject to the same conditions as the similar domestic product subject to the monopoly. On the other hand, both Article 95 and Article 37 of the Treaty are infringed if the charge imposed on the imported product is different from that

imposed on the similar domestic product which is directly or indirectly covered by the monopoly. (ECJ 45/75)

Hansen was yet another preliminary ruling relating to the German alcohol monopoly. As a result of the opening up of the German market and the consequent depression of prices (the consequence of earlier rulings which we have discussed) the monopoly found itself obligated to pay a price for the spirits (which had to be delivered to it) which was higher than that which it could obtain on resale. Consequently the consumption tax on spirits was raised and the proceeds thereof were used to finance the loss. In the absence of this aid or subsidy (which enabled domestic products to be sold at an artificially low price) these West German supplies would have been priced out of the market. As for the Court of Justice its view was that:

> Any practice by a State monopoly which consists of marketing a product such as spirits at an abnormally low resale price compared with the price, before tax, of spirits of comparable quality imported from another member-State is incompatible with Article 37(1) of the EEC Treaty. (ECJ 91/78)

These rulings considerably strengthened the hand of the EC Commission in rooting out discriminatory (and in effect protective) practices. For example, following *Hansen* the EC Commission directed criticism at the French alcohol monopoly. It too was selling alcohol at what the Commission described as exceptionally low prices and subsidizing the operation from public funds. France was called upon to bring its monopoly into line with the *Hansen* ruling (ECC 1980a, 128).

We mentioned that despite *Manghera* two problems continued to concern the Commission. The second one related to the French and Italian manufactured tobacco monopolies. The Commission was concerned among other things about the lack of independence of licensed retailers. This it felt might lead to them being pressurized into not dealing in imported products. This is one of a number of matters about which the Commission continues to express dissatisfaction and as yet these problems have not been resolved.

State monopolies are not so explicitly provided for in the Paris Treaty. When the old High Authority had to wrestle with one it based its action on Article 86 which obligates states to do what is necessary to accomplish the Treaty's aims and to refrain from measures incompatible with the common market. The case arose in connection with the Association Technique de l'Importation Charbonnière (ATIC), a body to which the French government had granted the exclusive right to import coal. Even the largest buyers of imported coal, such as French steel firms, could not conclude contracts independently with, say, their Ruhr suppliers but had to do so via ATIC. The High Authority felt that this limitation on the buyer's freedom was incompatible with the Treaty and, after protracted litigation, was able to secure the French government's agreement to ATIC losing its power to veto contracts in respect of coal imported from other Community countries.

Administrative barriers

The movement of goods across frontiers is still considerably burdened by various administrative procedures and requirements. In what can only be described as an angry outburst the EC Commission in 1981 observed that twenty-three years after the formation of the EEC the fact that 'the elimination of frontier formalities is still lagging behind that achieved in the Nordic Union must raise doubts as to the success of the internal market' (ECC 1981a). The Commission has drawn attention to the fact that customs clearance procedures within the Community are scarcely different from customs procedures with non-member countries. There are too many documents and there are unnecessary complications with VAT and the collection of statistics. A real attempt should be made to create simpler conditions which are closer to those which apply to domestic trade. The Commission estimates that the present excessive procedures increase the cost of goods by 5–10 per cent. In earlier days the High Authority had to contend with these problems in connection with ECSC goods.

4 Non-tariff barriers – cartels

Introduction

In this chapter we shall be dealing with cartels. The word cartel can have a very specific meaning but we intend it to cover a wide range of phenomena which are often referred to as restrictive business practices. We shall regard these two terms as interchangeable. Here we are concerned with collusive arrangements between otherwise independent firms in which they restrict their competitive behaviour, one against the other. We must also take account of behaviour which takes the form of the imposition of restrictions upon the market activity of other firms. An example of the former would be a price fixing agreement. The latter is exemplified by an agreement between a producer group and a dealer group in which they both agree to deal exclusively with each other and thus exclude producers and dealers not party to the arrangements. Such exclusions may be imposed individually as well as collectively. For the most part, and in contrast to the previous chapter, the phenomena under scrutiny will be private in character. The caveat 'for the most part' is necessary because from time to time we may encounter cases where state-owned enterprises join forces with the private variety in order to restrict competition.

In this area of policy the EC Commission is dealing with an extremely wide and sometimes complex range of practices. While we cannot identify all of them it is appropriate that we highlight the more important kinds of problem with which the Commission has to deal. It is important to recollect that under the Rome Treaty only those restrictive business practices which may affect inter-state trade fall due for consideration. The Paris Treaty, as we noted earlier, contains no such limitation.

High on the list must be agreements which fix prices. Here we are thinking of horizontal arrangements in which firms at one stage in the chain of production and distribution come together to fix the prices at which they will sell to enterprises further down the line. The object may be to achieve a collective market power which enables the firms concerned to raise prices above the competitive level. However it does not follow that the inevitable objective of such arrangements is to exploit consumers to the maximum. Rather the intention may be to secure a degree of market stability. In any case we need to recognize that a policy of extracting the maximum from the consumer may prove to be only a short-run advantage. If there are firms outside the agreement, or firms waiting to enter the industry, then short-run profit maximization may induce existing outside competitors to expand production and new firms to enter the industry. Even if all existing and potential EEC suppliers are party to the agreement we have to acknowledge the existence of competitors in the European Free Trade Association (EFTA) and elsewhere who enjoy tariff-free entry into the Community and of course enterprises in countries such as Japan and the USA may be able to offer effective competition even though they have to sell over the common external tariff.

Price fixing may occur within national export cartels. Here a group of suppliers located in one member state collectively determine the price that they will charge when exporting to other member states. In passing we should note that national export cartels, relating not just to prices but also to other matters such as markets to be supplied, often enjoy a privileged status in domestic antitrust laws. The latter frown on price fixing, for example, which affects domestic consumers but foreigners are regarded as fair game! However in the Community foreigners in other member states are not fair game although foreigners outside the Community are. Price fixing may indeed be truly international. In such a case firms from more than one and possibly all member states collude as to the prices to be charged in intra-Community trade. We shall encounter an example later in which firms achieved this object by respecting (i.e. not undercutting) the price set by the national price leader in the member state to which they were exporting. Within the Community it has not been uncommon for prices to be fixed by a common selling syndicate or agency – a company owned by the producers to which they assign their output. The syndicate eliminates competition between the producers, sets the price for the combined output and pays them in proportion to deliveries to it.

In economics it is recognized that control over price may be direct, in which case the demand curve determines the quantity that will be purchased at that price. But equally control may be applied directly to the quantity supplied in which case the demand curve indirectly determines the price at which that quantity can be sold. It follows that cartels aiming to raise prices may seek to achieve that objective by a control over the amount supplied. A horizontal cartel which applies absolute production or sales quotas may so curtail the collective size of those quotas as to enhance the market price. Quotas however may be cast in proportionate rather than absolute terms, perhaps with penalties for over-fulfilment and rewards for under-fulfilment. Here the apparent effect is to share sales at the going price rather than to influence it. It is however possible that such an arrangement will help to keep the price level up since in order to keep within their proportionate quotas firms will be inclined to limit their competitive sales efforts. The proportionate quota may of course be ancillary to a price agreement, having the purpose of deterring secret sales below the agreed price level. A more radical approach may be adopted in which parties are required to take existing plant out of production and to desist from creating replacement capacity. It is sometimes argued that the latter may be justifiable where chronic excess capacity exists.

This brings us to market sharing, which may be geographic or by type of customer. Where this is practised by a national export cartel it merely eliminates any competition from cartel partners when the firm, to whom the foreign market has been allocated, exports its goods. A market sharing agreement may however be international in membership. In which case if all suppliers participate the arrangement confers upon individuals or groups a sole or collective monopoly (ignoring third country supplies) in a particular segment of the market. This will facilitate a control over price in each market segment.

We must also take account of exclusionary practices. These take several forms. Aggregated rebates may be employed in which customers enjoy a progressive rebate scale which is related to their purchases from the group *as a whole*. This tends to induce customers to concentrate their orders on the group at the expense of outsiders who may be located in other member states. Another important phenomenon is collective exclusive dealing which we discussed earlier. Here a group of suppliers persuades a group of dealers to sell the suppliers' goods only – if the group of suppliers is also bound to sell only through the group of dealers then the arrangement would constitute *reciprocal* collective exclusive dealing. Obviously the possibility exists that the suppliers shut out could be located in other member states.

We have already moved from the horizontal to the vertical since collective exclusive dealing is an arrangement between producers and dealers and not between producer and producer or dealer and dealer. Mention should also be made of the vertical practice of sole dealing since this is of particular relevance in the EEC context. When conducting sales domestically and in other member states, individual suppliers may undertake to restrict their supplying at the wholesale stage to an appointed sole dealer. Such an undertaking may be accompanied by territorial protection or what is sometimes called the no poaching provision. That is to say, dealers will be required, as a condition of their appointment, not to supply the retail trade in the territories of other concessionaires.

Our earlier references to arrangements relating to prices, quantities supplied, productive capacity, markets to be supplied, and so on, were all examples of agreements to charge certain prices, to sell certain quantities. But in addition we have to take account of information agreements. In such cases the parties do not, for example, *agree* about the prices to be charged but merely *inform* each other about the prices that have been charged, are being charged or will be charged. These arrangements can of course lead to results similar to those arising from price fixing. Thus one firm may act as price leader and the information agreement will provide the signals which the rest will follow. However although the information agreement may not explicitly refer to the fixing of prices it may provide a forum in which such collusion begins to emerge. The parties may seek to pass off the uniformity of price by alleging that it is the product of information exchange. These agreements are sometimes justified on the grounds that they enable sellers to deal with phantom competition, i.e. the quotation by customers of false low offers.

Not all agreements are necessarily motivated by a desire to restrict competition even though they may incidentally have that effect. Here we are thinking about various forms of what may be called efficiency-promoting agreements. In the case of specialization agreements firms may undertake not to produce a full range of products but to concentrate on certain lines and thus to enjoy more fully the economies of long runs. They may nevertheless supply each other with their specialisms in order to offer a full line to customers. Alternatively firms may come together to develop a new product or process and thus eliminate duplication of effort and expense – these are referred to as joint research and development agreements and are a form of joint venture.

Firms may also enter into standardization agreements in order to cut down wasteful and unnecessary profusion of specifications.

We must not neglect to mention agreements involving industrial and commercial property rights – i.e. arrangements in which patents, trade marks or copyrights are involved. The owner of a patent in one member state could license a firm in another member state to produce the patented goods. The licence could however preclude the licensee from selling the good in the territory of the patent owner. An inter-state effect is evident. Patents could be the basis of international cartels. Suppose there are several producers, each located in different states, who each possesses rival patents relevant to the production of a particular good. They could cross-license one another so that each in his own state had sole control over all relevant patented technology. The result would be a tight compartmentalization of national markets with no inter-state trade and competition.

EEC cartel rules and cases

THE MEANING OF ARTICLE 85

The key provisions are to be found in Rome Treaty Articles 3(f) and 85. Article 3 lays down the general objectives of the Treaty – internal tariffs shall be eliminated; there shall be a common external tariff against the rest of the world; there shall be a common agricultural policy, and so on. As we noted earlier Article 3(f) calls for the creation of conditions that guarantee that competition in the common market is not distorted – a provision which is of course relevant to other non-tariff barriers. It is however in Article 85 that the substantive law is to be found. That article, which is in three parts, is reproduced in the Appendix. We will look at each of these parts in turn. However, before we do so we should note that differences exist between national antitrust systems in their approach to restrictions of competition. Some laws regard the preservation of competition as paramount. A restriction of competition is *per se* illegal and no mitigating arguments will be accepted. The task of the antitrust enforcement agency is merely to satisfy those sitting in judgement that collusion exists and an adverse decision automatically follows. This is the posture adopted in US federal law. Other laws initially prohibit agreements, or as in the case of the UK regard them as contrary to the public interest, but then provide for the possibility of exemption in certain defined circumstances. Some laws adopt a neutral position: they declare neither in favour nor against restrictions of competition but provide for investigation and enable prohibitions to be handed down when abuse is found to exist. Some countries simply do nothing. As we shall see, the EEC law is of the second category.

Article 85(1) contains the basic prohibition while Article 85(2) goes on to declare that prohibited agreements are null and void. The latter implies that it would be illegal to operate them or seek to enforce them in the courts. Article 85(3) defines the circumstances under which an agreement, which would otherwise be prohibited, can in fact be exempted.

The Article 85(1) prohibition applies to agreements, to the decisions of associations of enterprises and to concerted practices. By casting the net so wide the Commission is empowered to catch most forms of collusive activity. An agreement obviously relates to those undertakings which can be contractually enforced in the courts. But it can apply where not all the characteristics of a civil law contract are present. In the *Franco-Japanese Ballbearings* case (OJ 1974a) there was an auto-limitation agreement between French and Japanese producers which was designed to take the edge off import competition by requiring the Japanese to raise their prices. As it happened the arrangement had implications not only for direct imports to France but also for Japanese ballbearings entering indirectly via other member states. More to the point the central feature of the agreement was an exchange of letters between the French and Japanese trade associations. In the *Quinine* case (OJ 1969a) the Commission's adverse decision quite explicitly addressed itself to a gentleman's agreement which, among other things, consisted of a written document that was not signed.

A decision of association of enterprises enables the Commission to deal with the quite frequent situation where restrictive measures are agreed within the ambit of a trade association. It will be assumed that each member has participated in the making of association decisions. Firms will not be able conveniently to plead that they did not agree with this or that particular association decision and are therefore not involved. It should be noted that a decision of an association of enterprises also covers a situation where a trade body makes a recommendation to members in which there is no obligation to comply. This was so in the *VCH* case (ECJ 8/72), where the Court of Justice argued that the recommended prices were not devoid of effect in that they permitted the parties involved to foresee with reasonable accuracy what the behaviour of their rivals was likely to be. There was, it should be added, an obligation to make a profit.

The concerted practice concept is of particular interest because it requires us to recognize that there are more subtle and less formal methods of concerting behaviour in the market-place. One firm may make a representation to another; such representation may, for example, be an indication of the price it intends to charge in respect of a particular transaction or class of transactions. The representation is intended as an inducement to the other firm to charge the same price, and the other firm realizes this and signals its willingness to conform by falling into line. Over time there may indeed emerge a sustained pattern of behaviour in which successive representations are made which successively induce matching responses. A parallelism of action emerges without there being a formal agreement. It is situations like this that have inspired the need for concepts such as the concerted practice and they enable antitrust authorities to deal with situations where the more formal kinds of collusion may not be admitted or indeed may not exist. The concept was first used in the *Aniline Dye* case in which the Commission produced evidence of equiproportionate price increases introduced by the main European dyestuffs producers within a few days of each other (OJ 1969b). Moreover the instructions addressed by the firms to their subsidiaries and representatives in some cases showed great similarity in drafting even to the extent of using exactly identical phrases. However the accused did not admit that an agreement existed but argued that the parallelism was the inevitable product of an oligopolistic market structure. The Commission for its part argued that the parallelism was the result of a concerted practice and when the matter was further considered on appeal it offered the following definition of such a practice:

> In order that there should be a concerting, it is not necessary that the parties should draw up a plan in common with a view to adopting a certain behaviour. It suffices that they should mutually inform each other in advance of the attitudes they intend to adopt, in such a way that each can regulate its action in reliance on its competitors behaving in a parallel manner. (ECJ 48/69)

The Court upheld the Commission's decision and in doing so observed that a concerted practice was 'a form of co-ordination between undertakings which, without going so far as to amount to an agreement properly so called, knowingly substitutes a practical co-operation between them for the risks of competition'. In the *Sugar* cases the Court amplified the concept saying:

> Although it is correct to say that this requirement of independence does not deprive economic operators of the right to adapt themselves intelligently to the existing and anticipated conduct of their competitors, it does however strictly preclude any direct or indirect contact between such operators the object or effect thereof is either to influence the conduct on the market of an actual or potential competitor or to disclose to such a competitor the course of conduct which they themselves have decided to adopt or contemplate adopting. (ECJ 40–48/73)

In short the Court lays emphasis on conscious efforts to evoke matching responses from competitors as opposed to mere parallelism of prices.

Indeed in *Aniline Dyes* the Court expressly declared that a parallelism of prices was not sufficient proof of the existence of a concerted practice although it constituted a strong indication that one existed, particularly when it led to prices above the equilibrium level expected from competition. This reluctance to accept price parallelism as a proof of collusion is well founded. Markets that are perfectly competitive, and which can indeed, in terms of the absence of market power, be said to be the very acme of competition, will exhibit a uniformity of price. But even markedly different structures, such as oligopoly, may also have the same quality. In such a market, price uniformity could in certain cases be said to be a product of commercial prudence rather than of conspiracy. Thus if a firm raised its price above the going level its sales would fall drastically, particularly if the products were not greatly differentiated. Such an increase might not therefore be ventured. Equally, lowering the price below the going level might provoke a matching cut which would render the initiating price reduction not worthwhile.

The various *forms* of collusion prohibited in Article 85(1) must have the effect of preventing, restricting or distorting competition in the common market. This provokes a whole series of points. First, we once more encounter drafting which enables most forms of effect to be caught. 'Prevent' is obviously the most serious and takes in a total preclusion. 'Restrict' refers to a less serious inhibiting effect. 'Distort' would cover behaviour such as the placing of other firms in unequal conditions. Second, the restrictive effect applies to buying as well as selling. Third, that effect applies to services as well as to goods. Fourth, the list of specific restrictions referred to in the article (see Appendix) is illustrative and not exhaustive. Fifth, the prohibition applies to restrictions of competition in the common market and not to restrictions by common market firms only. This has led the Commission to claim an extra-territorial jurisdiction for EEC antitrust law. At this point we should note that the antitrust laws of some countries (notably the US) claim to be able to exert a jurisdiction not only over companies located on their territories but also over companies, located outside, who by their actions have effects on those countries. This is basically what is known as the 'effects doctrine'. (It is of course one thing to claim such a jurisdiction and another to carry it into effect. Can the foreign company be compelled to come into court? Is there any way of effectively imposing a fine?) As we have seen in the *Aniline Dye* case companies involved in concerted practices were fined. Since ICI, a company incorporated under British law, was one of the firms fined, and this was prior to UK membership, an extra-territorial jurisdiction appeared to be claimed. Indeed, the Commission has always been firm on this point. In the *Aniline Dye* case it observed: 'This decision is applicable to all the undertakings which took part in the concerted practices, whether they are established within or outside the common market.' This gave rise to an appeal by ICI to the Court of Justice. The Commission could of course have addressed its prohibition merely to ICI's subsidiaries in the EEC, in which case a claim to an extra-territorial jurisdiction would not have arisen. In its appeal ICI did in fact plead that the prohibited behaviour was that of its subsidiaries and not of itself. The Court argued otherwise: the fact that the subsidiaries were distinct legal personalities did not dispose of the possibility that their behaviour could be imputed to the parent company. The subsidiaries being controlled by the parent, it was indeed reasonable to argue that what the former did was what the latter told them to do. In defence of this argument the Court observed as follows:

> The telex-messages relating to the 1964 increase which the applicant [i.e. ICI] had addressed to its subsidiaries in the Common Market, determined, in a manner binding on their addressees, the prices and other conditions of sale which they must impose in relation to their customers. (ECJ 48/69)

Although the point that subsidiaries do what parents tell them to do was a convenient way of justifying the imposition of a fine on the parent, and was consistent with a claim to an extra-territorial jurisdiction, it fell short of an unqualified application of the effects doctrine. What was needed was a case where a company, of a non-member state, that had no subsidiaries in the common market participated in an outside association that had restrictive effects upon the Community market. This is indeed what occurred in the *Genuine Vegetable Parchment* case (OJ 1978a). A Finnish company, Serlachius (a producer of wrapping paper for fatty substances), was a member of the Genuine Vegetable Parchment Association, an international trade association which had its headquarters in Sweden. There was no evidence in the Commission's decision that the Finnish company had any presence within the EEC; nevertheless it was fined for its participation in concerted practices affecting the EEC internal market.

Sixth, mention should be made of the fact that quite early on the EC Commission decided that competition had to be restricted to a noticeable or appreciable extent for Article 85(1) to be invoked. This idea can be traced back to the *Grossfilex* case (OJ 1964a) and was judicially confirmed by the Court in *Volk* v. *Vervaecke* (ECJ 5/69). This was followed in 1970 by a *Notice on agreements of minor importance* (OJ 1970b) which established a *de minimis* rule. Under the current provisions (OJ 1977c), if firms participating in an agreement have a market share that is not more than 5 per cent in a substantial part of the common market, and the aggregate annual turnover does not exceed 50 million UA, then the agreement does not fall under the Article 85 prohibition. Some flexibility above these limits is allowed.

Seventh, we should note that control of a subsidiary by a parent does not fall within the scope of the Article 85(1) prohibition. We are here thinking of situations where the subsidiary has no effective autonomy as regards its market operations: the parent and subsidiary will therefore be regarded as one economic unit. This point was established in *Christiani and Nielsen* (OJ 1969c) and has been confirmed in cases before the Court.

As we noted earlier for the Article 85(1) prohibition to apply the agreements which restrict competition must also be such that they 'may affect trade between Member States'. The word 'may' implies that this provision covers both agreements which actually do affect such trade and also those which have the potentiality to do so and may actually have that effect in the future even if not at present. The effect may be direct or it may be indirect. It would be direct if a group of firms in one member state agreed the prices which they charged for exports to other member states. It would be equally direct if various national groups decided to keep out of each other's national markets. It would be somewhat more indirect if producers and dealers in one member state agreed to deal exclusively with each other. Such an arrangement would not directly regulate inter-state trade but it would have the effect of inhibiting or even totally preventing the entry of third party supplies from without.

It would be easy to interpret the inter-state clause as meaning that the sin is to reduce the level of such trade below that which would obtain if the competitive restriction did not exist. However this is not true. An effect upon trade between member states also arises when a restrictive arrangement artificially stimulates it. In the *Cimbel* case (OJ 1972a) Belgian cement producers operated a price equalization scheme as between the home and other member state markets. The practical effect was to subsidize sales in the latter and thus to stimulate them. The Commission observed that the arrangement 'artificially distorts trade between the member states because exports which, if the agreement did not exist, would not take place or would be made to a country situated at a more favourable distance, are deflected from their natural channels'. In short trade must not be distorted one way or the other.

Most commentators would agree that the type of restrictions discussed above do run counter to the idea of economic integration based on competitive trade inter-penetration. But the reader is warned that decisions by the Commission and judgements by the Court indicate that the inter-state trade concept is capable of substantial whittling down. A good but by no means isolated example is provided by the *VCH* case. This involved a group of Belgian cement dealers who regulated the domestic sales of home-produced and imported cement. They did not totally monopolize such sales (since there were independent dealers) but they controlled two-thirds of the market. Originally the VCH dealers fixed the price for some categories of sale and recommended (as we noted earlier) prices in respect of others. The Court in finding against the VCH arrangement observed:

> An agreement which extends to the whole of the territory of a member-State has, by its very nature, the effect of consolidating a national partitioning, thus hindering the economic interpenetration to which the Treaty is directed and ensuring a protection for the national production. (ECJ 8/72)

It is undoubtedly true that the VCH system did *apply* to imports and thus affected them. Equally it can be argued that the restriction of dealer competition would have the effect of raising prices and therefore reducing the demand for imported cement. The effect however would be small since demand for cement is price inelastic. However it is crucial to recognize that the arrangements applied as much to domestic as to imported cement supplies. Because of that it could not be argued that the imported supplies were singled out for special price-enhancing treatment. Oddly enough the Commission, in a somewhat rambling decision, drew attention to the fact that imported cement was cheaper than the domestic variety and that the VCH system had the effect of equalizing prices and thus removing the competitive edge which the imports would otherwise enjoy. Curiously the Court did not explicitly seize on this point but dwelt upon the unamplified fact that the VCH arrangement had a large, although by no means total, share of the trade. It would be easy to dismiss *VCH* as a case of defective reasoning or poor drafting but there are other examples where a more tenuous approach has been applied. In this context the reader is invited to consider the more recent *Italian cast glass* case (OJ 1980e).

When we come to Article 85(3) we encounter the exemption aspect. In order for, say, an agreement to qualify for exemption four cumulative conditions must be met. (a) The agreement must contribute 'to improving the production or distribution of goods or to promote technical or economic progress'. (b) Then the consumer has to be considered – he must be allowed a fair share of the resulting benefit. Benefit may be a fall in price. In some specialization agreement cases (see the *Clima-Chappée-Buderus* case, OJ 1969d) the Commission has recognized that specialization would lower costs of production and has assumed that the competition still remaining would guarantee that the reduction of costs would be passed on in whole or part to the consumer. But benefit may also take other forms, such as a more rapid and easy availability of goods (see *Jallatte-Voss-Vandeputte* case, OJ 1966) or an improvement of quality and technical performance (see *Fabrique Nationale d'Armes de Guerre-Cartoucherie Française* case, OJ 1971d). The consumer has been interpreted by the Commission to include purchasers next in line as opposed to the final consumer. Thus in the *ACEC-Berliet* case (OJ 1968a) the operators of buses were regarded as recipients of the benefit derived from a co-operation and joint research and development agreement in the field of bus construction. (c) The agreement, in achieving the improvement and the fair sharing, must not impose restrictions that are not indispensable to the attainment of those objectives. (d) The agreement must not allow the parties to eliminate competition in respect of a substantial part of the products in question. Cartels which totally control the supply of a product will not be able to get by.

THE ENFORCEMENT OF ARTICLE 85

Enforcement powers are most important in this area of policy since those operating restrictive business practices are inclined to be secretive on this matter and are not in the habit of voluntarily presenting their handiwork for inspection by the antitrust authority. This implies a need for powers of discovery. Equally in order to assess the effects of an agreement the antitrust authority must be able to command those under investigation to supply information. At the end of the process if the authority decides to prohibit an agreement a power to impose sanctions will be necessary since in the absence thereof the parties to the agreement may be disposed to carry on as before.

This process of enforcement is in the hands of the EC Commission and various regulations have been introduced to equip it to discharge that function. The Commission has the formal power to prohibit, although as we might expect these formal decisions are subject to appeal to the Court of Justice.

The first and basic enforcement regulation was issued in 1962 (Regulation 17/62, OJ 1962c). It provided the Commission with a system of notification although unlike the British system notified agreements are not open to public inspection. Notification is clearly of assistance to the Commission in locating violations, but it is also helpful to businessmen in that it enables them to discover what is and what is not allowed. Although notification is not a duty, there is a strong incentive for companies to notify, since if they do not do so within the time limits that have been set there can be no question of their agreement being exempted. For example, in the *Quinine* case the parties were advised to notify but deliberately chose not to do so. Subsequently they were caught by the EC Commission (having previously been attacked by the US antitrust authorities) and, not having notified, they were denied the possibility of an exemption hearing and were indeed heavily fined.

When a group of companies introduces a new agreement they are well advised to notify immediately. If, for example, they introduce the agreement first and notify it at a later date, the act of notifying does not put an end to the pre-existing state of infringement. That is to say if, when the Commission comes to investigate the agreement, it decides to prohibit it then fines can be imposed for the period between entry into operation and the date of notification – see *Pittsburg Corning* case (OJ 1972b).

The Commission does not however rely on notifications in order to uncover possible transgressions. In the first case it keeps its eyes and ears open. If it has good grounds to suspect that an infringement is occurring it can call for information and if the firms do not comply the Commission can take a formal decision requiring the parties to submit to investigation. Commission officials can enter firms and inspect their books. Fines can be levied where enterprises refuse to provide information or provide incomplete information. These powers are provided by Regulation 17/62. Additionally a complaints procedure has been established in order that possible infringements can be submitted to the Commission. Such complaints can be submitted by member states, or by natural or legal persons provided they can show a legitimate interest. A supplier may find himself excluded from a dealer network by a collective exclusive dealing agreement. A dealer may be boycotted because he has not honoured a reciprocal agreement not to deal in the goods of suppliers outwith the agreement, or he may have been fined because he sold below the price stipulated by suppliers. Producers may suspect that they are paying prices for materials that are inflated by monopolistic devices. Complaints tend to be of these kinds. Finally, the Commission is empowered under Regulation 17/62 to carry out sectoral investigations when the flow of trade between member states is suspiciously small or in some way distorted. Early studies were concerned with the lack of trade in beer and margarine and more recently studies have been completed in relation to naptha for petrochemical use and jet aircraft fuel.

Let us now consider how the Commission actually deals with cases. It will be convenient to assume that a group of firms involved in, say, an agreement have made a timely notification. What consequences can follow? The Commission may decide to issue a negative clearance. Such a formal decision is made when the Commission finds that the contents of an agreement are not such as to render it subject to Article 85 – in other words the Commission finds no reason to intervene. It should be emphasized that before such a decision is issued the parties to the agreement may have had to modify it, stripping it of offending matter. Alternatively, agreements may (and this could include cases where some stripping has been attempted) offend under Article 85(1). In that case the only hope of the parties is to qualify for exemption under Article 85(3). If they succeed they can continue to operate the agreement. If exemption cannot be accorded then the agreement has to be dropped if sanctions are to be avoided. Parties may choose to abandon a hopeless case rather than press it to the point where a formal prohibitory decision has to be issued.

In most instances, before the Commission arrives at a decision hearings will be held at which the parties concerned and also third parties, provided they have sufficient grounds, have an opportunity to be heard. A draft decision is then submitted to the Advisory Committee on Restrictive Practices and Dominant Positions (this is drawn from member state experts) and promulgation takes place.

The power to fine under Regulation 17/62 has already been referred to. It could, as we noted earlier, be applied if, an agreement having been prohibited, the parties persisted in operating it. The power also comes into play when serious infringements are unearthed which, not having been notified, cannot be exempted. This was so in *Quinine* and *Aniline Dyes*. There is of course always the possibility that firms involved in a cartel may indulge in lines of conduct which simultaneously breach Community law and national law. Where that is so the principle of *non bis in idem* suggests that firms should not be penalized twice for the same act and this point has been accepted by the Court of Justice.[1]

It should also be mentioned that while the national antitrust authorities are empowered to hear cases under Articles 85 (and 86), the principle has also been established that once the Commission expresses an interest in a case the national authorities must halt their proceedings and accept the decision of the Commission. Having said that national authorities are empowered to act, it should also be borne in mind that the Commission alone can *exempt*.

THE SCOPE OF ARTICLE 85

Before we turn to review individual cases we need to consider the scope of Article 85. Article 87 provides for the Council of Ministers to adopt directives or regulations designed to give effect to Article 85 (and Article 86 – see next chapter). This is where Regulation 17/62 and the like play a critical role. Without the powers provided in those regulations the Commission would be gravely weakened. It would, for example, issue decisions but not having the power to impose penalties firms could ignore them. Indeed Article 89 makes it clear that the Commission would have to rely on member states to take remedial action and this is plainly less than satisfactory. It is also important to note that Regulation 17/62 was not limited in its application – all sectors of the economy were covered. However under Regulation 141/62 (OJ 1962d) transport of all kinds was exempted from the scope of Regulation 17/62. Subsequently Regulation 1017/68 (OJ 1968b) provided special rules relating to road, rail and inland waterway transport. They provide exemption for certain forms of agreement and for small and medium-sized firms participating in agreements. They also institute an enforcement system similar in some respects to that contained in Regulation 17/62. It will be apparent from all this that there is no implementing regulation in respect of air and maritime transport. Articles 85 and 86 do however apply to those modes see *Commission* v. *French Republic* (ECJ 167/73) but until implementing regulations are introduced Article 88 stipulates that abuses under Articles 85 and 86 have to be dealt with under the provisions of both domestic and Community antitrust rules. This seems bound to give rise to conflicts of law and to unevennesses of application. Manifestly it is unsatisfactory and it is therefore not surprising that in 1981 the Commission submitted draft implementing proposals designed to bring these transport modes directly under Community control.

It should also be mentioned that under Regulation 26/62 (OJ 1962e) the prohibition of Article 85(1) applies to production and trade in agricultural products but it does not apply to agreements which form part of a national market organization or are necessary to attain the objectives of the CAP as laid down in Article 39. The CAP is not of course based on free competition but upon market regulation and management and thus it is hardly surprising that such a derogation was necessary.

ARTICLE 85 CASES

The record of the EC Commission in applying Article 85 to horizontal cartels concerned with price fixing, output restrictions and market sharing is extremely impressive. No such cartel with significant market power has been exempted.

Price agreements have been consistently attacked. We have already referred to *Aniline Dyes* where exemption was precluded by virtue of the fact that the concerted practice had not been notified. Fines totalling 480,000 UA were ultimately imposed on the participating firms.[2] In the *Glass Containers* case the Commission dealt with an international arrangement operated by the International Fair Trade Practice Rules Administration, an organization registered in Liechtenstein. Manufacturers of bottles, jars and flasks in Germany, France, Italy, Belgium and the Netherlands were parties to the arrangement. The latter was quite comprehensive since it involved a common method of calculating prices, the general adoption of a delivered price system, exchange of information on prices and, perhaps most significant of all, the fixing of export prices on the basis of the domestic prices in the country of destination. The 'natural price leader' in a domestic market informed foreign producers as to his prices, and if they supplied in his market they charged his price. A restriction of competition and an effect on interstate trade were all too evident. No benefit accrued to the consumer and so an exemption could not be accorded. The parties were therefore ordered to bring the infringements to an immediate end (OJ 1974b).

Common sales syndicates are best treated as a form of price agreement and in so doing we should note that the Commission has taken a consistently hostile attitude where significant market power has been evident. Such syndicates have usually been encountered in markets where products are homogeneous and price-cutting activity could be fierce – i.e. fertilizers, cement, sulphuric acid. Several early cases concerned fertilizers. In, for example, the *CFA* (OJ 1968c) and *Cobelaz* (OJ 1968d) cases the arrangements covered both home and export sales, but modifications had to be made so that sales to other EEC countries were carried out independently by individual manufacturers. This having been done the Commission was able to grant a negative clearance.[3] Interestingly three leading French producers of fertilizers, who were involved in the *CFA* arrangement, also set up an export sales syndicate during the year in which the *CFA* decision was handed down. This was called Floral GmbH and handled their compound fertilizer sales in West Germany. In 1979 the Commission banned this arrangement pointing out that the legal position of common selling syndicates had been made abundantly clear to the firms in the 1968 *CFA* decision. However because Floral handled only a small proportion of their fertilizer sales the fine imposed (85,000 EUA) was a modest one (OJ 1980f). Where a common selling syndicate controls only a small proportion of the relevant market and thus has no appreciable market power the arrangement may be granted a negative clearance as it stands. This was so in the *SAFCO* case, which concerned a common selling agency operating on behalf of French exporters of canned vegetables. Without modification, the Commission granted a negative clearance because its supply represented such a small part of the market. For example, in West Germany (a major area of its export activity) it supplied, on average, only 1–2 per cent of canned vegetable production, and this of course ignored the existence of fresh vegetable supplies (OJ 1972c).

As we saw earlier restrictions of competition may take the form of limitations of output or sales through the agency of quotas. Again the Commission has consistently attacked these forms of activity. In 1972 in the *Cementregeling voor Nederland* case (OJ 1972d) the Commission attacked the remaining elements of a cement cartel which had been in existence for decades. The agreement between Dutch, Belgian and German cement producers shared out the Dutch market in the proportion 69 per cent, 17 per cent and 14 per cent respectively with an amount varying between 250,000 and 500,000 tonnes per annum being left to free competition. This case originally began in 1964 when the more comprehensive Noordwijks-cement-accoord was operating. It not only prescribed quotas but also fixed prices and prohibited the construction of new cement works. Gradually the restrictions were dismantled and in 1972 the Commission dealt the *coup de grâce*. Output controls may also relate to the range of products supplied. For example, in 1977 the Commission secured the termination of certain clauses in agreements between manufacturers of video cassettes and video cassette recorders. The parties were the Dutch firm Philips and seven German firms including Blaupunkt and Bosch-Siemens. These firms had undertaken not to manufacture or sell any such equipment other than that conforming to the system licensed by Philips. The arrangement was in fact underpinned by the cross-licensing of patents. If a firm broke the agreement it forfeited its licences under the patents of the others but they kept their rights under those of the terminating party (OJ 1978b).

Agreements relating to the creation of capacity have been considered by the Commission and have been regarded as coming under the ban of Article 85(1) – this was so in the *Cement voor Nederland* and *Cimbel* cases. This is hardly surprising since a collusive restriction on the amount of capacity can have just as powerful an effect as a collective restriction of output or sales. Then in 1978 a case arose which raised the issue of the status of capacity-controlling agreements in a particularly acute form (ECC 1979a, 49-50). This related to the synthetic or man-made fibre industry where it was estimated that 30 per cent of the capacity was unused, price competition was extremely intense and losses were piling up. It is reported that Commissioner Etienne Davignon (industrial affairs) persuaded the industry to establish a crisis cartel to deal with the problem. While the agreement was under negotiation Davignon and Raymond Vouel (Commissioner for competition) put forward the proposal that on the basis of Article 87 the Council of Ministers should be invited to agree to a regulation legitimizing crisis cartels. In the interim the cartel should be notified to the Commission in the normal way and if the regulation was acceptable to Council the cartel could be considered under its special terms. From this point on the scheme began to run into difficulties. The Commission as a whole did not like the Davignon-Vouel proposals for all kinds of reasons including the obvious one that it would be taken to be a precedent and other industries would besiege the Commission for special treatment and Article 85 would be severely undermined. As for the agreement itself this was found unacceptable. The Commission argued that the capacity reduction element did restrict competition but was capable of exemption. However the production and sales restrictions which were also included in the agreement were not acceptable.

This case raises a number of fascinating issues, not all of which can be discussed here. Two however stand out. First, how could a capacity reduction agreement embracing the eleven major European producers satisfy the conditions of Article 85(3)? That article requires that the agreement must not eliminate competition in respect of a substantial part of the products in question. It also requires the consumer to benefit. How would he benefit? Consumers gain from lower prices but the agreement would raise them. More tenuous arguments would have had to be deployed such as the notion that excessive competition would adversely affect R & D spending and that this would slow down the flow of new products. Second, why was it that as late as 1982 the status of the capacity limitation aspect had not been finally determined? The possibility exists that in truth the Commission was not absolutely confident that an exemption would survive an appeal. Moreover it is open to doubt whether the Commission wished to commit itself. If an exemption succeeded would not the Commission be inundated with requests for equal treatment? On the other hand if it failed to get an exemption through then the man-made fibre industry (and others as well) would be formally precluded from carrying out any concerted rationalization plan. Was it not best to hasten slowly – in the meantime the industry could rationalize itself and the Commission would jeopardize neither the position of Article 85 nor the ability of industries to extricate themselves from chronic excess capacity situations. If the latter speculation is correct then it suggests that while the clean bill of health referred to at the beginning of this section is strictly correct since it refers to exemptions, the position in reality is a little more complicated by cases where it has been felt prudent to do nothing or not do anything with indecent haste.

The Commission has been consistently opposed to territorial market-sharing arrangements. For example, in 1965 it dealt with an agreement between Belgian and Dutch producers of detergent – the *Savon Noir* case. Under the agreement the Belgian parties were forbidden to sell their detergent on the Dutch market and the Dutch producers entered into a reciprocal arrangement. In order to buttress the arrangement all parties undertook, on pain of penalties, to prohibit any reselling by buyers that might prejudice the division of the market. The Commission declared the agreement prohibited, exemption not being warranted (EECC 1965a, 71, EECC 1966, 17). More recently the Commission brought about the abandonment of a long-term arrangement between a British and a Belgian producer of industrial sand. British Industrial Sand Ltd (BIS), a subsidiary of Hepworth Ceramic Holdings Limited, and Sablières et Carrières Réunies (SCR) had, for certain kinds of sand, assigned the UK market exclusively to BIS and the rest of Europe to SCR. Two other aspects of the case are of particular interest, namely the agreement not to supply machinery, or excavate, in each other's territories and an exchange of directors in order to maintain close contact and to supervise the undertakings (ECC 1977b, 69–70).

Exclusionary practices which protect national markets have been attacked in a long line of cases. One of the earliest was the *Convention Faience* case (ECC 1972, 36). This was a collective reciprocal exclusive dealing arrangement between Belgian dealers in, and layers of, wall and floor tiles and tile manufacturers in Belgium, the Netherlands and Germany. Basically manufacturers could deliver only to approved dealers party to the agreement and the latter could not purchase goods from manufacturers outside the arrangement. In addition new trade associations of dealers and layers could join only with the unanimous consent of existing members and new manufacturers could join only by unanimous consent of the manufacturers already party to the agreement. This type of arrangement obviously restricts competition and an effect on inter-state trade is obvious – in this case manufacturers in states other than Belgium, who were not party to the agreement, were barred from dealing with Belgian dealers and layers party to the agreement. Such arrangements are also not likely to provide any Article 85(3) benefits. *Convention Faience* was a long-drawn-out affair but in 1971 following Commission criticisms it was finally terminated. Since that case the Commission has consistently ruled that such exclusionary arrangements are incompatible with Article 85. Similar restrictions were subsequently successfully attacked notably in the *Dutch Sporting Cartridges* (ECC 1974a, 50-1), the *Bomée-Stichting* (OJ 1975e) and the *Dutch Stoves and Heaters* (OJ 1975f) cases. Exclusion from national markets can also result from aggregated rebate arrangements and these have in the past been a common device. Such a system was encountered in the *German Wall and Floor Tile* case. The rebate offered by a number of German producers was payable only on purchases from the group and progressively increased with the volume of orders. The effect of this was to induce purchasers to concentrate their orders on the German group, and outsiders had to make significant price concessions in order to draw custom away. The effect on interstate competition was clear. The Commission *inter alia* objected that the rebates should relate to purchases from individual producers, in which case they had the possibility of reflecting actual savings. Moreover, if the aim was to favour tiles relative to substitute products, then purchases of foreign tiles ought to be taken into account. The arrangement was not capable of exemption (OJ 1971e). This too was an important landmark decision.

A number of instances of information agreements have been encountered by the Commission. Some of these have related to prices and are sometimes referred to as open price agreements. The information may however relate to other matters such as sales. In the *Paper Machine Wire* case firms organized in national associations in Germany, France and the UK and in the International Association of Paper Machine Wire Manufacturers operated an information agreement relating to plastic and metal paper machine wires used for draining water from pulp. Members supplied the international secretariat with lists setting out their current prices, discounts, payment terms and also with copies of invoices which gave full details of the firms supplied and the terms of the individual sales. Apart from using this data to prepare market statistics national associations or individual firms could contact the secretariat in order to find out if a particular price had been paid by a particular customer. This was intended to prevent users from playing one supplier off against another – i.e. to prevent phantom competition. Following an intervention by the Commission the firms agreed to terminate the practice of supplying each other with price lists and details of individual sales (ECC 1977b, 75-8). The Commission subsequently stated its general view on information agreements. It is not opposed to the collection and dissemination of general data but it is opposed to the supply of information which enables parties to identify the competitive behaviour of other parties. Such exchanges are particularly dangerous in oligopolistic markets. The Commission also notes that buyers are usually excluded from this information and are thus not able to exploit 'concealed competition' (ECC 1978c, 18-21).

When the Commission first embarked on the business of handing down decisions in restrictive practice cases its initial concern was not with the major horizontal cartels but with distribution arrangements. In particular it concentrated much effort on (vertical) sole or exclusive distribution agreements. Indeed, the first occasion on which it exercised its power of prohibition was in connection with such an arrangement in the *Grundig-Consten* case. This was to prove to be a key case since it led to a regulation for the block exemption of certain forms of sole distribution agreement. In *Grundig-Consten* the West German firm Grundig appointed Consten, a Paris firm, as its sole dealer in France at its particular stage in the distribution chain – i.e. importer/wholesaler. Grundig also banned all its sole dealers in other states from delivering Grundig goods into the French market and thus undermining Consten's position. This is referred to as territorial protection. In fact a rival French firm UNEF obtained supplies from German wholesalers and a preventative legal action was then commenced by Consten which, given its importance for Community law and the need for clarification, brought the Commission into the case. The Commission in fact prohibited the entire agreement (OJ 1964b) but an appeal was made to the Court of Justice with a number of member states joining in. In the event the sole distribution aspect was upheld, the offence being narrowed down to the element of territorial protection (ECJ 56/64, 58/64). The latter buttresses the sole dealer's monopoly in the chain of distribution and, by compartmentalizing the common market, gives rise to differences in prices for the same goods in the different member states. Goods that have entered into trade must be allowed to move freely across frontiers in the hope that interstate price differences will be ironed out. Here we are of course referring to parallel imports, a concept which we identified in Chapter 2 when discussing the *Dassonville* case.

The Commission followed this up by a number of decisions in which pure sole distribution agreements were exempted. Such agreements do fall under the prohibition of Article 85(1) in that there is a restriction of competition (each party agrees to restrict its dealings to the other) and there is an effect on inter-state trade. Nevertheless because they have advantageous effects in helping firms to penetrate markets, they are capable of exemption. Moreover by being pure (i.e. by virtue of the absence of territorial protection) parallel imports are possible. This prevents the compartmentalization of the common market to which both the Commission and Court are fundamentally opposed. The Commission was in fact paving the way for the block exemption of this type of agreement. Regulation 19/65 (OJ 1965b) provided a power of block exemption and under Regulation 67/67 (OJ 1967d) bilateral sole dealing agreements (between two enterprises in two states), provided they are not accompanied by territorial protection, were accorded block exemption status. At the time of writing (1982) the Commission is proposing the adoption of a new block exemption regulation which will tighten up the rules so as to preserve parallel imports but will make cross-frontier distribution easier for smaller firms.

Those firms that seek to prevent parallel imports within their European distribution systems run the risk of severe penalties. In 1979 in the *Pioneer* case Pioneer Electronics Europe, a subsidiary of a Japanese multinational ranking among the world's leading suppliers of hi-fi equipment, was together with its sole distributors in France, Germany and the UK fined substantially for operating what were in effect export bans. The collective fine imposed by the Commission amounted to no less than 6,950,000 EUA (OJ 1980g).

Up to this point the Commission has been presented as a guardian of competition. But there is another side to EEC competition policy whereby certain forms of business co-operation can be viewed in a favourable light. In its 1968 *Notice on Co-operation* the Commission intimated that it was anxious to encourage certain forms of business co-operation. It pointed out that certain competitively innocuous practices were acceptable but also indicated that it intended to address itself to situations where competition was affected but where certain offsetting gains to efficiency or technological progress could arise. There then followed a number of favourable decisions which were concerned with specialization and joint research and development. Specialization is advantageous because it enables firms to produce longer runs of particular products and thus to spread fixed costs over a greater volume with an attendant improvement in efficiency. On the other hand such an arrangement is restrictive of competition since the number of producers is reduced. There may however be enough competition left in the market to guarantee that some at least of the gains are passed on to consumers in the form of lower prices. If of course each specialist supplies its partner with the results of its specialization so that each can offer a full line, *and each leaves the other free to determine the price of the other's specialisms,* then competition is not reduced. Examples of cases where exemptions have been accorded for specialization arrangements are *Jaz-Peter* (OJ 1969e) and *Clima-Chappée-Buderus* (OJ 1969f) cases. In the latter a French and a German producer of air-conditioning equipment agreed to rationalize their production – each undertook to produce only certain types of equipment. In order to offer a full line to customers, each supplied the other with equipment they had ceased to produce themselves. The fact that each was to be an exclusive distributor in its own home market constituted a restriction of competition, but this was not thought to be a significant drawback given the intensity of competition remaining in each domestic market.

Decisions such as these paved the way for another block exemption regulation. Regulation 2821/71 (OJ 1971f) provided general powers to block-exempt standardization, joint research and development and specialization agreements. Regulation 2779/72 (OJ 1972e) provided a specific power for the latter. Current limitations require that the market share in a substantial part of the common market must not exceed 15 per cent and the annual aggregate sales must not exceed 300 million UA.

Joint research and development agreements – these are a form of joint venture – can also lead to economic gains by eliminating duplications of expenditure. On the other hand it seems inevitable that there will be a sacrifice of potential competition in that each might otherwise have developed the product and been rivals in the market.

Arrangements of this kind may however have a stimulating effect on competition. It might be that an agreement would enable smaller or less well-entrenched suppliers to offer more effective competition to those more fully established. A good example of this is the approved agreement between Vickers and the French firm Sopolem for the joint development of microscopes (OJ 1978c). The European market for microscopes is dominated by German and Japanese producers, while the collaborating parties had only a small share and had not been able to break out of their home markets on any scale. The agreement also envisaged rationalized use of their distribution networks and possible specialization in production.

Thus far no reference has been made to the impact of EEC competition rules in situations where industrial property rights (i.e. patents, trade marks and copyrights) arise. Since however both Articles 85 and 86 can be relevant to such issues we shall postpone our discussion until we have discussed the meaning and implication of Article 86 – see Chapter 5.

ECSC cartel rules and cases

The relevant provisions of the Paris Treaty are to be found in Article 65 (see Appendix). Article 65(1) declares that agreements, decisions of associations of enterprises and concerted practices which prevent, restrict or distort competition within the common market are prohibited. There is, as we noted earlier, no inter-state commerce clause of the kind found in Rome Treaty Article 85. Article 65(1) singles out for special mention in its prohibition agreements, etc., which (a) fix or determine prices; (b) restrict or control production, technical development or investment; or (c) share markets, products, customers or sources of supply. The EC Commission is however required under Article 65(2) to authorize specialization, joint selling or joint buying agreements provided that a number of conditions are fulfilled. First, the arrangement makes a substantial improvement in production or distribution. Second, the arrangement is essential if these improvements are to be achieved and is no more restrictive than is necessary for that purpose. Third, the arrangement does not allow those involved to determine the price or restrict the supply of a substantial part of the products in question in the common market or does not shield them from effective competition from other enterprises in the common market. Article 65(3), (4) and (5) provide enforcement powers including the ability to fine.

Clearly these rules have a certain amount in common with Article 85 of the Rome Treaty but the reader will note three differences. Article 65(2) stipulates that the EC Commission *shall* authorize specialization and other agreements whereas Article 85(3) declares that it *may* exempt agreements. Article 65(2) singles out specific forms of practice for authorization whereas Article 85(3) does not indicate any preferred form of practice. The third contrast is that the conditions for authorization under Article 65(2) make no reference to the need for the consumer to share in any benefit arising. When actual cases are reviewed and compared with those based on Article 85 the impression emerges that the above differences are not unimportant. The stance of Article 65 seems to be somewhat more accommodating although, given the lack of an interstate commerce clause, its remit is wider.

Before we proceed to discuss actual cases it is necessary to draw attention to the fact that since the mid-1970s competition policy in the ECSC has been under a cloud. The acute difficulties experienced by steel producers have meant that various plans have been introduced to assist steel firms to weather the economic storm. Firms have been expected to co-operate in the implementation of official plans involving reduction of deliveries of particular products in order to temper competition and enable the steel industry to survive. Trade associations, and firms involved in permitted forms of agreement, have been instrumental in helping the Commission to carry out the plans. In effect the whole of the ECSC steel industry became part of an official cartel. More will be said about the latter topic in Chapter 7.

Joint selling agreements have been submitted for consideration by the old High Authority and the EC Commission on a number of occasions and have been authorized in a significant number of instances. One of the earlier decisions by the High Authority concerned the joint selling of coal in the Ruhr. At the time when the Paris Treaty came into operation the supply of Ruhr coal was dominated by the joint selling agency Gemeinschaftsorganisation Ruhrkohle GmbH (GEORG). GEORG did not actually control prices – these were fixed by the German government. However the power to do so was there should the price control powers lapse (perhaps under pressure from the High Authority) since GEORG was responsible for 50 per cent of ECSC coal production and for 93 per cent of West German coal. Cartels had to notify the High Authority of their existence and quite clearly the High Authority could not sanction GEORG's continued existence. It therefore decided that GEORG should be transformed into three selling agencies – they became known as Geitling, Präsident and Mausegatt although there was to be a joint office to deal with those who bought more than 50,000 tonnes per annum. Each agency was to be independent of the other and to achieve this end individual mining companies could only be members of one agency. Each agency would balance orders among the constituent mining companies and the joint office would balance large orders among the three categories (OJ 1956).

This decision has attracted a lot of criticism. It represented a climb down on the part of the High Authority since the Allies had previously established six selling agencies with GEORG as a co-ordinating body. However by the time the High Authority came to act it was GEORG, rather than the six supposedly independent agencies, which was selling the coal! It was also open to doubt whether the joint selling really led to the kind of improvements which Article 65(2) demands. Also if there were benefits to be derived from co-operation were they not capable of being obtained without going so far as to sanction the continuance of common sales agencies? Moreover although no mining company could be a member of more than one agency there was indisputable evidence of substantial proprietorial ties between companies involved in supposedly separate agencies. There was also room to doubt whether competition would emerge given that the co-ordinating agency provided a possible forum for discussions on prices.

The 1956 decision did not appear to be a great success. In 1957 the European Parliament began to press the High Authority about the simultaneity in the price changes of the three agencies. When the 1956 decision came up for renewal the High Authority indicated that it intended to continue with the arrangement although the Ruhr producers indicated that they wanted a monopoly sales agency which they proposed to call the Ruhrkohlen-Verkaufsgesellschaft GmbH. They continued to press and when the High Authority continued to refuse they appealed to the Court of Justice.

In 1962 the Court delivered its judgement (ECJ 13/60) and in so doing upheld the Commission's refusal. The judgement was a landmark decision in that the philosophy contained therein has continued to be relevant to the ECSC approach not only to cartels but also to concentrations (see Chapter 5). Two particular implications stand out. The first is that in coal and steel perfect competition is not feasible.

Large units are inevitable and therefore oligopoly is the order of the day. Moreover technological progress may dictate larger units and perhaps an even greater degree of oligopoly. (In the following quotation the reader should be aware that Article 66 relates to mergers and firms in a dominant position.) The Court observed:

> The technological and economic development leading to greater and greater economic units and every day reinforcing the oligopolistic character of the coal and steel market has not been ignored by the drafters of the ECSC-Treaty; instead, the provisions of article 65, para. 2, and 66, para. 2 justify the conclusion that they did not intend to oppose this development, provided that it serves the purposes of the Treaty and does not eliminate the minimum of competition that is necessary to satisfy the fundamental requirements of article 2, namely 'progressively to establish the conditions which by themselves safeguard the most economic apportionment of the production at the highest standard of efficiency' and to 'safeguard, that there will be no interruption in employment and to avoid heavy and lasting disturbances in the economies of the Member states'.
> ... nothing justifies the argument that the Treaty intended to prohibit the large production and sales units typical for the coal and steel market or at least to object to their formation. It would be closing one's eyes to reality and denying the necessities of technical progress to attempt the restoration of an atomistic market in this realm, which is quite unthinkable for the products in question. (ECJ 13/60)

The Court also advanced the critically important notion that in granting an authorization to a cartel the criterion (that a substantial part of the market should not be thereby controlled) should not be judged from the point of view of the percentage share of the market attained by the group in question but by reference to the relationship between that percentage and the percentage attained by other groups. A sales agency or agreement could not be authorized if it had a disproportionate effect in the market. In short oligopoly is an established fact and policy must be directed towards keeping a balance between oligopolists. Taken to an extreme 25 firms with 4 per cent of the market is no doubt desirable but 4 firms with 25 per cent each also preserves a balance. Economists would of course feel that the first structure was competitive but the second is likely to exhibit oligopolistic parallelism and indeed to facilitate clandestine collusion. Such a reduction in numbers would be acceptable only if efficiency and progress benefits were available as a trade-off.

It should be noted that the Court's view about disproportionate influence was of course related to the fact that if a Ruhr agency had been allowed it would have been much larger than any existing rival – it would, for example, have controlled twice the production of its next largest rival Charbonnages de France. Because of this the Court supported the High Authority in its refusal to accede to the Ruhr coalowners' request.

As a postscript two points remain to be made. In 1963, despite its earlier success, the High Authority decided to authorize two Ruhr agencies although this time it dealt with the proprietorial link problem. This move prompted the Dutch government to appeal but the Court upheld the High Authority's decision (ECJ 66/63). By 1972 the EC Commission had allowed one agency – Ruhrkohle AG – to secure control over 90 per cent of coal output in the Ruhr basin. However the Commission was quick to point out that this was acceptable because the energy market had changed radically. Coal had become a minority supplier of energy which had to contend with oil and natural gas – the relevant market had widened dramatically.

Joint selling has also been a feature of the steel industry. In 1967, for example, the then High Authority issued four decisions relating to the joint selling of rolled products by West German steel enterprises. The major West German producers were allowed to form four joint selling systems – the Western Group, the Northern Group, the Westphalia Group and the Southern Group. The object was to utilize the production facilities of each of the parties through specialization and joint distribution. In defence of the authorization the following official statement was made:

> In assessing what improvements might result in the production or distribution of the products in question (the test of Article 65 (2a)), the High Authority noted the following points: simplification of ordering by customers, lower freight costs, better utilization of production capacity, streamlining of production programmes and aligning of rolling programmes. The High Authority found that considerable economies could be made, but it ruled that the firms involved must produce within two years evidence of improvements obtained by rationalization. (ECC 1968, 47–8)

In short joint sale, which in effect provides for the tightest form of collective market control, is not in itself acceptable unless tangible benefits arise. The High Authority also had to consider whether the agencies would control a sufficiently substantial part of the market to be in a position to control prices. The answer was apparently No. In support the High Authority noted that the market was already oligopolistic and that the sales agencies would not upset the oligopolistic balance – this has a familiar ring. However the High Authority was being a little charitable since there were some proprietorial overlaps between the groups – this too has a familiar ring – and in some cases the group share of particular product markets was admitted to be on the high side.

Before we leave the topic of joint selling it is pertinent to observe that while this form of activity has found favour in coal and steel it has not been acceptable under the Rome Treaty except in circumstances where the common selling agency controlled such a small share of the market that it was of no practical significance. The EC Commission has not found that joint selling produces economies of the kind which qualify the arrangement for exemption under Article 85(3).

Subsequently the four agencies were transformed into specialization agreements (OJ 1971g). Authorizations under this heading have been quite common. More recently the Commission has accepted that such agreements are an acceptable way of coping with the steel crisis. When demand is low, as has been the case since 1975, firms have found themselves producing at low volumes with a consequent sacrifice of economies of scale. The obvious response has been for firms to enter into agreements whereby each sheds particular product lines so as to enable the other firm or firms to produce such products at a more economic volume. In effect specialization agreements have been mutual capacity reduction agreements.

Then in 1976 the four agencies were dropped and two groups – a Northern Group and a Southern Group – were formed from the original participants although some limited changes of membership were apparent. The two new arrangements were described as cooperation and rationalization agreements. They involved joint production, specialization and some joint selling of rolled steel products. The Commission considered that the structure of the market was such the firms involved would not have the power to determine prices. The Commission also noted that these groups would be instrumental in organizing the anti-crisis delivery programmes which we referred to above (ECC 1977b, 75–8). The possibility therefore exists that these arrangements found favour at least in part because they offered the possibility of more effective crisis management.

Joint buying has also been approved on a number of occasions. In 1975 the Commission authorized several French steel producers to set up a common buying agency to purchase pre-reduced iron ore (a high quality substitute for scrap) for use in electric steel furnaces. Pre-reduction is a relatively new process. The Commission approved the arrangement on the ground that the common buying would enable the firms to order greater tonnages and thus reduce supply costs. A power to determine prices would not be apparent since prices were determined by world supply and demand conditions and were also influenced by the relative prices of scrap and pig-iron (OJ 1975g). Joint buying has also been approved in respect of firms dealing in, as opposed to producing, ECSC products. In 1977 the Commission allowed forty German stockholding companies jointly to buy rolled steel products. The Commission justified this renewal of an arrangement first approved in 1967 by referring to the fact that it gave rise to economies of scale in buying, carriage and stocking and enabled these small and medium-size firms to compete more successfully with the large steel stockholders (ECC 1978c, 100).

By contrast to all that has gone before straight collective price fixing and the collective application of quotas have no counterbalancing advantages to offer and are likely to be prohibited and indeed to attract fines. In 1980 the EC Commission issued three decisions of this kind. One applied to a group of French special steel producers who fixed prices and applied quotas in the French market. Another related to German special steel producers who had behaved in a similar manner in the German market. The third involved both French and German special steel producers who had concluded an interpenetration agreement whereby they limited deliveries into each other's national market. In fixing the fines the Commission took account of the unfavourable financial position of the producers but observed that difficult market conditions did not justify the breaking of treaty rules (ECC 1981b, 74-5). In the same year the Commission required an association of German steel stockholders to terminate a price information system (ECC 1981b, 75-6).

5 Non-tariff barriers – concentrations and other issues

Introduction

It is traditional in antitrust policy to distinguish between the restrictive business practice, or cartel, dimension and the industrial concentration aspect. In the former otherwise independent firms acquire an influence on the market by virtue of a concertation of behaviour. By contrast the concentration problem emphasizes the point that individual firms may in their own right possess or come to possess a degree of market power. The most obvious phenomenon under the concentration heading is monopoly. It should however be emphasized that a true monopolist is not as common as the use of the word monopoly might suggest. The reasons for this are that the conditions for the existence of such a market position are quite rigorous. There must be only one supplier of a good and there must be no close substitutes to which consumers can switch if the monopolist chooses to raise his price.

A more common phenomenon is market dominance and it is significant that it is this concept rather than monopoly which is expressly recognized in both the Paris and Rome Treaties. We shall not attempt at this point to provide a comprehensive definition of the phrase market dominance. While a monopoly is obviously an extreme example of market dominance, the latter also embraces situations where more than one firm may be supplying a particular product but nevertheless for various reasons, including the fact that one of the firms supplies a preponderant part of the supply, that firm may possess market power. It may, for example, be able to exert a significant effect on the price level in the market in which it sells.

In practice neither monopoly nor the wider concept of market dominance is purely structural in character. That is to say it is not just the share of the market and so forth which is significant. There is also a restrictive practice dimension and the reader will thus appreciate that a hard and fast line between restrictive business practices and the concentration problem is impossible to maintain. Firms which in their own right enjoy a preponderant influence in the market may employ predatory and exclusionary practices in order to maintain it. Thus a firm which dominates a national market, and supplies a well-known brand, is in a position to require dealers to deal exclusively with it. Such an arrangement would make it difficult for firms in other member states to penetrate the tied national market. We can thus see how dominant firm behaviour could offend under the Rome Treaty although such an inter-state trade effect does not have to be present before the relevant Paris Treaty provisions can be invoked.

In practice the predominant structure of most manufacturing industry and mining in modern Western economies is not characterized by monopoly or market dominance but by oligopoly. Oligopoly refers to a situation where a few suppliers exist. There is of course a demarcation problem here. An industrial structure where one firm is dominant may also be one of fewness. However the oligopoly problem emphasizes situations where there are a few suppliers *between whom there is at least a rough parity of influence.* It is not immediately apparent why this should give rise to an anti-competition problem. Quite the contrary: the existence of a number of independent centres of initiative in the market suggests that a competitive outcome could well be expected. However the fewness factor tends to force firms to recognize that they are highly interdependent. In making, say, a price move a firm recognizes that other firms supplying the good will be significantly affected. Therefore reactions are possible and the nature of them has to be taken account of before the price change is introduced. This can leave the firms in a kind of impasse and in turn it may induce them to seek some form of *modus vivendi*. The latter may be collusive in character and certainly fewness enables such an arrangement to arise with the minimum of formality. Alternatively it may be of a price leadership type. (Either way the degree to which price can be raised above the competitive level depends on other factors such as whether barriers to entry exist and if so how high they are.) Straightforward collusion is of course covered by the cartel provisions of the treaties. However we have recognized that the relationship between oligopolists may be a good deal less formal than that. We know in the light of the *Sugar* cases (see Chapter 4) that a recognition of interdependence is not a crime. For a concerted practice to be proved to exist there must be evidence of conscious efforts to act in a collective manner. How conscious those conscious efforts have to be is not totally clear. Whether the concerted practice concept enables the EC Commission to block all oligopolistic anti-competition loopholes is open to some doubt.

Mergers are clearly a relevant phenomenon. The most obvious problem arises when firms at the same stage of production or distribution amalgamate. This is referred to as a horizontal merger. Such mergers do not automatically produce a monopoly or a dominant firm. However they do reduce the number of firms and thus help to oligopolize the market and if pressed far enough create dominant or monopoly firms. Attendant problems may then arise. From the point of view of the Paris Treaty, where an effect on inter-state trade is not specified, such mergers obviously pose a potential problem. The Rome Treaty does as we know require that there should be an effect on trade. It is not difficult to see how such an effect could arise. Suppose that firms in two separate member states decide to merge. Each firm may have previously exported to the others' national market. After the merger such competitive trade flows are almost inevitably likely to cease.

Vertical mergers occur when firms take over other firms further back or further forward in the chain of production and distribution. They too may pose problems. These may take the form of the denial of supplies to non-integrated competitors. Alternatively the vertically integrated firm may operate a price squeeze, enhancing the price of the inputs it supplies to non-integrated producers and depressing the price of the subsequent product. To be successful both these practices require the existence of horizontal dominance on the part of the firm denying or squeezing. We shall encounter cases below where an already existing condition of vertical integration has been associated with charges involving these types of anti-competitive conduct. Vertically integrated firms may also foreclose outlets to non-integrated producers. Mention must also be made of conglomerate mergers. Pure conglomerate mergers are amalgamations of firms with different product lines. In recent years much attention has been focused on this phenomenon. The fact that it involves firms engaged in different markets raises a doubt as to why such mergers should be regarded as a problem. Possible (and it is necessary to emphasize the word 'possible') anti-competitive effects may arise. To cite an example, the conglomerate may use the monopoly profits obtained in one market to make, or threaten to make, competitive forays in other markets in which it operates. This may confer upon a conglomerate a dominating position in those other markets.

Mention must also be made of joint ventures. This kind of arrangement was discussed in Chapter 4 when we reviewed the various kinds of restrictive business practice or cartel. Under the Rome Treaty joint ventures which take the form of agreements will be considered under Article 85. However there may be a transfer of assets in which case it will be treated as a merger. In which case the Rome Treaty's concentration article – Article 86 (to be discussed below) – will apply. It is possible that in complicated situations both Articles 85 and 86 will be applied simultaneously. Under the Paris Treaty it is theoretically possible that joint ventures could equally be regarded as agreements or as concentrations. In the big cases in which commonly owned steel plants were created (e.g. SIDMAR) the old High Authority recognized that while the joint venture did not involve a merger of the promoting companies, it was unlikely that, where those companies produced similar products to those produced by the joint venture, the promoting companies would compete with their joint venture. For competition purposes the promoters and the joint venture could be regarded as an almost homogeneous group and thus considered under the concentration article – Article 66.

The Rome Treaty

DOMINANT POSITIONS

Article 86 contains the relevant provisions – see Appendix. For an offence to arise three conditions must be fulfilled. (a) A firm (or firms) must be in a dominant position in the common market or in a substantial part thereof. The nature of a dominant position is not defined nor is any indication given of what 'substantial' means. This was inevitable since the conditions necessary for dominance to exist will vary from case to case – as we shall see. Equally what is substantial ought in principle to vary from product to product – as we shall also see. (b) Dominance itself is not the sin. Rather it is the abuse of the dominance which is declared to be incompatible with the common market. This is the approach which is almost invariably adopted in monopoly and dominance laws. There are several reasons for this but an obviously important point is that a firm may possess market power, and indeed may be a monopolist, because it is simply more efficient than its rivals. Its market power is thrust upon it. It would not be legitimate to attack it because it was excellent. Then again economies of scale may dictate a size in relation to the market which automatically implies at least an element of market power. For reasons of this kind monopoly and dominance laws do not normally condemn market power but seek to outlaw (i) abnormal business methods employed in the acquisition and maintenance of such power; and (ii) abusive exploitation of the dominant market position. These two may overlap. Article 86 provides some illustrations of abuse. They include the imposition of unfair selling *and buying* prices; the limitation of production, markets and technical development to the prejudice of consumers; the application of dissimilar conditions to comparable transactions, thereby placing those concerned at a competitive disadvantage (price discrimination); the application to contracts of supplementary clauses which would not normally be found in such contracts (tie-ins). These are illustrative and not exhaustive. (c) Abuses are incompatible with the common market only in so far as they may affect trade between member states.

The enforcement powers provided in Regulation 17/62, etc., are of course applicable to abuses of dominant positions. Notification however is not applicable. Detection of abuses therefore depends on the Commission being constantly watchful and upon sectoral investigations and complaints.

We turn now to a more detailed analysis of the meaning of Article 86. Obviously the first question must be, what is a 'dominant position'? A firm is in a dominant position when it enjoys significant market power and we shall argue that such market power expresses itself partly in relation to customers and suppliers and partly in relation to existing and potential competitors.

Where conditions of perfect competition exist there is a large number of firms producing a homogeneous product. Each supplier can exert no influence on the price of the product – the price is determined by market forces. By contrast in conditions of monopoly the supplier can exert market power in the sense that being the sole source of supply, he exercises discretion over the level of price. Market dominance however refers to situations where there are some competitors. Nevertheless it is still possible to imagine that the dominant firm will not, for example, be deterred from independently raising price even if it felt that its rivals would not follow it up. To take an admittedly extreme case, suppose that a dominant firm has a 90 per cent market share and suppose that it has four competitors who each have a 2.5 per cent share of the market. Let us assume that the dominant firm raises its price to such a degree that customers decide to desert it and offer their custom to the other firms that have not raised price. For the dominant firm to suffer a decline in its market share to 80 per cent it would, ignoring imports, be necessary for each of its rivals on average to be able to increase individual outputs by 100 per cent. This is improbable. If they could increase output only by 10 per cent then the dominant firm would find its market share only falling to 89 per cent. Certainly *in the short run* such a firm could largely ignore its rivals although presumably its disposition to do so would *ceteris paribus* decline as its market share declined. Dominance may also manifest itself in terms of the ability of the dominant firm to influence the price of the products which it *buys*. In a perfect market the buyer must take the price of supplies as given but where a firm dominates the market for supplies it can mobilize a large block of business in a way which is likely to secure price concessions.

But the dominance of a firm reflects itself not merely in its ability to influence price, e.g. the price of the products it sells, but also in its ability to influence the share of the market which it enjoys at that price. Its share will depend on the degree to which existing rivals and potential new entrants can be kept at bay. (This is most important since if the dominant firm uses its position in selling and buying to enhance profits it is likely to tempt existing rivals to increase their market share and to attract new entrants.) Existing rivals and new entrants may be kept at bay by the ability of the dominant enterprise to indulge in exclusionary and predatory practices. Customers may be induced to deal exclusively. Tie-in clauses may be required as a condition of receiving supplies. The size of the dominant firm may enable it to finance costly price wars. The dominant firm may also be protected by barriers to entry. While some of these may arise by virtue of factors outside the control of the dominant firm (e.g. economies of scale), others may be deliberately engineered (e.g. the deterrent effects of highly advertised products, control over vital patents and raw materials, etc.).

The Commission and Court of Justice have themselves made several attempts to define the concept of a dominant firm. Although there are important nuances in each definition, the common denominator seems to be the power of independent action – the dominant firm is not constrained by its consumers, suppliers or competitors. In the *Continental Can* case the Commission considered, and the Court impliedly accepted, that

> undertakings are in a dominant position when they have the power to behave independently, which puts them in a position to act without taking account of their competitors, purchasers or suppliers. (ECJ 6/72)

In *United Brands* the Court declared that Article 86 related

> to a position of economic strength enjoyed by an undertaking which enables it to prevent effective competition on the relevant market by giving it the power to behave to an appreciable extent independently of its competitors, customers and ultimately of its consumers. (ECJ 27/76)

Much the same definition was adopted by the Court in *Hoffman-La-Roche* when it declared:

> The dominant position thus referred to [by Article 86] relates to a position of economic strength enjoyed by an undertaking which enables it to prevent effective competition being maintained on the relevant market by affording it the power to behave appreciably independently of its competitors. (ECJ 85/76)

How then does the Commission and Court determine whether and to what degree a firm is dominant? They have employed several indicators of market power. A critically important one has been market share. In *Hoffman-La-Roche* the Court observed:

> Furthermore although the importance of the market shares may vary from one market to another the view may legitimately be taken that very large shares are in themselves, and save in exceptional circumstances, evidence of the existence of a dominant position. (ECJ 85/76)

The Court then went on to deploy a line of argument which we adopted a little earlier:

> An undertaking which has a very large market share and holds it for some time, by means of the volume of production and the scale of the supply which it stands for – without those having much smaller market shares being able to meet rapidly the demand from those who would like to break away from the undertaking which has the

largest market share – is by virtue of that share in a position of strength which makes it an unavoidable trading partner and which, already because of this secures for it, at the very least during relatively long periods, that freedom of action which is the special feature of a dominant position. (ECJ 85/76)

The market share can however be determined only when the relevant product market has been identified. For example, it may be that a firm is deemed to be in a position of absolute dominance because it controls the whole supply of a particular product. But it may be that there are close substitutes to which consumers can turn if the price of the product in question is raised. In other words to be absolutely dominant at any moment in time a firm must have total control over all the products which are substantially interchangeable.

The *Continental Can* case although concerned with a merger illustrates this type of approach. The case concerned the activities of the Continental Can Company Inc., a large US multinational manufacturing metal containers, other packaging materials and machines for the manufacture and use of containers. It acquired a majority shareholding in a large West German producer of light-metal containers, Schmalbach-Lubeca-Werke AG of Brunswick. Continental Can then transferred its holdings in Schmalbach to a holding company, the Europemballage Corporation. It also agreed to make an offer for the shares of the large Dutch can producer, Thomassen and Drijver-Verblijfa NV of Deventer – actually the offer was made by Europemballage. This was accomplished and thus control of both Schmalbach and Thomassen came to be vested in the one holding company created by Continental. The EC Commission then intervened. It saw the acquisition of Schmalbach as being a violation of Article 86. This was a controversial interpretation of Article 86 since it was being applied to a merger.

Essentially the Commission was arguing that Schmalbach had a dominant position in the West German market for light containers for preserved meat and fish and metal caps for preserve jars. The Commission also argued that the extinguishing of Thomassen's competition, via the acquisition, was an abuse within the meaning of Article 86. An effect on interstate trade was likely in that Thomassen would not now sell competitively in the West German market, nor for that matter would Schmalbach sell in the Benelux market. The case is instructive since much turned on the question of whether Schmalbach really had a dominant position in West Germany.

The Court in fact found against the Commission. In doing so it did not invoke any particular market share as being critical but pointed to the existence of other sources of ongoing or potential competition, such as containers made of plastic or glass and suppliers of metal containers for other goods who could turn their attention to the meat and fish-container market. In short the Commission had defined the market too narrowly and had thus exaggerated the market share enjoyed by Schmalbach.

Identifying the relevant market is of course only the first step on the road to proving the existence of dominance. We are still left with the question of what proportion of the relevant market has to be attained in order that a firm be dominant. In *Continental Can* no particular percentage was specified but the Court did emphasize as a test the idea that 'the remaining competitors could not constitute an adequate counterweight'. Obviously an absolute monopoly (i.e. a 100 per cent share) as in the *GEMA* case (OJ 1971h) will qualify since there is no counterweight whatsoever. In *Sugar* (ECJ 40–48/73) Raffinerie Tirlemontoise, with 85 per cent of the Belgian–Luxembourg market, was on this test not surprisingly regarded as dominant. But the market share can fall to as little as 40 per cent. In *Hoffman-La-Roche* the company's share of the vitamin A group was only 47 per cent but it was declared to be dominant. In the *United Brands* case the share of the banana market held by United Brands (UB) was only 40 per cent.

Why have firms with these relatively low market shares been declared to be dominant? The answer is that the share of the market has not been the only factor which has been taken into account. Barriers to entry have also been important. In *Continental Can* one reason why the Commission had overestimated Schmalbach's power was its failure to recognize that food producers could enter the container market – they could produce their own containers. In *United Brands* the barriers to entry were regarded as high – there was a need for large investments and numerous sources of supply, market penetration costs were considerable and scale economies were present. In *Hoffman-La-Roche* the Court felt that Roche's technical lead and the existence of overcapacity would deter entrants. Another factor in both these cases was the structure of the fringe of existing rivals. In both cases they were small and thus offered a diminished competitive threat. In the case of UB its main rivals were Castle and Cooke with only 9 per cent of the market and Del Monte with only 5 per cent.

Earlier we noted that dominance also has a geographic (as well as a product) dimension. A firm may be dominant in a substantial part of the common market. This is of course essential because the market is sometimes geographically segmented. Where, for example, transport costs are high only the firms and thus the supply structure within a particular region will be relevant in determining the degree of competition therein. The Commission and Court have indeed been prepared to consider areas which were much less than the whole common market. The territory of one member state has on several occasions been deemed large enough to be 'substantial' – it was West Germany in *GEMA* and *Continental Can* and it was Belgium when the Court dealt with a copyright dispute (*BRT-SABAM* case (ECJ 127/73)). In *Sugar* the Commission treated the Netherlands on its own and Belgium and Luxembourg as substantial parts of the common market.

We have already noted that the sin is not to have a dominant position but to abuse it and to abuse it in a way which may affect trade between the states. In the examples below the latter effect was present in all instances. In actual cases one of the main forms of abuse encountered has been the granting of fidelity rebates. In *Sugar* two large West German sugar producers had in concert offered rebates that were conditional upon buyers taking all their supplies from them. In *Hoffman-La-Roche* the Commission took Roche to task for a similar practice in respect of supplies of vitamins for bulk use in medicines, foods and feeding stuffs. The Commission observed: 'Whether to compensate for the exclusivity or to encourage a preferential link, the contracts provided for fidelity rebates based not on differences in costs related to the quantities supplied by Roche but on the proportion of the customer's requirements covered.' Moreover, Roche was able to extend its power to products where it was not dominant, since the rebates were not calculated separately for each particular group of vitamins but were aggregated across all purchases.

In the more recent *NBIM* case (OJ 1981c) Michelin's subsidiary in the Netherlands was accused of abusing its dominance by employing a system of distributive bonuses which had the effect of tying tyre distributors to Michelin products. The bigger the proportion of a distributor's sales which were Michelin products, the better the bonus. In practice to earn the same level of bonus as in the previous year distributors had to turn in a better performance than that of the previous year. As the Commission observed: 'As a result, great pressure is put on dealers to outdo themselves each year in their sale of Michelin tyres.'

The Commission has also attacked the practice of refusal to supply. This arose in the *Commercial Solvents* case (ECJ 6-7/73). Commercial Solvents, a monopolist of a raw material needed to produce a particular drug, decided (through its subsidiary) not to supply the raw material to an existing producer of the drug. The Court of Justice stated that an undertaking that is in a dominant position in the supply of a raw material, and is thus in a position to control the supply to producers of products manufactured from that material, cannot refuse to supply such a customer with the effect of eliminating all competition therefrom. We shall return to the subject of the supply obligations of dominant firms when we discuss ECSC dominance cases below.

In the *GEMA* case the Commission objected to the activities of a performing rights society which in fact enjoyed a monopoly of the German market. GEMA was established to protect the rights of member composers, authors and publishers. Rights were assigned to it and it exploited them in return for royalties. GEMA had imposed unduly restrictive terms on its members: they had to assign to it all existing and future rights in all respects and in all countries, for a minimum period of six years. The Commission objected to the universality of the assignment required of members. It felt that they should be free to assign only a part of their rights and be able to retain the other part for individual exploitation. The Commission also singled out for criticism the exclusion of non-residents – a provision that was apparently designed to consolidate the market power of other national societies.

A not dissimilar instance of the imposition of unduly onerous terms arose in the *Eurofirma* case (ECC 1974, 60-1) in 1973, which was settled without the need for a formal decision. A company on behalf of six national railways invited tenders for the development and supply of passenger carriages. The company inviting the tenders inserted a provision giving it unrestricted rights to use the designs, patents and so forth that arose from the execution of the contract. The Commission took the view that the company had a dominant buying position and that the unrestricted right of sole exploitation was an abuse.

In the *United Brands* case a number of abuses were singled out for attack. A central issue was the charging of different prices, in different parts of the common market, for the same product. On appeal the Court took the view that price should be related to cost and should not be set at the various levels that the different national markets would bear. Also singled out for criticism was the fact that UB refused supplies to a distributor who had advertised a rival brand. Again more will be said on this latter aspect when we come to discuss ECSC cases. It should be noted that in *United Brands*, as in some other dominance cases, a heavy fine was imposed.

MERGERS

On the face of it the Rome Treaty contains no provision dealing with the control of mergers. However from at least 1965 the Commission consistently maintained that Article 86 did apply. It was of the opinion that if a dominant firm took over another and so established a monopoly then that was an abuse within the meaning of Article 86. The view that Article 86 does apply to mergers was put to the test in *Continental Can*. As we have seen the Commission lost the case because it did not do its homework properly in defining the relevant product market. Nevertheless the case caused something of a sensation because the Court did accept that Article 86 could be applied to mergers. In so doing it took a position which was dramatically opposed to that suggested by the Advocate General who saw Article 86 as relating purely to the abuse of an existing dominant structure and not being applicable to changes in structure of the kind represented by a merger. The case exemplified a continental as opposed to a British approach to the interpretation of law. The Court noted that a prime aim of the treaty was the achievement of conditions of undistorted competition (Article 3(f)). It was therefore essential to see Article 86 as being applicable to mergers. If this was not so the treaty would be undermined. If control of a market via collusion between independent enterprises was blocked by Article 85, that Article could be side-stepped by those companies amalgamating. In this context the Court was of the view that:

> There may therefore be abusive behaviour if an undertaking in a dominant position strengthens that dominant position so that the degree of control achieved substantially obstructs competition i.e. so that the only undertakings left in the market are those which are dependent on the dominant undertaking with regard to their market behaviour. (ECJ 6/72)

Article 86 is therefore now applied by the Commission to mergers and from time to time it reports on the outcome of its scrutiny of particular amalgamations. Subsequent to *Continental Can* there has been no formal decision prohibiting a merger under Article 86. However in 1980 the Commission did report that it had opposed certain acquisitions by the British glass group Pilkington. These concerned Pilkington's proposed purchase of the French group BSN-Gervais-Danone's flat glass subsidiaries outside France. These included subsidiaries in Belgium and the Netherlands as well as Flachglas AG in Germany. The Commission felt that this would have unduly strengthened Pilkington's dominant position in the north-west of the Community. The Commission sent a warning to this effect. It did not however object to the acquisition of Flachglas only (ECC 1981b, 122).

Article 86 is unfortunately less than perfect as an instrument of merger control since it cannot be activated until a dominant position exists whereas it might be desirable to prevent such a position from emerging in the first place. Because of the inadequacy of Article 86 the Commission submitted a draft merger control regulation to the Council of Ministers as long ago as 1973 – for the background to this proposal see Chapter 6. Mergers would be declared incompatible with the common market if the parties involved acquired or enhanced a power to hinder effective competition in the common market, provided also that the concentration affected inter-state trade. Only large mergers would be subject to control. Pre-notification would be required in certain cases. No efficiency trade-off was provided for but mergers, essential to the achievement of certain objectives which were given priority treatment by the Community, could be exempted. Considerable problems have been encountered in securing agreement to this proposal. In 1981 the Commission put forward a modified proposal but this seems likely to be significantly watered down and even so it is by no means certain that the necessary agreement will be forthcoming.

The possibility exists that EEC merger law could conflict with other merger laws. This point will be dealt with later when we have reviewed the ECSC approach to concentrations.

The Paris Treaty

DOMINANT POSITIONS

There are two articles which are relevant to undertakings having a dominant position in Paris Treaty products. First, we should mention

Article 66(7) which applies to private or public undertakings which hold or acquire a dominant position which shields them from effective competition in a substantial part of the common market. If such an enterprise uses that position for purposes contrary to the objectives of the Treaty, the EC Commission is required to make recommendations designed to prevent that misuse. Clearly the existence of a dominant position is not the offence. The offence lies in the abuse thereof although unlike Rome Treaty Article 86 no illustrations are provided. Equally there is no inter-state commerce clause. The article also provides that if the recommendations designed to terminate the abuse are not implemented satisfactorily then the Commission, in consultation with the government concerned, can prescribe prices, conditions of sale, production or delivery programmes as appropriate. Failure to comply can lead to financial penalties under the provisions of Articles 58, 59 and 64.

Firms in a dominant position are also subject to Article 60 although that article is not reserved solely for application to such firms. Article 60 relates to pricing. Section 1 prohibits unfair competitive practices, in particular (a) purely temporary or purely local price reductions which tend towards the acquisition of a monopoly position in the common market; and (b) the application of discriminatory practices whereby dissimilar conditions are applied to comparable transactions, especially on grounds of nationality. Enforcement powers, including the ability to fine, are provided for.

Surprisingly, considering that there are several nationalized concerns and a number of large private units within the ECSC, there have been few conventional dominant firm cases under ECSC law. One of the earliest concerned the Oberrheinische Kohlenunion (OKU). The *OKU* case was one of the earliest ECSC antitrust actions. OKU was a common selling syndicate which dominated the South German coal market – it supplied two-thirds of all solid fuels sold in that area. Although it was owned by a mixture of mining and wholesaling companies, in practice mining companies had substantial ownership ties with wholesalers and as a result OKU was directly or indirectly controlled by mining companies in the Saar, Lorraine, the Ruhr and Achen. OKU sold directly to customers who consumed 30,000 tons or more of solid fuels annually. It sold to wholesalers who themselves dealt with smaller consumers. The High Authority considered that the division of the clientele between OKU and wholesalers, with the latter being confined to dealing with the smaller customers only, was an offence under Article 66. It issued a decision which required OKU to take 'appropriate measures to eliminate practices contrary to Article 4 of the Treaty' (OJ 1953). It will be recollected that Article 4 bans discrimination and the sharing of markets. This action was only a holding operation for in 1957 the High Authority compelled a complete reorganization of OKU – it was transformed from a common sales agency to a common *purchasing* agency of wholesalers – the coal-mining firms were compelled to withdraw.

More recently an interesting case – *National Carbonizing* – involving Article 66 arose in a British context. In 1975 the National Carbonizing Company Ltd (NCC) laid a complaint before the EC Commission in which it alleged that the National Coal Board (NCB) was indulging in an unfair competitive practice, within the meaning of Article 60(1), and was misusing its dominant position, within the meaning of Article 66(7). The NCC produces coke from coal. It had a 7 per cent share of the UK hard coke market and a 9 per cent share of the domestic-type coke market. Its main competitor was National Smokeless Fuels Ltd (NSF) with shares of 84 and 80 per cent respectively. Of great significance were the facts that NSF was owned by the NCB, that NSF was the UK coke price leader and that NSF and NCC both obtained the coal needed to produce coke (i.e. coking coal) from the NCB. The NCB controlled the coking coal price to NCC and, via NSF, it controlled the coke price. It should be added that the UK government for social reasons was anxious that domestic coke prices should not rise. The NCC was in a very vulnerable position. From time to time the NCB raised the price of coking coal but the NSF did not increase the price of domestic-type coke. In order to preserve the profitability of domestic-type coke production a rebate was given on the price of coking coal but this was not always sufficient to offset fully the rise in the price. The NCC was thus caught in a price squeeze. Indeed the margin between the two prices had become so thin that the NCC was forced to consider closing its two coking plants.

Part of the NCC complaint related to the squeeze. But in addition it also accused the NCB of discrimination on the grounds that although the Board granted a rebate on the price of coking coal which was turned into domestic-type coke destined for the UK market, it did not rebate the price of coal which was used to produce domestic-type coke for sale in the rest of the Community. The Commission approached the Board on the latter point and the Board undertook to abide by the requirements of Article 60(1) and apply equal treatment. However on the subject of the abuse of the dominant position (i.e. the price squeeze) the Commission had some interesting things to say. It acknowledged that an undertaking in a position such as the NCB, which had the power to influence input and output prices, would abuse its position if it acted in a way which eliminated competitors such as NCC. Such a dominant enterprise therefore had a duty to arrange its prices so that a 'reasonably efficient' producer, who was in the kind of position NCC was in, would be able to survive in the long term. The Commission however concluded that the NCB had not abused its position. Assuming that in so finding the Commission was not implying that it was the UK government's fault and not the NCB's, it seemed to follow that the Commission had concluded that the problems of NCC were not due to NCB action but were the result of NCC being less than reasonably efficient (OJ 1976c). This was hardly gladsome tidings for NCC!

NCC decided to appeal to the Court of Justice. It claimed that there was an abuse and it requested the Court to require the Commission to secure redress. In the interim the NCB should assist NCC to survive. The Court agreed to the latter point and the Commission duly required the NCB to reduce temporarily the price of coking coal. It should be added that the NCC also attacked the UK government whose policy of price control it quite rightly claimed was highly material to the case. The matter of the abuse took longer to consider. But when eventually the Court came to deal with it, it was announced that the NCC had withdrawn and the case was accordingly dropped (ECJ 109 and 114/75). Why the NCC failed to press its case was not revealed. It may have felt that it had at least achieved some satisfaction on the discrimination issue, although it is not clear that it benefited financially from the resulting change introduced by the NCB. Perhaps more important was the announcement by the Board that NSF was going to raise the price of domestic-type coke – that was of material benefit to NCC. NCC was also bound to draw some comfort from the point that bodies such as the NCB were obliged to arrange their prices in a way which would allow dependent enterprises, provided they were reasonably efficient, to survive. The Commission had served notice on the NCB to that effect and the NCC could breathe a little easier. In its *Seventh Report on Competition Policy* (ECC 1978c, 30–1) the EC Commission drew attention to the growing body of cases relating to the supply obligations of firms in a dominant position. *NCC* is one which was referred to and others, which in a Rome Treaty context were also said to be germane, included *Commercial Solvents* and *United Brands*.

MERGERS AND JOINT VENTURES

Mergers (and joint ventures which are similar in character) are governed by the provisions of Article 66. Article 66 actually employs the word 'concentrations'. It applies provided at least one of the parties to the concentration is an enterprise producing goods which fall within the purview of the Paris Treaty – it is therefore possible that the other party, or parties, may be producing an EEC product rather than an ECSC product. Both horizontal and vertical concentrations are covered. That is to say a horizontal integrating concentration between, for example, two steel producers[1] would be caught but so also would, for example, a backward integrating concentration between a steel producer and a raw material (coal, iron ore) supplier or a forward integrating concentration between a steel producer and a steel dealer or steel user. For a concentration to occur a firm or firms must control another firm or firms. Obviously this control can be achieved in situations where less than the whole of the voting stock is acquired. A holding of 51 per cent will suffice but in the *GKN-Miles Druce* case (OJ 1974c) the Commission concluded that a 39.9 per cent holding would enable GKN to control Miles Druce on the basis of probability that only 60 per cent of the voting stockholders would be present at an extraordinary general meeting.

Concentrations must not be consummated until they have received the prior approval of the Commission. If a concentration occurs prior to the Commission being consulted, but proves acceptable on later examination, a fine can be imposed because of failure to follow proper procedure. When a concentration takes place prior to Commission scrutiny, and is then found unacceptable, the Commission can require a divestiture. Approval of concentrations can be subject to the attachment of conditions – we shall return to this point later.

Article 66 says that the Commission *shall* authorize concentrations provided certain conditions obtain. The first is that the undertakings concerned do not as a result have the power to determine price, to control or restrict production or distribution or hinder effective competition in a substantial part of the market for the products covered by the concentration. The second is that the undertakings involved are not as a result able to evade the rules of competition, notably by being placed in a privileged position which involves a substantial advantage in access to supplies or markets. The first condition obviously relates to horizontal arrangements; the second to vertical situations. In the application of these two conditions the principle of non-discrimination requires that the Commission when considering the size of undertakings must seek to avoid unequal competition. This seems to suggest that if the Commission lets some firms get bigger then other firms will feel they have a right to similar treatment. It also follows that individual decisions could lead to sympathetic industry-wide structural changes.

Article 66 clearly employs a single test – whether or not the concentration will confer a degree of market power which enables enterprises to do certain things such as determine prices and hinder effective competition. In order to do this the normal processes of identifying the relevant product and geographic markets obviously apply. It has however been evident ever since the judgement in 1963 in relation to the Ruhr coal cartel GEORG (see Chapter 4) that sizeable market shares would be tolerated. The reader will recollect that the GEORG judgement recognized that oligopoly was inevitable. But the Court went further and asserted that the further concentration of an already oligopolistic market did not imply a lessening of competition. 'On the contrary a smaller number of competitors may result in intensified competition.' This view undoubtedly prepared the way for a series of sizeable mergers and joint ventures of which the coming together of the German firms August Thyssen-Hütte and Phoenix-Rheinrohr and the creation by a group of Belgian, French and Luxembourg enterprises of SIDMAR are just two of an impressive list of examples which could be quoted.

Of course lying behind this somewhat optimistic view of the competitive consequences of greater degrees of oligopoly was a recognition of the need to accept that larger-scale operations were inevitable. That was apparent when the Court pronounced on GEORG. It was even more apparent in the late 1960s. In 1969 the EC Commission reappraised the structural needs of the industry and came to the conclusion that further rationalization was needed. It envisaged a situation in which there would be about a dozen large groups of independent enterprises, the largest of which would be allowed to represent 13 per cent of the Community's output of crude steel. There then followed a further flush of concentrations which within the space of the two years included the merger of two Belgian enterprises Cockerill-Ougrée-

Providence and Espérance Longdoz, the merger of two German enterprises Salzgitter and Peine, the merger of two French enterprises Creusot and Loire, the merger of two Italian enterprises Fiat and Piombino, the cross-frontier merger of Luxembourg's Arbed and Germany's Rochling and the joint control of Acieries de Pompey by a group of French and German iron and steel enterprises.

In connection with all this merging activity it is pertinent to note that while Article 66 refers only to the need to protect competition and does not explicitly provide for an efficiency trade-off (i.e. an economies of scale, and so forth, justification for mergers), in practice the need to allow firms to grow to the optimum size dictated by technological development has undoubtedly been an important consideration in the minds of the old High Authority, the Commission and the Court. Such a position could no doubt be justified by reference to the efficiency objective referred to in Article 2. Individual cases also indicate that economies of scale are invoked in defence of large market shares. This was so in the *Krupp-Stahlwerke Südwestfalen* case (OJ 1975h). Here Friedrich Krupp Hüttenwerke AG (a partly owned subsidiary of Friedrich Krupp GmbH) acquired the major part of the shares of Stahlwerke Südwestfalen AG. The concentration was important because both firms produced rolled products from special steels and in respect of cold rolled alloy sheet the merged firm was expected to have a market share in West Germany, the main sales area, of about 50 per cent. The Commission in defence of its approval pointed out that there were significant economies of scale in the production of this product which justified the high market share of 50 per cent.

We have now touched upon some of the features of ECSC concentration policy but the reader should be aware of one major problem. Appraisal of competition policy is greatly facilitated by the existence of cases in which particular forms of behaviour or activity are condemned as well as approved. While it could not be said of ECSC concentration policy that it exhibits no case in which a concentration was not allowed, it must be admitted that the published decisions consist of an almost endless stream of approvals! Inevitably the suspicion arises that the policy may have been too accommodating to business interests. The standard reply is that the published decisions provide a biased picture – the High Authority in the past and the Commission more recently have on occasions said 'no' but that has been done informally. Perhaps that is so but it is odd that there has been a marked absence of appeals against such refusals. In fairness it must be conceded that approvals to merge and to create joint ventures have frequently been accompanied by the attachment of conditions designed to eliminate inter-enterprise links which would reduce business rivalry. Shareholdings in other enterprises and seats on other boards have had to be relinquished, and so on. For example, in the case of the Krupp decision discussed above both companies involved in that merger were prohibited from having a seat on the board of any other steel enterprise and of acquiring shareholdings, above a certain size limit, in competing special steel producers without prior Commission approval.

When discussing EEC merger law we noted the possibility that a particular Community merger law could conflict with other merger laws. This is indeed true. Cases can and do arise in which both Article 86 of the Rome Treaty and Article 66 of the Paris Treaty have to be applied simultaneously. Equally it is possible that cases can arise in which either or both of those laws is applicable but in addition a member state may also seek to apply its own merger law to the concentration. Even more fascinating is the possibility that simultaneously *both* Community laws may be applicable and also more than one member state may rule as well. The latter arose in the *GKN-Sachs* case.[2] The acquisition of a controlling interest in Sachs AG by GKN fell under Article 66 because of GKN's steel interests. It was considered under Article 86 because both firms produced motor components, notably clutches. The EC Commission decided that there were no grounds to intervene under either provision. However the West German authorities prohibited the merger under the Act against Restraints of Competition of 1957 (as amended in 1966 and 1973). To add to the complication it was also considered under the UK's Fair Trading Act but the Director-General of Fair Trading decided to advise the Secretary of State for Prices and Consumer Protection that it was not appropriate to refer it to the Monopolies and Mergers Commission. The EC Commission noted that there was no conflict with Community principles in the fact that Germany banned a merger which was deemed to be inoffensive under Community law. However it has observed that where the Community bans a merger but the national authority is disposed to allow it, Community law would be paramount. The merger would have to be dropped (ECC 1981d, 106).

Industrial and commercial property rights

This brings us face to face with the topic of patents, trade marks and copyrights[3] which we are now in a position to consider having dealt with all the various provisions which relate to the free movement of goods and the maintenance of competition. Two points arise immediately. First, these are not matters which have given rise to problems in the ECSC – they are however extremely important in the EEC context. Secondly, property rights are complex matters and we shall do no more than concern ourselves with the broad principles.

The basic problem is simple. The EEC is based on the free movement of goods and Article 30 *et seq.* reminds us of that fact. Equally Articles 85 and 86 seek to create and maintain competition and it is possible to envisage agreements involving patents which conflict with that objective and also interfere with the flow of inter-state trade. On the other hand, as we noted in Chapter 2, Article 36 allows member states to restrict imports in order to protect industrial and commercial property (provided there is no arbitrary discrimination or that the action is not merely a disguised restriction of trade). The basic problem is how can these two be reconciled? Is it the freedom of trade or the protection of industrial and commercial property which must prevail?

The broad answer seems to be that a distinction has to be drawn between the *existence* of a property right and its exercise. Let us consider a patent. The existence of such a property right in so far as it is a monopoly to manufacture is untouched (the national legislatures decide on these matters). But the exercise of the right is subject to Community law. For example, a patent owner might attempt to prevent the import of the patented product which had been legally put into circulation in another member state by the patent owner himself or by his licensee. Such action comes within the ambit of Community law and would in fact be a breach of it. The territorial protection aspect of patents, trade marks and copyrights has indeed been dealt a mortal blow by a number of decisions and judgements.

In the *Grundig-Consten* case, discussed in Chapter 4, the prevention of parallel imports was achieved partly by the territorial protection arrangements which we discussed earlier, but also by the West German firm Grundig assigning its trade mark GINT (Grundig *Int*ernational) to the French sole dealer Consten. This was condemned by the Court of Justice on the ground that it helped to reinforce the compartmentalization of national markets. The *Sirena-Eda* case (ECJ

40/70) also concerned trade marks. An American company Mark Allen, specializing in shaving creams had registered a trade mark Prep in Italy. Later Mark Allen transferred the trade mark to an Italian company Sirena. Mark Allen also allowed a German company to use its mark. As a result both the Italian and the German firms produced the toiletries under the Prep mark and no problem arose while each kept within its own national territory. However an import–export company Novimpex SRL obtained supplies of the German product and began to sell them on the Italian market. At this point Sirena took action in the appropriate Italian court, seeking to prevent the import of a good bearing a trade mark in respect of which it claimed it had a monopoly in Italy. The matter was referred to the Court of Justice for a preliminary ruling. The case was considered under Article 85 since an agreement existed in connection with the assignment of the trade mark. The Court concluded:

> Article 85 therefore applies where, by virtue of trade mark rights, imports of products originating in other member-States, bearing the same trade mark because their owners have acquired the trade mark itself or the right to use it through agreements with one other or with third parties, are prevented. (ECJ 40/70)

In another case – *Deutsche Gramaphon* v. *Metro* (ECJ 78/70) – which in effect concerned copyrights, a conclusion with similar territorial consequences was reached.

On the other hand in the *Parke Davis* case (ECJ 24/67) a holder of a Dutch patent for a pharmaceutical product was allowed to prevent the import of an identical product from Italy. However the circumstances were special in that in Italy no patent protection for pharmaceuticals is possible and so the Dutch patent was itself clearly under threat. In the *Centrafarm* v. *Sterling Drug* case (ECJ 15/74) this kind of protective behaviour was not allowed. Sterling Drug possessed parallel drug patents in several member states including the UK, Germany and the Netherlands. It licensed its *subsidiaries* in the various member states to manufacture or to sell the drug. The case arose because a Dutch firm Centrafarm obtained supplies of the drug in Germany and the UK and offered them for sale in the Netherlands. Sterling sought to prevent the import of the drugs on the grounds that it infringed its Dutch patent rights. The case was referred to the Court of Justice for a preliminary ruling. The Court was of the view that an attempt by the owner of a patent to prevent the import of a product, protected by that patent, which had been marketed in another member state by the patent owner was incompatible with the concept of the free movement of goods. The Sterling subsidiaries had exhausted their rights in the first marketing of the goods. If the party who had acquired them then sought to sell them in another territory where a parallel patent existed that was perfectly compatible with the common market. It should be noted that in this case there was no agreement of the Article 85 type because all the firms enjoying the patent rights were subsidiaries of the patent owner. Article 85 did therefore apply. Instead the Court of Justice based its conclusions on the free movement of goods requirement contained in Article 30 *et seq*.

What general interpretation do we put upon policy in this area? Tentatively it would appear to take the following form. The patent is a reward for the inventor – that reward is undermined if persons other than the patent owner, his subsidiaries and licensees can illegitimately market the product or process in question. Equally the reputation of the owner of a trade mark, his subsidiaries and licensees could be undermined if the mark was illegitimately attached to goods which might turn out to be of inferior quality. Similar considerations would apply in the case of copyrights. Article 36 could presumably be legitimately invoked to protect the owners of industrial and commercial property, their subsidiaries and licensees against such illegitimate imports. What the property owners, their subsidiaries and licensees cannot do is to prevent the free circulation of goods which they themselves have legitimately put into circulation. Having put them into circulation they have exhausted their rights in the goods. Obviously, if these property owners charge different prices in different markets then they are bound to create conditions which are likely to encourage arbitrageurs to shift goods from low price to high price markets. The attitude of the Commission and Court would appear to be that such arbitraging is an essential feature of a common market and is desirable since it helps to eliminate discrimination between national markets – the reader will note the comparable role of parallel imports in sole distribution situations. It follows that if property owners wish to prevent such arbitrage they will have to arrange matters so that prices are equal as between the various national markets and they will have to supply fully the national demands at that equalized price. The fact that the common price may be inflated is a property of the market imperfection which is inherent in the patent or trade mark. In practice the extent to which that imperfection can be exploited will depend on the degree of competition, if any, offered by substitutes.

The reader is also referred to Chapter 6 where the provisions of the Common Market Patent Convention and the proposal for a European trade mark are discussed.

Public enterprises

The Paris Treaty has no special provisions relating to such enterprises. As far as competition policy is concerned they come under the same rules as private enterprises. For example, we have seen that Article 66(7) was in principle as much applicable to the NCB, a public corporation, as to the Oberrheinische Kohlenunion AG, a private company. By contrast the Rome Treaty contains specific provisions and the ones we are concerned with at this point are contained in Article 90.

Article 90 recognizes that there are public undertakings and that there are undertakings to which the state grants special or exclusive rights. The former would, for example, include what in the UK are called public corporations or, to use another term, nationalized industries. The latter are private undertakings to which the state grants some concession. Thus a private railway company might be granted the right to provide a public service. Then again private firms might be given authority to supply water or gas.[4] It is quite apparent that both these categories are governed by the rules of competition. Such a conclusion follows from the following points. A cursory glance at the Rome Treaty shows that Article 90 falls within a section of the Treaty entitled 'Rules on Competition'. Moreover it comes under a heading entitled 'Rules applying to undertakings'. It is quite clear that by virtue of the absence of the word 'private' those rules apply to *all* undertakings and not just *private* undertakings.

With the above points in mind we can now consider the details of Article 90. Article 90(1) requires that in respect of public undertakings and undertakings to which member states grant special or exclusive rights, the member states shall not 'enact or maintain in force' any measure contrary to Article 7 (non-discrimination), Articles 85 to 89 (cartels and dominant positions) and Articles 92 to 94 (state aids).[5] The reason why this stipulation was included is as follows. If a public corporation behaved in a way which, for example, breached Article 7 or Article 86, there would be little point in commanding the corporation to desist if the statutory terms under which it operated (as laid down by the member state in question) required it to behave in a way which broke the rules. Because of that, Article 90(1) commands states not to breach the specified articles *at the same time as it requires the enterprises not to do so.* There is a double duty here.[6]

Having placed such enterprises quite firmly under the controlling influence of the non-discrimination and competition rules (the latter of course extend beyond Articles 85 to 89 so as to include Articles 92 to 94), Article 90(2) of the Treaty recognizes two limited exceptions. These exceptions apply to undertakings entrusted with the operation of services of general economic interest and undertakings having the character of a revenue-raising monopoly. (Since the word 'private' is not used it follows that these may be public or private.) The former are usually taken to refer to utility undertakings supplying water, gas and electricity. The latter have already been encountered in Chapter 3 when we discussed state monopolies of a commercial character as, for example, those concerned with alcohol and tobacco. Article 90(2) declares that these two categories are subject to the rules of the Treaty, in particular those relating to competition. In other words Articles 7, 85 to 89 and 92 to 94 (to quote some obvious ones) apply to them too. But the Article then goes on to indicate that those non-discrimination and competition provisions apply only to the extent that they do not obstruct the performance of the tasks assigned to these two types of undertaking. There is also a further stipulation that this exceptional treatment must not cause inter-state trade to be affected to a degree which is contrary to the interests of the Community.

Article 90(3) empowers the EC Commission to ensure that the provisions of Articles 90(1) and 90(2) are applied and to that end it can address decisions and *directives* to member states.

One thing is clear from all this, namely that if a government nationalizes a firm or a whole industry which lies outside the special categories covered by Article 90(2), those nationalized entities are fully bound by the normal Treaty rules. Firms or industries in the manufacturing sector would, for example, seem automatically to be subject to the full rigour of the Rome Treaty. This is essential if equity is to be preserved since rivals in other member states may be privately owned and they would have no escape clause to take advantage of.

In Chapter 3 we discussed state aids and indicated that one category of assistance, namely aid to public corporations, had still to be discussed. We can now remedy that omission. As we saw in Chapter 3 the EC Commission has over the years developed a policy approach to aids and has applied it to the various categories of assistance. However state aid to public sector enterprises is a particularly sensitive issue although Article 90 makes it clear that in varying degrees Articles 92 to 94 apply to them. The Commission has for some time felt that Articles 92 to 94 ought as far as possible to be applied equally as between the private and the public sectors and it has been seeking a way forward. In 1980 the Commission took a controversial step in this direction when it adopted a directive on transparency in the financial arrangements between member states and their public undertakings (OJ 1980h). The Commission is obviously concerned about the distortions which can arise when member states provide capital on subsidized terms, provide finance to cover losses or forgo profits on the normal return on funds employed. (The fact that the wind was blowing in this direction was quite obvious when we consider the way in which the Commission reacted to the activities of the NEB – see Chapter 3.) Under the directive member states are required to seek data on such transactions for five years and to communicate such information to the Commission on request. The Commission has been anxious to point out that it recognizes that, in the light of Article 222, the Treaty does not prejudice the system of property ownership adopted in member states. In other words if member states choose to nationalize this or that industry they are free to do so. Equally the power to request information about the financial relationships between states and their nationalized industries does not prejudice the right to nationalize. On the other hand it requires little imagination to see that such information could lead to action on the part of the Commission which would curb the freedom of action of member state governments in relation to their public enterprises. Member state governments, particularly those which have recently shown a penchant for nationalization, may feel that the whole object of having public sector enterprises is to be in a position to require or allow them to behave differently from the private variety. They may fear that the Rome Treaty will allow the form of nationalization but will constrain the behaviour of that form to a degree which will render the nationalization exercise useless. The distinction between the existence of a right and its exercise is a well-worn theme in Community thinking – see the above discussion of property rights.

Not surprisingly this evoked a considerable amount of concern in certain quarters. Three countries with substantial public enterprise sectors – France, Italy and the UK – attacked the Commission for adopting the directive. On the other hand two countries where public enterprise is less important – the Netherlands and West Germany – supported the Commission. France, Italy and the UK in fact took the Commission to the Court of Justice in the hope that the directive would be declared null and void. In the event the Court supported the Commission.

6 Industrial policy – the EEC

The search for a policy

In this chapter we shall be concerned not only with industrial policy as a device for influencing industrial structures (i.e. the growth and decline of industries, the size of, and linkages between, firms, and so on) but also with science and technology policy. In short, following the approach adopted in Chapter 1, the phrase industrial policy will be taken to cover both these aspects. The science and technology dimension will incidentally require us to refer to the role of Euratom.

Perhaps we should begin by seizing the bull by the horns. The plain fact of the matter is that the reader will search the Rome Treaty in vain to find provisions which call for, and provide the juridical basis of, a Community industrial policy. If we are prepared to draw a distinction between competition and industrial policy, it is all too evident from what has gone before that competition policy is well provided for, but the reverse is true in the case of industrial policy. Having said that, it has to be acknowledged that the Community is not tied to the Rome Treaty blueprint. It is possible to identify further policy objectives and to provide the means to achieve them. For example, the Rome Treaty does not refer to the EMS or the Regional Development Fund yet both have been created. In the present context this point is of crucial importance since it was at the Paris summit of 1972 that the heads of state and of government gave an important impetus to the search for the structural and science and technology components of EEC industrial policy.[1] We shall first review the steps which led up to their formal acceptance. The subsequent sections will single out particular aspects and will consider what has actually been achieved. The reader is warned in advance that in some areas of EEC industrial policy the gap between aspiration and achievement is substantial!

As we pointed out in Chapter 1 the EEC was conceived in a period of expansion and optimism. The need to intervene in industry was not uppermost in the minds of those who drafted the Rome Treaty. The emphasis was on opening up the national markets and creating the greatest possible degree of economic unity based on competition and undistorted trade flows. Nevertheless in the mid-1960s certain developments provided a possible basis for a more interventionist strategy. The Union des Industries de la Communauté Européenne (UNICE)[2] and the Patronat Français pointed to the disparity in the size of EEC enterprises as compared with those of the US and to the rising tide of direct foreign investment in the Community, much of which was American. The conclusion they drew was that in a few sectors survival would depend on a programme of industrial concentration. The problem faced by Community industry was also emphasized in books such as that of Servan Schreiber (1967) which highlighted the American challenge. However the Commission's response was a good deal more guarded than that of UNICE and the Patronat. In a memorandum, *Industrial Concentration in the Common Market* (EECC 1965b), it opted for a policy of neutrality. Factors which artificially impeded the creation of larger enterprises and those which artificially favoured them should be swept away. In short the legal and fiscal factors which impeded cross-frontier mergers should be eliminated. Equally the cascade turnover tax which encouraged vertical integration should be replaced by VAT. The size of firms would then be determined by the interplay of genuine economic factors and if larger size was more efficient or effective, firms would gravitate in that direction. If real economic benefits were likely to arise from cross-frontier mergers and links then firms should be free to develop on that basis. The Commission, guided by its Competition Directorate (currently this is Directorate General (DG) IV), did not at this point put its weight behind a policy of positive merger sponsorship.

The weakness of the Community in the area of technology was recognized. The EEC Medium Term Economic Committee set up a Working Party for Scientific and Technical Research Policy (PREST) and it produced a report in 1967 in which it advocated a series of initiatives for stimulating research and innovation at national and Community level. Seven areas of technological collaboration were suggested – these were data processing, telecommunications, transport, oceanography, the metallurgical industries, pollution and meteorology. It also recommended the study at Community level of national and international research work and programmes in the nuclear, space and aeronautics fields. Additionally it advocated (i) the comparison of national R & D plans with a view to harmonizing policies; (ii) the development of common procurement policies for equipment having a high R & D content; (iii) the creation of a European system for the dissemination of scientific and technical information and of a centre for the utilization of sophisticated techniques; (iv) the development of a legal and fiscal framework which would stimulate research and innovation (this included the concept of the European Patent and the European Company). It was a seminal document. Also thrown into the discussion pot were memoranda by the Inter-Executive Working Party on Scientific and Technical Research and the French government. All this paved the way for the first Council of Science Ministers in 1967 which in turn adopted a number of resolutions. Council recognized the leeway which Europe had to make up, it affirmed its intention to press ahead with legal and fiscal developments which would stimulate research and innovation, it asked the Working Party to press ahead with the proposal for collaboration in the seven chosen areas and it envisaged the possibility that this latter collaboration might also extend to non-member states.

On the organizational plane PREST became the focus of R & D activity arising from the 1967 Council resolutions. PREST created a series of sub-groups to examine the seven chosen collaboration areas. Co-operation with non-member states was held back by political difficulties but eventually in 1970 the Council of Ministers established a framework called COST (European Co-operation on Scientific and Technical Research) through which the Community collaborated with a number of non-member states – the involvement of the latter in specific projects was decided on a case by case basis. Progress in getting collaborative projects off the ground was however exceedingly slow and it was not until 1971 that eight international agreements were signed – these incidentally were in the COST framework.

In respect of the period up to the end of the 1960s it is important to recognize that the Community was preoccupied with the task of setting on foot the many basic developments clearly specified in the Rome Treaty – the customs union, the common agricultural policy, the common transport policy. Central issues such as these together with the two attempts at enlargement and the majority voting dispute (and associated issues) monopolized the Community's attention.

However by 1970 the transition period was over and much progress had been made on basic issues. The Commission, as initiator of policy, then had an opportunity to take stock and contemplate what further developments were called for (and also what unfinished business still remained to be dealt with). The answer came forth in 1970 in the shape of two Commission documents – a *Memorandum on the Community's Industrial Policy* (ECC 1970a) (called the Colonna Report after the Commissioner who was in charge of DG III which had been formed in 1967 to look after industrial affairs) and a *Memorandum concerning Overall Community Action in Scientific and Technological Research and Development* (ECC 1971b). The latter emanated from DG XII – the directorate created in 1967 to deal with science, research and development. The science and technology memorandum was clearly a response to the fact that, as Commissioner Spinelli had to admit, despite the good intentions expressed in 1967, the resulting discussions and the supportive remarks of the heads of state and of government at the Hague summit of 1979, the Community still had precious little to show in the science and technology field.

The Colonna Report was an ambitious document. Its first section was concerned with the importance of creating a single European market. This implied pressing ahead with the harmonization of technical barriers, the elimination of discrimination in public procurement and the removal of tax frontiers. Common procurement of technologically advanced products – as we have seen this was not a new idea – was also advocated. The second section emphasized the importance of companies being able to organize their activities on a European scale. For this to be facilitated certain legal developments were called for including the adoption of a European Company Statute, the approximation of national company laws, the introduction by all member states of legislation relating to corporate groups and the possible introduction of new forms of business co-operation such as the Joint Undertaking (already in existence in respect of Euratom) and the Groupement d'Intérêt Economique (a type of organization which existed only in France). On the fiscal front there was a need to eliminate the discriminatory tax treatment accorded to cross-frontier mergers when compared with that applied to internal amalgamations. The financial structure in the Community was in need of improvement so that firms would be able to raise the capital needed for their expansion. The third part of the memorandum was more *dirigiste* in character. The Commission, recognizing the need for the Community to catch up on matters of technology, saw the transnational firm as being the vehicle which would enable this to be achieved. It therefore suggested that the Community should introduce development contracts with a priority being given to firms that were willing to carry out technological development on a transnational basis – i.e. by cross-frontier merger or cross-frontier agreement. (The reader should appreciate that although the EEC had been in existence for twelve years businesses had been remarkably slow to merge across frontiers.) The fourth section emphasized the importance of economic adaptation – new industries would have to be developed to create new jobs as existing industries declined. The emphasis was laid on the new industry element and stress was placed upon the importance of labour mobility, the application of new technologies (a topic to be dealt with in the sister memorandum) and the improved effectiveness of business management. The specific techniques to be applied to industries in decline were not discussed although the need to deploy the resources of the Community (e.g. those of the European Social Fund) so as to facilitate change were referred to. We shall see that in due course the detailed problems involved in coping with industries in decline or in difficulty became a major preoccupation of Community industrial policy. The fifth and final section called for the extension of Community solidarity into the field of external relations. A range of issues were introduced at this point including the need for fair competition when Community firms sold in third country markets.

The science and technology memorandum was largely concerned with organizational structures. The Commission was worried about the proliferation at Community level of bodies dealing with research and innovation. It suggested that a European Research and Development Committee (CERD) should be set up. It would consist of senior officials responsible for R & D policy in member states and would take over and develop the functions of the various existing working groups. This would include defining the areas for future Community research and innovation initiatives. The Commission was also concerned about the financing aspect. The existing Joint Research Centre (we shall discuss this later) needed to be financed on a multi-annual programme basis. Also the Commission suggested that it should set up a European Research and Development Agency (ERDA) to be supplied with Community funds. ERDA would provide the administrative backing and financial resources needed for the successful implementation of CERD initiatives.

Of the two documents the most controversial by far was the Colonna Report. It was discussed by COREPER (the Committee of Permanent Member State Representatives which endeavours to iron out national differences before proposals reach the Council table) but it was abundantly evident that there was general disagreement about economic philosophy. Some, notably the Germans, subscribed to a liberal market economy philosophy while the French particularly were inclined towards interventionism and planning. This cleavage was also apparent when the document was discussed by the Council of Ministers. At the end the ministerial discussion merely produced a list of ten topics for further study by COREPER. The outlook was thus bleak and those subsequent studies and other developments did nothing to lighten the gloom. However the darkness was significantly dispelled at the Paris summit of 1972. The resulting communiqué called for the establishment of a single industrial base – a concept for which the UK claimed some credit. This required the elimination of technical barriers to trade, the opening up of public purchasing, the elimination of barriers in the fiscal and legal fields which hindered mergers and closer links between firms, the rapid adoption of the European Company Statute and the promotion on a European scale of firms which were competitive in high technology. Whether the latter was to be achieved by a policy of removing barriers or by a more *dirigiste* policy of development contracts was not made clear. The communiqué also referred to the transformation and conversion of declining industries under acceptable social conditions – a reference no doubt to the use of Community instruments such as the European Social Fund and the newly agreed Regional Development Fund. Reference was also made to the need for fair competition within and without the Community – this seemed to pick up the point made in the fifth section of the Colonna Report. All this represented something of a triumph for the Commission since, admittedly, with some evasions on the potentially *dirigiste* issues, it covered similar ground to Colonna. The communiqué also envisaged a common policy in the field of science and technology, including the co-ordination of national policies and the joint implementation of projects of interest to the Community.

The Commission had good cause for satisfaction and in 1973 it took advantage of the more favourable climate and submitted to the Council two memoranda, one on the industrial base – *Towards the Establishment of a European Industrial Base* (ECC 1973a) – and one on science and technology policy – *Scientific and Technological Policy Programme* (ECC 1973b).

The industrial base document was a simpler, toned down, version of the Colonna Report. It emphasized the need to create a single market, to facilitate business integration and to promote enterprises of European scale. On the latter point a conflicting element was introduced in that the new memorandum also emphasized the importance of controlling mergers so that effective competition might be maintained within the common market. By 1973 the Commission was indeed drawing attention to the dangerously high level to which concentration had risen and to the need to be able to arrest the process. The memorandum drew attention to the fact that following the *Continental Can* case Article 86 was applicable to mergers. As we noted in Chapter 5 the Commission was at this point in the process of seeking to introduce a merger control regulation. The more *dirigiste* elements in the Colonna Report were either watered down or dropped. The idea of offering financial incentives in order to speed up structural reorganization was retained but in a muted form and as a kind of postscript to an exposition which laid emphasis on the less controversial ideas of removing barriers and creating new legal forms. The proposal that there should be a concertation of public procurement policies was not resurrected.

The science and technology memorandum reflected the businesslike stance of Commissioner Dahrendorf. It stressed the need for (i) co-ordination of national science and technology policies; (ii) joint execution of projects of Community interest; (iii) a more effective flow of scientific and technical information; (iv) technology forecasting; and (v) the creation of an effective organizational structure – the latter was a crucial element.

Programmes of future action in pursuance of these aims were adopted by the Council of Ministers at the end of 1973 in respect of the industrial base and early in 1974 in connection with science and technology. The beginning of 1974 represented a high point in the willingness of the Community to contemplate positive action in the broad field of industrial policy. We now turn to consider the degree to which that willingness has been translated into positive action.

Industrial base

This aspect of policy has already been dealt with in Chapter 3. The

Community has been pressing steadily ahead with the process of the harmonization of technical standards, assisted more recently by key cases such as *Cassis de Dijon*. It has also adopted directives relating to public works contracting and public procurement generally although there are some important areas which lie outside the latter directive. Not surprisingly common procurement, which would have been both a powerful aid to Community technological advance and a means of securing economies of scale, has failed to materialize.

Business integration

The Rome Treaty contains a number of provisions which relate directly to this topic. In Chapter 2 we discussed the right of establishment and it should be noted that Article 58 emphasizes that this freedom to move around also applies to companies. Article 220 goes on to require member states to enter into negotiations with a view to securing for their nationals a mutual recognition of companies and indeed in 1968 such a convention was signed by the original Six and became part of the *acquis communautaire* for new members. Article 220 also requires the member states to negotiate (i) the abolition of double taxation, and (ii) the creation of conditions which would make possible mergers between companies governed by the laws of different countries.

The facilitating of cross-frontier business integration required that action should be taken on both the fiscal and legal fronts. On the fiscal side it was essential that those factors which militated against cross-frontier mergers, and discriminated against companies which had subsidiaries in other member states, should be abolished. On the legal side it was equally essential that national company laws should be harmonized and Community-wide legal structures should be introduced.

We turn now to the specific *fiscal* problems which arose in the post-1958 period. Suppose that company X in member state A decided to merge with company Y in member state B. Let us assume that this was to be a true legal merger in the sense that two companies were proposing to amalgamate and that only one new legal entity would arise. This new legal entity would, depending on who was doing the acquiring, be subject to the company law either of member state A or of member state B - but wherever it was located it would be vested with the collective assets. (We shall at this point ignore the fact that the legal systems in the member states militated against such arrangements – we discuss this later. A major potential difficulty arose in connection with the taxation of so-called 'hidden reserves' – i.e. the real value of the enterprise which had not up to that point been taken into account by the relevant national tax administration. Where a merger involved two enterprises *in the same member state* the national tax administration might decide to leave this higher value untaxed since neither enterprise was leaving the country. Alternatively it might levy tax at a lower than normal rate and/or over a longer than normal period. But in a cross-frontier merger situation matters would be otherwise. For example, if company X was being merged into company Y, the national tax officials in member state A would be much less accommodating and would seek to squeeze out the maximum juice before the fruit disappeared from the national scene. A similar reaction would arise if company Y was being merged into company X. The national tax officials would seize the opportunity presented by the merger to tax all the real values which up to that point had not been taxed. The burden of such taxation might indeed deter the companies from going ahead with the merger and clearly cross-frontier mergers were at a disadvantage as compared with internal ones. There were however other problems. One arose from the fact that in such a situation one country loses a taxpayer. The other was connected with the tax treatment to be accorded to the establishments of the merging companies in third countries. In 1969 the Commission submitted a draft directive designed to deal with these problems. It proposed, for example, that the writing up of book values (the 'hidden reserve' problem) should attract tax treatment only if the assets were actually sold. This and other related provisions have however aroused serious differences of opinion and are still under discussion.

In 1969 the Commission also submitted to the Council a draft directive relating to the taxation of parent companies and subsidiaries in different member states. The object of the proposal is to create a common system for the tax treatment of dividend exchanges between a parent company in one state and a subsidiary in another. Profits that have already been taxed in the subsidiary would not be subject to further taxation when distributed to the parent – double taxation would thus be avoided. Again this proposal is still under discussion and progress is likely only when the merger taxation directive is adopted.

We turn now to the *legal* problems of cross-frontier mergers. Here again we are thinking of a true merger where two or more companies amalgamate in order to form one new legal entity. When the EEC came into existence major problems existed which quite simply prevented such mergers. The following illustrate the kind of obstacles which existed. Dutch law did not provide for mergers between domestic companies and *a fortiori* there was no possibility of a Dutch company merging with a company from another member state. German law precluded mergers between German companies and foreign companies – this applied equally to situations where the German company would be the new company or was the one which would cease to exist. A study of the legal systems of Belgium, France and Luxembourg indicated that when a company changed its nationality (as would be the case if in a merger it was proposed that the new entity should emerge in another member state) the unanimous approval of the shareholders was required. Given the highly dispersed nature of shareholdings such unanimity was virtually impossible to obtain – some patriot was almost inevitably going to protest! It should of course be recognized that these difficulties arose only in the case of genuine legal mergers – it was possible for cross-frontier link-ups to occur in other ways. For example, a company incorporated in member state A could obtain control (perhaps 100 per cent) of a company incorporated in member state B. In such a case both companies would continue to exist. These mergers, sometimes referred to as economic as opposed to legal mergers, have apparently not been subject to legal frustration.

In order to deal with legal obstacles to genuine legal mergers two approaches were advocated. The first, explicitly foreshadowed in Article 220, was to negotiate an international convention which would facilitate cross-frontier mergers. The second was to introduce a European Company Statute.

Negotiations towards a convention on international mergers were begun as early as 1965. A working group composed of six governmental delegations together with the Commission set to work and in due course formulated the *Draft Convention on the International Merger of Sociétés Anonymes* (ECC 1973b). Work was completed in 1972 and the draft was submitted to the Council of Ministers in 1973 although it was not then possible to invite member states to sign because of the adaptations made necessary by the accession of the UK, Ireland and Denmark. The convention provides for mergers by acquisition and by the formation of a new company. In the first case the company acquired is wound up but there is no liquidation procedure. The acquired company transfers the whole of its capital to the acquiring company. In the second case a new company is created and the two (or more) companies involved in the merger transfer their capital to the new company. Although, as we have noted, the basic technical work was completed by 1972, certain political problems were still outstanding. For example, should a company which was a subsidiary of a company set up outside the Community be brought within the convention arrangements? There were also problems arising from the fact that German workers play a role in company affairs by being members of the company supervisory board – the so-called *Mitbestimmung* or co-determination. The problem here was, what would happen to these rights in a merger situation? It was possible to imagine that if *Mitbestimmung* applied only to companies formed under German law, German companies would seek to escape the stricter German co-determination rules while non-German companies would not relish the prospect of being merged into a German company. The convention has not yet been signed.

The draft merger convention constitutes an attempt to facilitate legal mergers between companies subject to national company laws which are divergent in character and which either totally preclude or significantly impede such a form of amalgamation. The alternative was to create one company law which would be applicable in all member states, would exist in parallel with national company laws and would permit various forms of business integration including legal mergers. This is the objective of the European Company Statute. The idea goes back to the early years of the EEC and at that time the Commission was sufficiently interested to consult national industrial federations about the desirability of such a development. Unfortunately industrial circles did not evince any great enthusiasm and the idea failed to make progress until 1965 when the French government submitted a memorandum to the EEC Commission proposing that the Community should establish a form of European company which would facilitate mergers and concentrations within the Six. The Commission eagerly seized upon the proposal and in 1966 produced its own memorandum outlining two possible ways forward. One, which the French favoured, would have required each member state to enact a uniform law which would have been subject to interpretation by national courts. The other, favoured by the Commission, envisaged a more supranational approach – there would be a Community law under the aegis of the Court of Justice. The Commission also asked a group of experts, led by Professor Pieter Sanders of the University of Rotterdam, to produce a draft company statute. This was completed by the end of 1966. The matter was then handed over to the Council of Ministers. It referred the subject to COREPER, which in turn set up an *ad hoc* group of company law experts chaired by Professor Sanders. The group decided that the basic scheme was quite feasible but that there were some knotty political problems which would have to be resolved by the Council of Ministers. Top of the problem list were (i) the question of access (which persons were entitled to form a European company?); (ii) the extent to which the European company should be under the aegis of the Court of Justice; and (iii) the solution to be adopted in respect of *Mitbestimmung*. Thereafter the proposal became bogged down in political differences although the change in the French presidency and the heady atmosphere of the 1969 Hague and 1972 Paris summits gave grounds for hope of progress. In 1970, drawing upon the Sanders report, the Commission submitted its own scheme – *Proposal for a Council Regulation embodying a Statute for European Companies* (ECC 1970b) to the Council for approval. The new draft European company law envisaged three possible forms of cross-frontier business integration. (i) The merger of two or more companies, which were subject to the laws of different member states, into one European company. (ii) The setting up of a common holding company by two or more companies which were subject to the laws of different member states. These latter companies would be 100 per cent owned by the European company. As subsidiary companies they would keep their legal identities under domestic law but their shareholders would exchange their shares for those of the European company. The latter would be the decision-maker and the parent. (iii) Two or more companies, which were subject to the laws of different states, could set up a European company as a joint subsidiary. It is interesting to note that the proposal envisaged extensive worker representation on the supervisory board on the German pattern. Equally interesting was the point that the Commission intended that the law of the European company should be Community law and that the uniform interpretation of it should be the responsibility of the Court of Justice. In 1975 the Commission tabled an amended proposal – *Proposal for a Council Regulation on the Statute for European Companies* (ECC 1975b) which took account of suggestions made by the European Parliament, and the Economic and Social Committee, relating to access and worker representation. More recently a Council of Ministers working group has been subjecting the proposal to detailed scrutiny and on the basis of that fact the reader will appreciate that the European Company Statute has yet to be adopted.

The Colonna Report referred to the desirability of introducing other forms of business collaboration which would foster cross-frontier co-operation. In 1973 the Commission submitted a draft regulation to the Council designed to create a European Co-operation Grouping – *Proposal for a Regulation by the Council on the European Co-operation Grouping (ECG)* (OJ 1974d). This would not be a company as such but would provide a legal basis for co-operation. It would be available to individuals as well as to companies, would have a cross-frontier character and would be particularly helpful to small and medium-sized undertakings. A modified proposal was submitted in 1978 and is still under active consideration by the Council of Ministers.

Up to this point the reader will note that apart from the convention on mutual recognition of companies the business integration cupboard is bare. However there are three positive achievements to note – progress on the harmonization of company laws, the creation of a Business Co-operation Office and the emergence of two patent conventions.

The process of harmonizing national company laws should not be seen as a self-contained exercise unrelated to what has gone before. Quite the contrary: the greater the harmony between national legal systems the easier it will be to secure agreement on the kind of specific legal forms and arrangements which we discussed earlier. For example, we have noted that in the discussions concerning the merger convention and the European company statute the negotiations have run up against the problem of *Mitbestimmung*. Clearly if every country adopted *Mitbestimmung*, or something like it, then life would be easier for those who have wrestled with the international merger problem. The Commission has so far fired eight company law harmonization proposals at the Council of Ministers and several others are in process of consultation and drafting. Four directives have so far been adopted – they relate to the disclosure of information by companies (first directive – OJ 1968e), the formation of public limited liability companies and alterations of their capital (second directive – OJ 1977e); the protection of creditors, debenture-holders, employees and directions in the event of mergers of public limited liability companies (third directive – OJ 1978d); the disclosure, format and content of annual accounts and annual reports of public limited liability companies (fourth directive – OJ 1978e). The fifth directive is concerned with employee participation (the *Mitbestimmung* problem) and has been under discussion since 1972. In 1982 it successfully emerged from the European Parliament and at the time of writing is before Council for a formal decision. The sixth draft directive is concerned with the information contained in the prospectuses of companies wishing to have a stock exchange listing and has been before the Council since 1978. The seventh directive on consolidated accounts and eighth draft directive on the qualifications of auditors are currently before Council.

In 1972 the Commission decided to take the initiative and create what was then called a Business Liaison Office but is now called the Business Co-operation Office (BCO). It was initially established on an experimental basis for a period of three years. It proved so popular and useful that it became a permanent service providing information to companies on the economic, tax and financial aspects of cross-frontier co-operation and integration. In addition it acts as a 'marriage bureau' for small and medium-sized firms, putting potential partners in touch with one another and assisting in preliminary discussions. Such twinning arrangements have been popular with small and medium-sized banks but manufacturers have also found the BCO useful in connection with joint ventures, reciprocal distribution of products and the avoidance of duplication of trade fairs. In more recent years the Commission has been developing an interest in the problems of small and medium-sized enterprises (SMEs) although its role is inevitably bound to be largely indirect; that is to say it can take the interests of SMEs into account when particular policies (e.g. energy, competition, industrial and regional) are formulated.

The Community has also been instrumental in creating two inter-connected international patent conventions, the *Munich Convention for the Grant of European Patents* of 1973 (the European Patent Convention, EPC) and the *Luxembourg Convention for the European Patent for the Common Market* of 1975 (the Common Market Patent Convention, CMPC). The development of these conventions can be traced back to 1959 when the EEC Commission addressed two memoranda on the subject of the legal protection of industrial property to the governments of the Six. An expert group was duly set up and a preliminary draft agreement on a European patent law was produced – this was published in 1962. However political differences prevented any further progress until 1968 when the French government proposed that work on a European patent law should be resumed. In 1969 the Council of Ministers decided that there should in fact be two conventions – one in conjunction with non-member states, hence the EPC, and one confined to the Communities, the CMPC.

The main reason for the EPC was the desire to cut down the work involved in obtaining simultaneous patent protection in a wide range of European countries. Under the EPC it is possible, with one application filed at the European Patent Office, to obtain patent protection in all the states involved which, as we have noted, include non-Community countries. This European patent is in effect a batch of national patents. The CMPC gives rise to a Community patent and is valid in all the member states – an application for one state will automatically imply validity for all states. In order to conform to the free movement of goods principle of the Rome Treaty the kind of dividing up of the common market, which we discussed in Chapter 5, is precluded under Community patents. If a product is put on the market by a patentee, or his licensee, the patent right will be exhausted and it will not be possible to partition the common market into separate national markets by parallel patents or licences. (The CMPC also extends this principle to national patent laws.) Like the EPC, patents under the CMPC exist alongside national patents but each patent in the EPC batch is governed by the national law of the country concerned whereas the Community patent under the CMPC is governed by CMPC law.

In passing we should also note that in 1959 work began which led up to the publication in 1964 of a preliminary draft convention for a European trade mark. Thereafter because of international developments in the field of trade marks work was suspended at the Community level and thereafter the original draft convention was found to be outdated. Activity was revived in 1976 and in 1980 the Commission approached the Council of Ministers with a draft regulation for a Community trade mark.

Science and technology

The reader will now have recognized the truth of the warning issued at the beginning of this chapter to the effect that in some areas of policy the ratio of aspiration to achievement is high. This is undoubtedly true in the case of business integration policy. In the case of science and technology policy however it is possible to point to solid achievements. Having said that it is important not to exaggerate the size of the EC contribution in this area. It has been estimated that EC (i.e. all three communities) spending on R & D in 1980 was about 1 per cent of the total European (i.e. EC, governmental and industrial) appropriations. (In some sectors the EC contribution was much greater. Thus EC spending on energy Research, Development and Diffusion (R D & D) in 1979 was 8 per cent of total European energy R D & D.) On the other hand, it is essential to note that EC spending undervalues the EC contribution. This arises from two facts. First, the EC sometimes finances only part of the cost of a research programme and therefore EC appropriations are only a fraction of the total value of the programme which it is sponsoring. Second, in some cases the EC contribution is merely one of co-ordination and so again EC spending does not fully reflect the value of the R & D which it has facilitated.

In the opening section of this chapter we saw that at the beginning of 1974 the Council of Ministers adopted a programme of action in the field of science and technology. What has resulted from this commitment?

Some of the resulting developments have been organizational and institutional and so it is appropriate that we begin by reviewing the essential features of the decision-making system. This is extremely complex, there being a host of interconnecting committees. However clearly at the centre of the system are the EC Commission, which makes proposals relating to science and technology policy, and the Council of Ministers, which adopts them. As we noted earlier the Commission has a separate Directorate General for Science, Research and Development (DG XII). In 1981 all research activities including the Community's own Joint Research Centre (JRC) – to be discussed later – were brought under its wing. In 1973, thus predating the adoption of the action programme, the EC Commission created its own advisory committee – the European Research and Development Committee (CERD). The reader will recollect that a body to be called CERD had been envisaged in the Commission's 1971 memorandum. However the 1971 proposal anticipated that the membership would be drawn from national government experts. In the event CERD drew its membership from individuals, well known in the fields of science and technology, who were appointed in a personal capacity. In 1974, under the action programme, the Council of Ministers created the key committee in this field of policy – CREST. CREST advises the

Council of Ministers (and the EC Commission), is responsible for the co-ordination of national science and technology policies and also helps to identify those R & D projects which are of interest to the Community (and are thus candidates for Community financial support or sponsorship). It is composed of senior governmental officials from the ten member states together with two members from the EC Commission staff. In 1974, also in accordance with the action programme, the Commission participated in the establishment of the European Science Foundation. This body brings together the research councils and academic bodies both in the member states and in a number of non-member countries. It held its inaugural session at Strasbourg in November 1974. The COST framework, which facilitates joint research between the Community and non-members, has continued to operate fruitfully.

We turn now to the means by which the EC implements its programme of R & D. In practice there are three avenues open to it. The first is direct action and this relates to the activities of the JRC. This is the Community's own research centre which consists of four research laboratories which are located at Ispa (Italy), Geel (Belgium), Karlsruhe (Germany) and Petten (the Netherlands). Originally the JRC was called the Joint Nuclear Research Centre (JNRC). It was a product of the Euratom Treaty of 1957. Originally it was envisaged that the JNRC would carry out a collective R & D programme related to the development of nuclear reactors, the fuel cycle, reactor safety, the disposal of radioactive waste, and so on. In practice the larger member states became disaffected with the concept of collective R & D and instead began to develop their own individual nuclear energy programmes which in turn gave rise to industries based thereon. As a reflection of this trend, direct action via the JNRC declined and proportionately greater amounts of Euratom R & D appropriations were channelled into the member states. The JNRC fell under a cloud. In earlier days it enjoyed the benefits of multi-annual funding and this enabled it to plan ahead and support projects whose gestation periods were lengthy. Sadly in 1969 it was reduced to an annual programme basis. However in 1971 the Council of Ministers resolved that the joint centre should no longer be confined to atomic matters, hence the present title JRC. Then in 1973 the member states decided to restore the JRC to a multi-annual programme and funding basis. Programmes for the years 1973-6, 1976-80, 1980-3 were subsequently adopted. The 1980-3 programme was supported by a vote of 510 million EUA

– it is of course a charge on the Community Budget. The JRC in its more diversified role is now concerned with new sources of energy (e.g. solar power), protection of the environment, specific support for the EC Commission's sectoral activities, the operation of major installations as well as more traditional matters such as nuclear safety, the fuel cycle and nuclear measurement.

Direct action implies that the Community organ – the JRC – carries out the R & D. By contrast the Community can also procede via indirect action. This takes the form of research contracts concluded with national teams, institutes or laboratories. The Community pays for half the cost, the remainder has to be put up by the contractors in the member states. Again the Community contribution is a charge on the Community Budget. A particularly impressive example of indirect action is the research programme on thermonuclear fusion. This is concerned with the development of an energy generation system based on atomic fusion as opposed to the present fission method. If successful this method will produce abundant energy since the basic materials (lithium and deuterium) are to be found in vast quantities in the sea; the pollution problem (e.g. Three Mile Island) would be absent and there would be no security risks of the kind arising from fast breeder reactors which use and produce plutonium (the basic material of a hydrogen bomb). Thermonuclear fusion is the showpiece of Community R & D policy and relatively large amounts of money have been voted for it. Thus in the 1976–80 programme the Community allocated 124 million UA. Under the cost-sharing system this represented only a fraction of the cost of the programme – it was expected that the total resulting expenditure would be approximately 500 million UA. In addition in 1978, after a considerable amount of wrangling, it was decided to site the experimental facility – the Joint European Torus (JET) – at Culham in Oxfordshire. The object of JET is to produce a sustained and controlled fusion reaction using a system of magnetic confinement. The first phase of JET involved an estimated expenditure of 128 million EUA. The Community contributed 80 per cent (i.e. 102.4 million EUA), the host (UK) provided 10 per cent and the other 10 per cent was provided by other member states plus Sweden and Switzerland. Subsequently the Community allocations to the fusion programme and the JET facility were augmented. In passing it should be noted that the vehicle for JET activity is a Joint Undertaking – this is provided for under Articles 45 to 50 of the Euratom Treaty. Unlike the EEC Treaty the Euratom Treaty provides a specific means of cross-frontier collaboration and the JET Joint Undertaking was the first genuine application of that co-operation provision.

The Community also engages in concerted action. Here the Community's role is to co-ordinate national initiatives and the financial burden is limited to bearing the costs of co-ordination.

Finally we need to consider what kinds of research and development are promoted by the Community. The emphasis here is on internal (i.e. non-COST) indirect and concerted actions. In practice four priority areas have emerged. They are security of supply of resources; the promotion of internationally competitive industry; the improvement of living and working conditions and the protection of the environment.

The security of supply of resources covers energy (the Community is heavily dependent on imported energy), raw materials and agriculture. Energy appropriations have swallowed the bulk of Community research funds. We have already discussed the allocations for indirect fusion research. We should also note the four-year indirect action research programme, launched in 1975, concerned with new non-nuclear forms of energy – the topics covered were solar and geothermal energy sources, the utilization of hydrogen, energy saving and systems modelling. The programme was renewed for a further four-year term in 1979. On the raw materials front three multiannual indirect action research programmes were launched in 1978 – they related to primary raw materials, natural uranium exploration and extraction, and paper and board recycling. In 1979 a multi-annual indirect action programme was launched in the field of urban and industrial waste recycling. A multi-annual research programme was adopted in 1975 in relation to agriculture – it covered the period 1975-8. In 1978 Council adopted another programme for the period 1979-83.

The maintenance of an internationally competitive industry has attracted only a small proportion of the funds available. Some of the funding has been directed towards conventional technologies – small amounts being allocated for research in textiles and footwear. More emphasis has been placed on the development of new technologies. In 1974 the Council of Ministers resolved to stimulate development in the field of data-processing. In 1976 support for a number of projects was approved by Council, in 1977 a small multi-annual programme was approved by Council and in 1979 a much larger programme was adopted. The Commission has also emphasized the importance of the

Community keeping abreast in the field of bio-technology and in 1981 a four-year indirect action research programme was approved by Council. Recently emphasis has been laid on information technologies (novel information techniques covering computers, office equipment and communications) and microelectronics and indirect action programmes have been launched in both these areas.

A considerable number of small research programmes has been started in the areas of protection of the environment and of health – here the emphasis has been on concerted action and the financial cost to the Community Budget has thus been small.

Finally we should note that in 1978 the Council allocated 4.4 million EUA for the support of a five-year indirect research programme concerned with long-term scientific and technological forecasting (FAST).

Winners and losers

This is perhaps as appropriate a title as any for a discussion of Community policy towards the newer industries (spotting the winners) and industries in difficulty and decline (coping with the losers). As far as picking the winners is concerned we have in fact covered the topic. Community policy in this area takes the form of allocating funds for research. We must, for example, see nuclear fusion research as having the potential to give rise to a new industry just as the existing nuclear plant industry was one of the end products of atomic fission research – reducing energy import dependence is not the only end in view. Equally the stimulation of research in bio-technology, data-processing and microelectronics promises hard-nosed pay-offs in the newer industries. The Community tends to intervene at the research end. It does not itself put up capital to establish plants to produce the products based on the new technologies – interventions of that kind, if they occur at all, occur at the national level.

In practice the bulk of Community interventions in this general area of policy are concerned with coping with the losers – that is to say coping with industries such as textiles, clothing, footwear and shipbuilding. In the ECSC context the parallel problem is that of steel – see Chapter 7.

The important point to emphasize is that, given the nature of the Rome Treaty, the Community's room for manoeuvre is limited. The Community organs simply do not have the power (or the financial resources) necessary to step in and rationalize industries which are in difficulties. If rationalization takes place by virtue of intervention, rather than through the pressure of market forces, the interventions will emanate from member state governments. They possess the necessary powers or can take them. They have the necessary funds or can extract them from the taxpayers. Although Community action under the Rome Treaty is constrained by its limited power to act, it does not follow that the Community is absolutely powerless. It can exert two forms of leverage – it has the power to regulate state aids and it is in a position to control or influence imports from third countries. Textiles, clothing and shipbuilding exemplify the application of these forms of leverage.

Let us first consider textiles and clothing. Here the problem has been one of competition from NICs to which has been added the effect of general recessions of activity. However, it must be admitted that the degree to which these Community industries have suffered from NIC penetration has been variable. Victoria Curzon Price has pointed out that between 1972 and 1978 the ratio of EEC textile exports to imports fell from 1.23 to 1.10. In clothing the position was more serious – over the same period the ratio fell from 0.92 to 0.75 (Curzon Price 1981, 109-10). Moreover, as we pointed out in Chapter 1, the decline in employment in the clothing industry was not merely related to the displacement of Community production by imports. Rising productivity also played a key role although the stimulus to increased labour productivity obviously came partly from the competitive threat offered by NIC exports. Such an increased productivity effect was not of course confined to clothing; textiles were bound to follow a similar path.

In response to these problems the Commission published in 1971 its *Framework for Aid to the Textile Industry* (ECC 1972, 135-6) – the Commission seems to define textiles widely to include not only spinning and weaving but also making up into clothing. The Commission pointed out that the textile industry would have to face a situation in which it was increasingly open to cheap imports. Since demand was not likely to grow fast and the Community industry would be at a competitive disadvantage, it followed that textile production in the Community was likely to shrink. It was also likely, indeed it was already evident, that member states would seek to protect their industries by giving aid and of course that carried with it the possibility of distortions in intra-Community trade.

The Commission therefore established a series of rules. These were in effect a recipe for orderly and non-distortive adjustment. In issuing these rules the Commission was not in any way seeking to indicate that aid giving was necessary but it did recognize that in certain acute situations it might be inescapable. What it did say was that aids which merely consisted of subsidies to price were unacceptable – they would merely prop up industries which in fact might have no prospect of independent viability. In so far as aids were permitted they should not add to capacity – there was likely to be too much already. Rather aids should reduce existing excess capacity (thus giving the remaining capacity a chance to survive) and should facilitate diversification away from the areas of acute competitive pressure. Aids to existing activities were to be permitted but they should be designed to enable the industries to become competitive. Had the last element not been present the rules would have been exclusively designed to facilitate the contraction of the industry.

What we are therefore recognizing is that the Commission did not dispose of the power itself to step in and adapt the industry to increased NIC penetration. Nevertheless what it could do was to regulate the aids which states were giving in such a way that only those which slimmed the industry down or made it more competitive would be allowed. Aids which permitted firms to avoid the need to take such adaptive action were outlawed.

In 1976 the rules were revised (ECC 1977b, 124-6) although it is difficult to detect any great change in philosophy. Aids which added to productive capacity would still be opposed although this was to be confined to sectors where there was structural over-capacity or demand was stagnating. By implication aids which added to capacity would be acceptable provided they applied to the more buoyant areas of activity. Presumably this was designed to allow member states to speed up the shift of employment from the declining to the more buoyant sectors. In those sections of the industry where prices had collapsed because of low demand or over-capacity, aid should be granted only to companies converting to other activities. Aid giving to increase competitiveness *vis-à-vis* the NICs was still allowed.

In applying these rules the Commission became engaged in tussles with several member states. Italy was a notable transgressor. The Commission successfully contested operating aids (reductions in the contributions made by firms to family allowances) granted to the textile and clothing industries under a law introduced in 1971. The

Commission objected that the law merely provided an operating aid to all firms and was not selectively granted to those who took steps to remedy the structural difficulties of the industry (ECC 1974, 85). In 1976 the Commission returned to the attack when the Italian government introduced a scheme for subsidizing export advertising campaigns for textiles and clothing as well as other industries (ECC 1977b, 124-6). In the case of the UK the Commission took exception to the programme of aid for the clothing industry instituted in 1975. The scheme involved a 20 per cent grant for the purchase of new plant and machinery and a 50 per cent grant for the use of consultants and the establishment of a productivity centre for the industry. The latter two were acceptable but the 20 per cent grant was rejected on the grounds that the firms were not required to restructure their plants or to give undertakings that they would not add to capacity. The programme had to be resubmitted in the light of the Commission's criticism and the aid was made conditional on programmes of rationalization proposed by the firms (ECC 1976a, 79-80).

Man-made fibres have also encountered acute difficulties. This was partly a reflection of the problems experienced by the Community clothing and textile industries. It was however also a product of what may be termed self-inflicted wounds. First, the Italian government via the Instituto per la Riconstruzione Industriale (IRI) poured vast amounts of money into the creation of fibre producing capacity although it was warned by the Commission that market conditions and prospects did not warrant the expansion. Second, chemical companies in Europe but also the US and Japan sold plant and technology to the NICs and Eastern Europe and as a result the growth of their textile and clothing activities did not generate a demand for European fibre output.

In order to avoid further exacerbation of the excess capacity problem in 1977 the Commission requested member states to refrain from granting aid which would have the effect of adding to man-made fibre capacity. Aids were however approved where the effect was to reduce capacity (ECC 1978c, 147-8). In 1979 the Commission noted some improvement in the position but renewed the moratorium for a further two-year period (ECC 1980a, 104-5). Subsequently however the situation deteriorated as a result of economic stagnation and the temporary effect of imports of cheap American fibres. The moratorium was therefore extended yet again (ECC 1982a, 133).

Man-made fibres are indeed an excellent example of the fact that *internally* the Commission's approach to declining industries must be indirect – it can call the shots over the kind of aid which is allowable but a more direct and *dirigiste* approach is ruled out. The point is well illustrated by the fact that although DG III (industrial affairs) was prepared to give its support to the man-made fibre firms introducing a cartel to eliminate excess capacity (see Chapter 4), the Commission as a whole did not agree to a crisis cartel regulation and in fact up to 1982, despite the Commission's view that such crisis arrangements were capable of exemption, it had not formally taken that step. At the end of the day the competition principle enshrined in the Rome Treaty prevailed. Whether it stopped the firms from going through with their plan is a different matter!

We have noted that in the early 1970s the Commission envisaged that the Community market for textiles (broadly defined) would be increasingly open to imports from third countries. This was reflected in the Arrangement Regarding International Trade in Textiles, more familiarly known as the Multi-Fibre Arrangement (MFA), the first of which was negotiated in 1973 and ran until the end of 1977. It related not only to textiles but also to fibres and clothing. The parties to it were the developed countries such as the EEC, US and Japan, which were major markets for the above products, and a large number of supplier countries which for the most part could be called developing or newly industrializing countries. By agreement both parties accepted that textile exports should be taken out of the GATT framework of tariff-regulated trade and placed under a system of trade regulated by quotas. The first agreement was a fairly generous arrangement. It did not allow the penetration of developed industrialized markets to proceed in a totally unregulated manner but did, subject to certain exceptions, allow for a liberal growth in imports of 6 per cent a year.

However by 1977, when the negotiations for the second MFA were beginning, the mood of the importing countries had changed. The penetration by the NICs and recession had taken their toll. Between 1973 and 1978 the Commission later claimed that 422,000 jobs had been lost in textiles and a further 278,000 in clothing – 4200 firms had gone out of business. The attitude of the EEC and the other importing parties stiffened. Discussions within the EEC in 1976 revealed considerable pressure at national level for a more restrictive arrangement. In the event although the second MFA (to run until the end of 1981) maintained the import growth ceiling at 6 per cent, it also provided for a 'most sensitive product' range where there was to be virtually no growth. Just how restrictive this could be was demonstrated by the UK where the most sensitive product range accounted for 61 per cent of imports (Farrands 1979, 30). When in 1981 the Commission adopted a Communication and Recommendation to the Council of Ministers it proposed that there should be a further MFA but the slow growth rate of the Community and the obstacles faced by Community exports on the world market ruled out a generalized import growth rate of 6 per cent. A much more restrictive and selective approach should be adopted. In the event a potentially more restrictive arrangement was provided for. At the end of 1981 a Protocol was agreed which extended the MFA to the end of July 1986 and in it a clause was inserted which allowed for differential treatment. Dominant (otherwise described as most developed and competitive) suppliers would have to enter into negotiations about access reductions. A clause was also inserted preventing import surges within under-utilized quotas.

It is important to note that the EEC Commission regarded the much more restrictive approach adopted in the second and third MFAs as being a temporary stance. In both cases the justification was that the Community textile industry needed a breathing space. The external protection was therefore a positive element in the Community's policy of textile adjustment. Just when the protection is to be phased out has not been made clear although in 1981 the Commission, in arguing for a five-year period for the third MFA, considered that such a period would enable the Community industry to make new progress in its restructuring efforts. The Commission however stopped short of saying that such a period would be sufficient to do the trick.

Shipbuilding is another industry in which state aids have been a notable feature. In order to understand the aid rules it is necessary to appreciate that the problems of the Community industry have changed over time. In the early days the main problem was the production subsidies given by third countries, notably Japan, to their shipyards. As a result member states felt impelled to follow suit – subsidies were given to offset the competitive disadvantage arising from this outside aid giving. Since the Japanese shipyards, for example, competed for orders placed by Community shipowners and not just for the orders of third country owners, member states were forced to offer subsidies when their shipyards tendered for orders emanating from shipowners in other member states. There was therefore a real possibility of different levels of subsidy being offered by the various member states which would then distort intra-Community trade in ships. As a result a harmonized level of offsetting subsidy was agreed in a series of directives, the first of which was adopted in 1969 (OJ 1969g). Credit terms were also harmonized on OECD levels. As aid directive succeeded aid directive the permitted level of subsidy was reduced until by the third directive of 1975 an end to subsidies was eventually envisaged (OJ 1975i).

However a new phase then emerged. Following the oil crisis of 1973 there came a recession of economic activity, a slowing down of world trade, a fall of freight rates and a consequent fall in orders and shipbuilding activity. Between 1976 and 1979 vessel completions in Community shipyards fell by 42 per cent – world-wide the fall was something less being 37 per cent (Bredimas and Tzoannos 1981, 111). The industry found itself saddled with a great deal of excess capacity and not surprisingly competition on the international market was extremely fierce.

The Commission was forced in its fourth directive (OJ 1978f) to rewrite the aid rules – the anticipated final phasing out of production aids now had to be indefinitely postponed. Aid was permitted but it had to be associated with a restructuring of the industry – the latter implied that excess capacity would have to be eliminated and diversification into more profitable areas of activity and greater efficiency encouraged. Temporary aid was allowed, so that bankruptcy could be avoided, pending the introduction of positive restructuring programmes. Production subsidies were allowed – they were referred to as crisis aids – but it was stipulated that this kind of assistance should be progressively reduced and it too had to be linked to the introduction of restructuring programmes. Sectoral investment aids which created new shipyards or added to capacity in existing yards were banned and general and regional investment aid schemes were required to respect this objective. Thus we see that, as in textiles, the Commission sought to control aids so that they facilitated the adjustment of the industry. This general approach was continued in the fifth aid directive (OJ 1981d).

On the external side there was also a parallel with textiles. Quantitative restrictions on imports were not introduced but in 1977 the Commission did negotiate a 5 per cent increase in ship prices with Japan and that, together with a strengthening yen, was expected to give the industry a breathing space during which adjustment could take place.

In 1979 the Commission did endeavour to persuade the Council of

Ministers to adopt a somewhat more *dirigiste* approach to the shipbuilding problem. In that year it addressed a Communication to Council proposing a scrap and build programme for ocean-going ships (ECC 1979b). A one for one (in terms of compensated gross registered tons) scrapping and building arrangement would have increased the orders flowing into Community shipyards but equally obviously it would not have made any contribution to reducing the excess capacity in the existing shipping fleet. A reduction of the latter was desirable since it would raise freight rates and would therefore increase the incentive to shipowners to order new ships. In order to achieve these objectives the Commission therefore proposed a two to one scrapping to building ratio with the possibility of Community involvement in the financing of the scheme. The Commission thus envisaged an arrangement which had a threefold virtue – it would create more work for the yards, it would eliminate surplus shipping capacity and it would modernize, and thus increase the competitiveness of, the Community's ocean-going fleet. Unfortunately the scheme still lies upon the Council table.

7 Industrial policy – the ECSC

Introduction

In Chapter 1 we pointed out that while the EEC and the ECSC have much in common, they nevertheless exhibit significant contrasts. While it is true that the Paris Treaty envisages a system of economic integration based on competitive trade, that Treaty is significantly more *dirigiste* than its 1957 successor. It is this *dirigiste* character which we emphasize in this chapter. By virtue of the powers of intervention industrial policy is much more firmly rooted in ECSC than in EEC economic policy.

We shall first proceed to discuss the nature of these powers. We shall then see how they have been applied in the steel industry which in recent years has been the ECSC industry experiencing difficulties and thus the one giving rise to interventions both by the Commission and the member states. By contrast coal has had to take a back seat in recent years. The rise in the price of energy after 1973 gave the coal industry a breathing space although, as we recognized in Chapter 3, the industry has still been in receipt of aid. Taking a long view the crisis periods for coal were the early years of the Community when the industry was accommodating itself to free trade (as that stage the Belgian sector got into difficulties) and the period of cheapening oil after 1956. The interventionist responses to these problems were also discussed in Chapter 3.

In our discussion of the steel industry we shall first consider the causes and manifestations of the difficulties which it has experienced. We shall then recognize that the policy response can be divided into three phases – as phase succeeded phase the degree of intervention was increased.

Treaty powers

In deciding to launch the European steel industry on the high seas of international competition the founders of the Community recognized the difficulties which such a course entailed. In the pre-war period the industry had been cartelized and there was a fear that there would be a tendency to cartelize again. One way of preventing this from happening was to build antitrust provisions into the Treaty – see Chapters 4 and 5 above. The other was to provide powers which would help to prevent conditions from arising which would induce steel producers (and governments who might have to finance losses) to press for cartelization. Given the lumpy nature of investment in the steel industry the possibility exists that left to themselves companies and corporations could mature investment plans which would collectively lead to the creation of excessive production capacity. In countries where steel is nationalized the tendency to over-investment might be a product of state pressure. If the reader has any doubts on the latter score let him consider the role of the Italian government in the creation of man-made fibre capacity – see Chapter 6. If capacity is chronically excessive competition will be ruinous, prices will fall, unit costs will mount (since fixed costs are heavy in steel production) and losses are likely to emerge. The solution devised to deal with this problem reflects the influence of Jean Monnet. Article 46 provides for a system of indicative planning although the article actually describes the process as one of laying down General Objectives. General Objectives are forecasts of the medium to long-term development of the demand for steel products and the medium-term development of productive capacity. In describing them as part of an indicative planning system we are referring to the fact that the published General Objectives are designed to influence company and corporate plans but as we shall see the Commission has other ways and means of influencing investment activity.

The purely indicative aspect of General Objectives can best be appreciated if we look at a specific example. In October 1976 the Commission published the General Objectives for steel for 1980 to 1985 (OJ 1976d). The document begins by trying to estimate the Community's internal demand for steel in 1980 and 1985. Within the framework of the expected growth of the Community economy this involved trying to estimate the growth of demand arising from the main steel-using sectors. To this had to be added the trade component.

The Community steel industry is an important exporter – in 1972 its share in world export trade in steel (excluding intra-Community exchanges) was 31 per cent although by 1976 this had fallen to 27 per cent. Exports add to the demand placed on the Community's supply capacity but of course the Community is also a steel importer (as we shall see below) and as a result some of the demand arising from Community steel-using sectors does not fall upon the Community steel producers. The nature of the trade balance (exports minus imports) obviously depends on a number of factors such as the emergence, capacity and competitiveness of third country steel producers. The forecasted steel demand (internal demand plus exports minus imports) was broken down into product groups. As we shall see below the Commission has to be notified about major investment projects and in addition it carries out an annual investment survey. On the basis of its information about projects in progress, projects definitely decided and projects only planned the Commission was able to build up a picture of the likely level of production potential in 1980. It was then able to compare this with its estimate of likely demand. In practice the comparison gives rise to a forecast of the likely rate of capacity utilization in the various sectors. If production potential is expected to rise faster than demand, the rate of utilization will tend to drop and vice versa. In the former case the Commission would assume that the published forecast would cause projects such as the 'only planned' category to be deferred. In the latter case it would be assumed that the forecast would encourage companies and corporations to implement the 'only planned' category and indeed to add to it. (We are of course assuming that at the point of departure the capacity utilization ratio was already optimal.) The demand forecast for 1985 was also intended to have an indicative function but, since in 1976 long-term capacity plans for 1985 either did not exist or if they did were so tenuous as to be meaningless, no production potential data was published for 1985.

Earlier we hinted at the existence of other means of influencing investment activity. Here we are referring to the fact that under the powers provided by Article 54 investment projects (above certain minimum size limits) have to be notified to the Commission before construction work on them is commenced. The Commission then gives a reasoned opinion on the projects in the light of the General Objectives. The company or corporation is notified of the opinion and the opinion is also brought to the attention of the relevant member state government. Lists of opinions are also published. Clearly if the project is not in conformity with the General Objectives the opinion is likely to be adverse. We should immediately note that the Commission has no power to prohibit investments but certain consequences are likely to flow from an adverse opinion. First, the Commission, under the Paris Treaty, has the power to borrow on the international capital market. Under the provisions of Article 54 it can lend on to the steel (or coal) industry. It is a first-class borrower and can reflect its ability to borrow at keen terms in its subsequent lendings – it is also empowered to lend at subsidized interest rates for projects which it regards as being of particular importance. Clearly the Commission would not lend money to support projects about which it had rendered an adverse opinion. Second, it may be doubted whether any other lender would be prepared to provide finance when an adverse opinion had been issued. Of course if the company or corporation is using internally generated funds then these lending influences will be incapable of preventing it from proceeding with the project. Having said that it should be noted that Article 54 provides that where the financing of a project involves subsidies, protection or discrimination contrary to the Paris Treaty the Commission can prohibit the enterprise from drawing on resources other than its own funds to carry out the programme. Such a case appears to have arisen in 1978 at a time of chronic excess capacity. The Commission stopped the construction of a huge new steel complex at Gioia Tauro in Calabria, the grounds being the massive state aid which the Italian authorities proposed to pour into the project.

The Commission's power to withhold finance should not be overrated. Taking the Community as a whole its loans provide only a modest proportion of investment funds – between 1977 and 1981 the annual proportion ranged from 5 to 18 per cent. These global figures do however conceal a much more significant level in some states – for example, in 1978 45 per cent of Benelux investment was based on ECSC loans and in 1980 the French proportion was 35 per cent (ECC 1982b). The Commission has made the point that its influence via loans may be enhanced in periods of intense competition when because of declining profitability internal funds dry up. The timing of investment notifications has attracted some criticism and in 1981 the Commission indicated that the rules would be changed so that it had an opportunity to comment on them before firms had taken a definitive position on their projects (ECC 1981c). In 1976 the Commission also indicated that its investment opinions might have more effect if they were more widely known in influential circles – oddly (given the requirements of Article 54) governments were mentioned as well as banks and trade unions (ECC 1976b).

Before we leave the subject of the Commission's borrowing and lending activities we should briefly note that by virtue of Article 56 the Commission can also lend in order to create new employment possibly outside the steel (and coal) industries in order to assist redundant workers within ECSC industries. This power has been of practical relevance in the recent steel crisis which we discuss below. (In passing we should also note that the Commission can make and has made grants to retrain redundant steel workers.)

The discussion so far has primarily centred around the influencing of investment decisions. In addition the Commission has attempted to influence the supply emanating from existing capacity. This it has done by producing forward programmes, which have taken the form of estimates of expected demand levels as indicated by surveys of expectations in the steel using sectors. Again the purpose has been to prevent over-supply spoiling the market. In earlier days these were produced on a quarterly basis. The Commission then appears to have moved to an annual basis – i.e. demand forecasts for the coming year. However as the steel crisis developed apace in 1975 the market situation was changing so rapidly that the annual forecast became very out of touch with market realities and it was decided to move back to a quarterly basis.

The Treaty also provides for three other forms of official influence. First, a system which governs the way in which pricing offers may be made in the market; second, provisions for controlling prices and outputs in periods of crisis; third, powers to control the quantity and price of imports. The last point was discussed in Chapter 2 and we shall not repeat the details here; instead we shall concentrate on the first two.

Article 60, which we referred to in Chapter 6, prohibits unfair competitive and discriminatory practices. The pricing rules are designed to prevent these and notably the second item which is singled out for special mention in Article 4. These rules call for price publicity. The published prices must also relate to a particular geographical point – this is called a basing point.[1] Since there are a number of basing points in use over the territory of the Community we are indeed discussing the properties of a multiple basing point system. When an enterprise makes a quotation to a customer it takes the form of the published basing point list price plus transport costs from the basing point to the customer. As in the case of basing point prices, transport rates are supposed to be transparent – i.e. published and therefore known to all other suppliers and to customers. Were this the full extent of the system, it would follow that an enterprise, having named its basing point price, would be totally precluded from making any competitive deviation. However in practice there is considerable scope for competition. This arises from the alignment rules. Internal alignment relates to the meeting of competition from other Community producers. External alignment refers to the meeting of competition from offers from outside the Community.

Let us consider internal alignment first. Suppose that there is a recession and that an individual producer wishes to obtain a particular sale. What is the lowest price that he can offer? The answer is that he can align his bid down to *match* the lowest delivered price which any other producer (operating on a different basing point) could offer. Such an offer does not need to have actually been made – it is sufficient that it could be made. In other words knowing all the prices of all other producers (operating on other basing points) and knowing the transport charges of all those producers to the customer in question, he can push his quotation down to the lowest of those theoretically delivered prices. Such an alignment involves the producer in absorbing some of his freight costs and is referred to as freight absorption. It should be emphasized that we are here referring to full alignment – i.e. the producer is making the fullest use of the alignment possibility. In practice he might not need to go so far in order to secure the order, perhaps a more limited reduction – partial alignment – would be sufficient to do the trick.

The reader will note that in discussing the scope for making competitive offers the emphasis has been laid on alignment. What, it may be asked, is there to preclude our producer from making a more attractive offer by lowering his basing point list price? The answer is that notice of price changes must be given to the Commission and there is a waiting period before new list prices can become operative.[2] However having become operative the producer then has the scope to make a lower list price plus transport offer. Indeed if full alignment would not do the trick, lowering the list price would be the sole remaining way of legitimately meeting competition. We employ the word legitimately because of course in times of severe recession, when there is a desperate scramble for orders, prices are sometimes secretly quoted which are below those provided by the rules.[3]

In the case of external alignments (i.e. a Community supplier meeting competition within the common market from a non-Community source) the rule is that the Community supplier can align down only to meet an *actual* offer. The Commission has to be notified of such transactions.[4]

These rules really provide for a system of controlled competition. The control lies partly in the publicity element but also in the requirement which sets a limit to how far alignment can proceed together with the stipulation that competition can be met but not undercut. There are some critics who have doubted whether such a system can be regarded as competitive. Does not the fact that producers in particular countries tend to use the same basing point and must publicize prices lead to price leadership or cartelization? Do not the rules, with their limits on reductions and the stipulation to meet but not to undercut, take the edge off the system? The answer to these questions lies in considering the evidence. Certainly in times of recession, and in contrast to cartelized systems, competition has manifested itself in sharply falling prices. Community producers have endeavoured to fight off low-priced imports by vigorous use of the external alignment provision. Internally national groups have via the alignment rule taken advantage of differences in national price levels to make competitive incursions into each other's markets. Under pressure list prices have themselves been reduced.[5]

An understanding of the steel pricing rules is essential in order to appreciate the way in which the steel industry may respond to a recession or slump. For an understanding of the crisis policy measures however it is more important to appreciate the crisis powers which the Commission disposes of under the Paris Treaty. By virtue of Article 61 the Commission (having consulted the Council of Ministers, the ECSC Consultative Committee and in certain instances trade associations) can fix maximum and minimum prices within the common market and also maximum and minimum export prices. In the context of recent policy the important power here is that which relates to minimum prices. Then under Article 58 the Commission can (after consulting the Consultative Committee and with the assent of the Council of Ministers) impose a system of production quotas on Community producers. Both these powers refer to a manifest crisis (which is not defined) but the price powers can be invoked when such a crisis is imminent as well as present whereas the quota power applies only when the crisis is actually in existence. Article 58 also indicates that the application of quotas can be accompanied by protective measures of the kind provided by Article 74. The reader will recollect that the Commission can recommend the application of quotas or any other measure to imports. Clearly the internal price and quota provisions give the Commission substantial powers of intervention of a kind which are not generally available under the Rome Treaty.

The nature of the steel crisis

1974 was a good year for the Community steel industry. Demand was high, production was the highest since the Community began and the utilization of production capacity was at the extremely favourable level of 85 per cent. Thereafter the economic background deteriorated as the Community economy and the rest of the world felt the impact of the recession which followed the oil crisis. The course of the Community economy is reflected in the unemployment percentage which in 1974 was 2.9 per cent. The rate rose steadily until 1978 and 1979 when it stabilized at 5.5 per cent. Thereafter it progressively deteriorated yet again, this time to about 9.5 per cent in 1982. The experience of steel did not exactly mirror the general movement of the economy but like the latter it was continuously under a cloud after 1974. In 1975 the industry was plunged into crisis. Output fell by 20 per cent on the 1974 level and capacity utilization declined to 65 per cent. By the October internal prices had fallen by 35-40 per cent on the 1974 peak level and in the export market the fall was 50 per cent. Not surprisingly producers began to make losses. The main cause of the difficulties was the weakening of demand both internally and on the world market. At this stage the problem was thought to be cyclical and not structural - in time the steel industry would turn round. In 1976 there were some signs that this diagnosis might be correct since production recovered by 7 per cent on the 1975 level and with it went the utilization rate which improved marginally to 67 per cent. Prices however remained depressed both internally and on the world market. This was partly a reflection of the foreign trade position - as we can see from Table 7.1 exports fell, in the face of intense competition notably from Japan, and imports rose, thus provoking matching downward price alignments. The slight improvement of 1976 was however a brief interlude. In 1977 the crisis deepened. Production fell by 6 per cent on

Table 7.1 Community imports and exports of steel products ('000 tonnes)

	Imports	Exports
1974	4198	24,289
1975	6145	20,815
1976	9768	16,474
1977	9949	21,497
1978	8856	25,770
1979	9416	24,708
1980	8992	22,189

Source: Statistical Office of the European Communities (1982) Tables 5.1 and 5.2

the level of 1976 and the rate of capacity utilization dropped to 60 per cent. The latter was not helped by the fact that extra capacity, which had begun to be laid down in the more prosperous period, was now coming on stream. Price competition was intense, partly because of an internal scramble for orders but also because of a marginally greater penetration by imports. Prices were particularly low in some sections – for example, in February 1977 reinforcing rods were being sold for 56 per cent of the price that they had commanded in November 1974. Not surprisingly losses were being made by almost all producers. Even the relatively efficient German firm Saltzgitter was losing $20 per tonne and likewise Luxembourg's Arbed. The British Steel Corporation was losing $46 per metric ton but this was less than the French firms Usinor and Sacilor who lost respectively $54 and $78. The Community industry as a whole lost nearly $3000 million. Increasingly now the analysis suggested that the Community industry was suffering from a structural problem. If it was to survive it would have to become more efficient. Unfavourable productivity comparisons abounded. It was, for example, pointed out that in the UK in 1976 it took 30 man-hours to produce a tonne of steel. It took 18 man-hours in West Germany. But in Japan only 4 man-hours were needed.

We have in fact now set the scene for the first batch of recovery measures which we shall discuss below. In the years 1978 to 1982 the industry continued to be relatively depressed. Output did pick up in 1978 and again in 1979 but in 1980, reflecting the second twist in the general recession, the demand situation deteriorated and in the last quarter of that year capacity utilization fell to the all-time low of 58 per cent. This was the year of manifest crisis – we shall also discuss this below. In 1981 the position eased marginally but we are speaking of an improvement of capacity utilization only to about 63 per cent. Not surprisingly over this period the industry shrank. In December 1974 the Community steel industry (excluding Greece) employed 795,000 workers – the comparable figure for December 1981 was 550,000.

The response – the Simonet Plan

The short-term reaction to the crisis was to do very little. As the recession deepened consideration was given to the declaration of a manifest crisis but the Commissioner concerned with industrial affairs – Altiero Spinelli – decided against such a move. Instead the Commission contented itself with more modest measures. The forward programme for steel for 1975 was revised and as we noted earlier the programme was placed on a quarterly basis. Later in 1975 the Commission decided to institute an *ex post* surveillance of imports so as to obtain a clearer picture of their volume and prices. At more or less the same time consultations were initiated on the subject of fixing minimum prices (Article 61) but the perking up of prices in the early part of 1976 took some of the steam out of this initiative. In 1976 Spinelli left the Commission and was replaced by Henry Simonet. In July 1976 a plan for steel was tabled by the Commission – it came to be known as the Simonet Plan. It was concerned with achieving market discipline among Community steel producers – no consideration was given at this time to actually introducing import restrictions. The basic feature of the plan was that the forward programme for steel should be made operational. Instead of merely acting as a guide to producers, producers, in co-operation with the Commission, would agree to restrict their deliveries in line with the programme guidelines. In short voluntary sales quotas would be introduced (Article 58 would therefore not need to be activated) and it was hoped that by preventing the market from being swamped prices would be pulled back up. The Commission was in effect organizing a collective monopoly. The quotas were introduced at the beginning of 1977 for a four-month period which, as we shall see, was later extended.

The response – the Davignon Plan, phase I

At the beginning of 1977 Simonet was replaced by Count Etienne Davignon who approached the steel portfolio with considerable energy.

The reader will recollect that 1977 was a disastrous year for the industry. Output and prices fell and horrendous losses were made. It was the year in which the Commission came firmly to the conclusion that the problem was not merely a cyclical one which would go away when the cycle turned up. It was likely to be prolonged and in substantial degree it was structural in character. It was also soon obvious that the Simonet Plan was inadequate. Eurofer, the newly created association of iron and steel producers,[6] pointed out that a proper crisis plan would have to address itself to the role of imports – they would have to be cut back. There was much logic in this observation. It is a well-known feature of both price and output restricting cartels that the more effective they are in raising prices, the more they are likely to attract interlopers who will undermine the system. To be effective price and output cartels need to be buttressed by exclusionary practices. It should also be added that in certain areas, notably reinforcing bars, market discipline had not in fact been established – not all producers were playing the delivery game.

A package of new proposals, which formed the core of what came to be known as the Davignon Plan, was therefore put to the Commission and approved. Consultations followed with the Consultative Committee and the Council of Ministers and in May 1977 the new crisis measures were published in the *Official Journal* (OJ). The essential message of the plan was that if the industry was to survive it would have to be restructured. This meant concentrating output on new, well-located plants and getting rid of old, inefficient and badly located plants and excess productive capacity. Given the difficulties faced by the industry, states were likely to be involved in giving aid to keep firms afloat and to help bring about the new structure.

The achievement of this new efficient structure gave rise to two requirements. First, aid rules should be devised which guaranteed that state assistance was firmly channelled towards restructuring as opposed to merely bailing out and propping up firms in difficulty. The Community should equally deploy its financial assistance with this aim in mind. Second, and as a temporary measure only, the industry should be cushioned from the full effects of competition. This implied protection from cheap imports and controls over the market behaviour of Community producers. We will discuss the measures devised to achieve these ends in reverse order and it is important to note that some of the ideas lying behind them had been part of thinking which took place in the Simonet period.

In May 1977 the Council agreed to the application of *mandatory minimum* prices in the case of reinforcing bars. In order to make this more effective Community producers were forbidden to align down on the import prices of reinforcing bars (rebars) and the minimum prices were also made binding on stockholders. As from the beginning of 1978 minimum prices were also applied to hot rolled wide strip and merchant bars. The voluntary delivery targets introduced under the Simonet Plan were continued and for the products involved *guidance* prices were also prescribed.

On the external side automatic import licences were introduced. As their name implies such licences were always granted on request but the price data thus supplied made it possible to determine more quickly whether dumping was taking place. Later in the year it became increasingly evident that the internal price level was being undermined by low priced imports and it was therefore decided to institute a system of external protection. The outline of the system was described in Chapter 2. The Commission was charged with the task of negotiating bilateral agreements with third countries with a view to them restricting their exports to the Community – these came to be known as voluntary restraint agreements.[7] In the interim a fast track anti-dumping system was introduced which conformed to GATT rules. A basic import price was fixed which reflected the 'lowest production costs in third countries in which normal conditions of competition existed'. If the price of imports was less than the basic import price a countervailing duty was applied to make up the difference. Ultimately under GATT rules it would be necessary to prove that the imports damaged the steel industry. However if a voluntary restraint agreement came into being the protective system would be dropped. Community firms would be banned from aligning on the imports from the restraining country, and since the agreements provided for prices below Community levels it followed that the restraining country had a price advantage *in respect of its restrained quantity*. The basic import price system would however continue to apply to third countries which did not negotiate agreements. By 1979 the Commission had entered into or extended agreements with seventeen countries.

Given the structural diagnosis it was also important that action should be taken to restructure the industry. The Commission therefore made it known that aids which were solely for the purpose of preserving the present structure were to be avoided. It would however look kindly on assistance which contributed towards modernization, rationalization and research designed to improve productivity. Aid which was intended to save steel-making companies was permitted but the Commission would expect that the companies were being saved because there was a plan to make them independently viable within the new structural context.

In 1978 the Commission also produced new General Objectives for 1980-85-90 and it emphasized that it attached great importance to these new objectives since they pointed the way the Community industry would have to go in its pursuit of restored international competitiveness.

When in 1979 the Commission reviewed the measures to be taken to combat the crisis it emphasized that its reaction to aid schemes and to notified investment projects would depend on whether or not the schemes and projects helped to achieve structural changes in conformity with the General Objectives. Equally all Community financial assistance would be limited to projects which contributed to the desired restructuring (ECC 1979c). We have of course got to bear in mind that although the Paris Treaty is more *dirigiste* than the Rome Treaty, the Commission is not thereby empowered to step in and carry out the restructuring. That depends on the companies and corporations as well as the governments who control and/or finance them.

In 1978, thanks partly to the Davignon measures, prices improved – the Commission referred to a rallying of 20-25 per cent. In 1979 some further improvement was evident but this was selective in character. Coils and cut plates were weak. Long products, notably rebars and light sections, were considerably improved. The improvement in prices was partly the result of the Commission's vigilant attitude towards companies who broke the rules. In May 1978 it imposed fines on the French firm Usinor and on four Italian producers of rebars. The latter were located around Brescia. They were small, privately owned, profitable and by implication efficient. There were 81 such Bresciani. These Italian firms had not joined the big boys club – Eurofer – and while the latter had restricted deliveries the Bresciani underquoted them and thus enlarged their sales. Much of the weakness in rebar prices was laid at the door of these freebooting spirits. While the recovery measures were voluntary there was little that could be done. However when mandatory minimum prices were introduced the Commission descended upon the Bresciani for undercutting the prescribed prices and fines were imposed. The firms appealed to the Court of

Justice but the Court basically found for the Commission although some of the fines were reduced slightly (ECJ 154/78). Apparently the firms subsequently agreed to channel their sales through an agency which was run with the help of Commission staff. They also agreed to cut back drastically their exports to other member states (Curzon Price 1981, 89). The Bresciani had finally been tamed.

The response – the Davignon Plan, phase 2

The internal discipline of voluntary undertakings on deliveries plus minimum and guidance prices was continued in 1978, 1979 and into 1980. But in 1980 the severe depression of demand placed enormous strains on the voluntary aspects of the system. Market discipline crumbled as steel producers scrambled for a share of the shrinking market. Prices fell by 13 per cent at a time when production costs had increased by 5 per cent. The Commission was therefore forced to recommend the declaration of a manifest crisis under Article 58. The Council assented on 30 October. The Commission then proceeded to impose mandatory quotas on firms although in 1981 it was able to shift some sales on to a voluntary quota basis. In order to maintain profitability the Commission was subsequently forced to cut back the quotas – for the last quarter of 1982 the level of output was planned to be no greater than that which on a quarterly basis had been produced in 1951 – the year the Paris Treaty was signed! Towards the end of 1982 there was also considerable pressure, notably from the UK, for a further restriction of imports. These were expected to be of the order of 11.2 million tons in 1982 as compared with 8.3 million tons in 1981.

Although in 1980 the Commission had assumed a monopolistic control of the industry and thus appeared all-powerful, this did not in itself do anything to solve the underlying structural problem. All it did was to provide the industry with a sort of breathing space in which it could adapt. *Pressed too far* the insulation from market forces could indeed be counter-productive – why should firms bother to modernize if, with or without state handouts, they could scrape along with the existing structure? Critics could also argue that what appeared to be triumphs of market management were indeed long-term disasters – would it not have been better if the new Italian plant at Gioia Tauro had been built in place of existing old and inefficient capacity?

When early in 1981 the Commission addressed a Communication to the Council of Ministers on the subject of restructuring policies (ECC 1981h), it noted that in the previous five years much had been done to grapple with the problem of over-capacity.[8] But it also drew attention to the fact that the need to declare a manifest crisis was an indicator of what yet needed to be done. It pointed to existing surplus crude steel capacity of 40 million tons. On even the most optimistic assumptions there would by 1983 be a surplus of 25 million tonnes – for which there would be no market at the going levels of cost and price. By September 1982 Count Davignon was reported as estimating the Community's installed capacity at 200 million tons (a figure which had also been quoted for 1980!) while output in the third quarter of 1982 was running at an annual rate of less than 100 million tonnes. The Count dispelled any hopes of returning to the output levels which had been experienced in the mid-1970s – i.e. 130–150 million tonnes. Restructuring of course did not just imply getting rid of surplus capacity.[9] It also required that the remaining capacity should be of high efficiency. Without that the return to international competitiveness would not be accomplished.

Given the important role of state aids it was essential that new guidelines should be agreed. In June 1981 Council agreed to a new code. Undertakings benefiting from aids had to be engaged in implementing a systematic and specific restructuring programme. Such programmes should lead to an overall reduction in production capacity and should not add to capacity in areas for which there was no growth market. Aids should be progressively reduced – the code envisaged the final phasing out of aid-giving by the end of 1985. The Commission was given the task of closely supervising the application of the code. Only time will tell whether it is successful in helping companies, corporations and governments to tread the path to the sunny uplands of internal competition and external competitiveness.

8 Concluding assessment

Although the major part of this book has been devoted to competition policy, we shall in fact begin by reviewing the role of industrial policy in the EEC and ECSC.

Industrial policy

Before we turn to consider in detail the role of industrial policy in the EEC it is important to note the change of emphasis which has occurred in recent years. Although this change is most obvious in the case of the EEC, a similar trend is evident in the ECSC where powers which remained unused for many years have been invoked more recently. In the early 1970s the debate within the EEC about industrial policy centred on three lines of development. There was a call for the creation of a European industrial base – that call was concerned with matters which in this book have been treated under the heading of competition policy. The remaining two elements related to the facilitating of cross-frontier business integration and the establishment of a common policy in the field of science and technology. By contrast relatively little was said about industrial restructuring both in terms of encouraging the development of new industries (spotting the winners) and managing the contraction of older ones (coping with the losers). By the second half of the 1970s it was evident that the centre of gravity had changed. While the original three policy elements remained on the table, activity was increasingly dominated by the restructuring issue. This need to restructure was above all a response to competition from Japan and the NICs, problems which either did not exist or were less evident in the earlier years of the Community. Competitive pressures were forcing the Community to face the inevitable need to abandon certain traditional industries and to replace them with up-market and higher technology activities. Coping with losers and spotting the winners to replace them increasingly came to dominate industrial policy thinking. Interestingly and perhaps ironically the element of temporary protection which was designed to facilitate the transition from the old to the new technologies and structures proved to be much more of a unifying element within the Community than some of the proposals which the Commission espoused in the early 1970s.

While in theory restructuring is as much concerned with growth as with contraction, in practice Community policy has been concerned overwhelmingly with the problem of how to cope with industries that are in decline. However we have noted that the Commission's role in this context is essentially negative. For example, it can forbid aid which is not linked to rationalization. What it cannot do, even under the more *dirigiste* Paris Treaty, is to step in and itself positively restructure industries in difficulty. From time to time it is evident that the Commission feels some understandable frustration with its essentially negative role.

The point which therefore arises is this. Is it feasible and desirable that the Commission should be able to act in a more positive manner? If by that we mean actually stepping in and directing the restructuring then the answer is No – for a variety of reasons. One is that the Commission is not staffed to a level which would enable it to perform so complex a function. It employs only 10,000 or so individuals, many of whom are translators.[1] When the officials, as opposed to translators, are divided among the many Commission portfolios, relatively few are available to deal with problems such as industrial restructuring. The staff of the Commission could of course be increased but there are other objections which render further consideration of little value. One is that member states would almost certainly be opposed to giving the Commission such a positive interventionist role. But undoubtedly the major argument against lies in the way the Community would be likely to approach the process. Once the Council of Ministers came into the picture, and we can well imagine that the Council would demand a say, politics would fly in at the door and economics would fly out of the window. In short there would be a temptation for each member state to demand a continued presence in particular industries with the need for economic efficiency being a secondary issue. If indeed states were allocated particular shares of an industry, and some of, or parts of, those shares were relatively inefficient, a continuation of state aid would be implied since only by that route could the various entitlements be sustained.

It can be argued however that the lack of a positive power of intervention does not mean that the Commission is denied an effective role in the restructuring of particular industries. The Commission disposes of a number of important powers and enjoys considerable influence. It can seek to provide a breathing space during which industries can mature and implement rationalization plans. Here there are two possibilities which are not in any way mutually exclusive. First, the Commission can control the competitive pressure exerted by imports from outside the Community (as in the case of steel and textiles). In both the EEC and the ECSC the Commission can press the member states to agree to the imposition of external protection and in certain instances the Commission can itself initiate protective measures. Second, although in both Communities aid-giving is subject to control, it has come to be recognized in recent years that firms have to be kept afloat while rationalization plans are devised and executed. The latter may take a substantial time and in the recent depressed conditions the possibility of rapid absorption of redundant labour is very slight. Therefore if severe social shocks are to be avoided the process of rationalization has to be extended over time. It is of course essential that the possibility of such a breathing space should not be taken as an excuse for the indefinite retention of outmoded structures and technologies. It is in this respect that the Commission discharges a crucial role. It can and must insist that aid to keep firms afloat is accompanied by, or is rapidly followed by, aid designed to restructure the industries in difficulty. Equally it is essential that ultimately aid should cease. On the external side the Commission can opt for a policy of never completely insulating the problem industries from the pressure of foreign competition and it can seek progressively to restore that pressure. This approach *if resolutely adhered to* has the advantage that the nature of the new industrial structure is determined not by political horse-trading but by the application of the principle that in the context of a free international market only those who are efficient will survive in the long run.

There is in fact scope for a partnership between the Commission and the member state governments. The devising of detailed restructuring interventions is best left to member state governments. The role of the Commission is twofold. It must insist that aids do not merely bail out but contribute to rationalization. The provision by the Commission of a broad framework indicating what kind of aids are acceptable is an essential feature of such an approach. The other aspect of the Commission's role relates to competition. It must press for the progressive removal of aids and the restoration of external competitive discipline. Such an approach underlines the point that industrial intervention and competition can be complements rather than rivals.

It is evident from the content of Chapters 6 and 7 that the Commission is not engaged in picking winners in the sense of sponsoring the creation of new production facilities. In so far as the Commission does step in it tends to be at the research end. Moreover its major initiative, JET, is an example of an entirely legitimate venture. The project is so speculative and long term in character that it is difficult to envisage private enterprise shouldering the burden. Equally it would be the height of folly for the member states to duplicate such research. Elsewhere the Commission appears to see its role as surveying the technological developments of the member states and comparing them with achievements outside, thus identifying gaps in the Community's armoury. Having done that it seeks to interest the member states in filling them, possibly on a collaborative and non-duplicating basis. The above general approach to research seems worthy of encouragement. The resources devoted to it (outside the energy sector) have been disappointingly small.

It is also interesting to speculate as to whether aspects of the more *dirigiste* ECSC approach to industrial policy could be beneficially applied to industries covered by the EEC treaty. Two possible candidates stand out – the crisis powers and the General Objectives. The first would give rise to difficulties of a kind which we have already discussed. While the taking of such powers would not raise any great staffing problem, the operation of them would. As we have seen in the case of steel, the Commission has in fact found itself being forced into acting as a cartel organizer. In times of severe recession, when numerous industries might claim to be afflicted by a crisis, the administrative task could be overwhelming. It is of course doubtful whether the member states would be prepared to contemplate such an extension of the Commission's influence. It should also be added that it is questionable whether such powers are desirable. *Dirigisme* of the kind which emerged under the Simonet and Davignon Plans is not without danger from the point of view of the preservation of competition. Little wonder that in 1977 the then current steel proposals prompted the European Parliament to invite the Commission to exercise 'particular vigilance so as to ensure that the maintenance or restoration of competition is not prejudiced, either by the effects of the short-term measures adopted on deliveries and prices or by the risks of re-cartelization' (OJ 1977e). Although the Commission may have seen Eurofer as an ally in time of crisis, it may be difficult to shake out the Eurofer habit when the immediate crisis is over. The pure cartelization approach is also open to criticism on the grounds that it is unselective. Rather like the CAP, the common price is manipulated in order that the least efficient can enjoy a degree of shelter under the price umbrella. It would be more preferable (and somewhat less damaging to steel-using industries) to allow prices to settle at a lower level and to assist firms selectively according to the magnitude of their difficulties. Not only is this more economical but also it helps to avoid the development of harmful collusive habits.

By contrast the General Objectives system, stripped of the associated lending arrangements, could without undue effort be usefully extended to EEC industries where the size of plant is large and the bunching of investments could be destabilizing. There is indeed some evidence that, as in the case of Italian man-made fibre capacity discussed in Chapter 6, the Commission already discharges this role on an informal basis.[2]

In Chapter 6 we noted that in the early 1970s the Commission secured the agreement of the Council of Ministers to the development of an industrial policy in which one of the major ingredients was the facilitating of cross-frontier business integration. This was regarded as a highly desirable objective. Given the existence of a common market consisting of 10 states and 268 million people it is essential that businesses should be able freely and without inhibition to organize themselves on a European scale. The policy proposals that have been outlined have partly followed the Commission's earlier approach of neutrality – i.e. that factors which artificially impede or stimulate cross-frontier business integration and organization should be swept away. In addition it has been envisaged that specific instruments would be provided which would act as vehicles for cross-frontier and collaborative activity. Businesses would not be compelled or induced to go down that path but the path would be available to those who saw economic advantages in following it. In practice, and despite the fact that long ago the heads of state and of government gave their blessing to this endeavour, there is little to show by way of achievement. Here there is a real need for progress.

Competition policy

In this book competition policy has been given a broad definition. It encompasses policies which have a bearing on both external and internal protection. In respect of internal protection, which has been the prime focus of attention, competition policy has been taken to include not only tariff and quota disarmament but also the attack on all forms of non-tariff barrier and not just the antitrust variety.

It is important to recognize that competition policy is a key element in the European edifice. That judgement is based upon an appreciation of its *political* as well as its economic impact. Even a cursory glance at the activities of the European Communities reveals that while there are a considerable number of separately identifiable policy areas, they are by no means of equal significance. With the best will in the world it is difficult to pretend that, for example, social policy really amounts to very much. By contrast competition policy is one of the main areas of Community activity – it competes with the CAP and external trade and development as a policy area of the first rank. On a wide range of issues the competition provisions of the Paris but particularly the Rome Treaty have compelled member states to establish at Community level mechanisms for the creation and maintenance of competition across the frontiers and have required them to come together, again within the Community framework, to take decisions which modify national laws and circumscribe domestic policies. All this focuses attention upon the Community as a forum and method for formulating and implementing economic policy. The political impact of this policy-making process has been heightened by the success which has been achieved in particular areas. In this respect antitrust has been outstanding. Some of that success is reflected in the attention which is bestowed upon it by business circles both within and without the Community. It is interesting to note that the concepts and approaches of Community antitrust have and still do excite considerable interest abroad and are cited in foreign judgements. It is also no exaggeration to say that throughout the world antitrust lawyers who advise companies having trading links with the Community neglect the implications of Articles 85 and 86 of the Rome Treaty at their peril. EEC antitrust policy is a force to be reckoned with.

Of course one of the most valuable properties of the integration process is that it offers economic advantages. The fact that in practice trade creation has outweighed trade diversion is only part of the picture and a small part at that. More important are the benefits of the larger market. These include the fuller exploitation of economies of scale, the intensification of business rivalry as enterprises in one member state compete for business with enterprises of other member states and the greater choice available to consumers. In addition the existence of a large market can act as a powerful magnet for foreign investment. There is, for example, more than one way of redressing the trade imbalance between the EC and Japan and one approach would be for Japanese industry to produce in Europe rather than to export to it. At the European end the balance of payments would have to bear the burden of profit repatriation but would benefit from a reduction in the import of Japanese goods and of course employment prospects in the Community would improve. If all these benefits are to be enjoyed to the full, it is essential that a truly common market for goods should be established and we should not neglect to add that there is a need for businesses to be free to supply services across frontiers and also to establish themselves on other national territories. The task of accomplishing this is what competition policy is all about. It is one of the most crucial functions which the Commission has to discharge.

Competition policy is one of the Commission's relative success stories. This is certainly true of the EEC and as we indicated earlier it is particularly true of the antitrust dimension. By contrast we must be a little reserved about ECSC antitrust achievements. When the EEC first came into existence some commentators expressed some scepticism about the likely success of Articles 85 and 86. In casting doubts they had in mind the less than impressive record of the old High Authority on the basis of Articles 65 and 66. While it is true that the High Authority was not without its successes, the suspicion tended to arise that it was somewhat inclined to cast around for good reasons why it should do little or nothing in situations which seemed to some to call for firm action. Concern still remains – the Commission has tended to find virtue in cartel arrangements which have not been blessed under the Rome Treaty and in Chapter 5 we noted a marked absence of merger refusals. Given that since 1967 the operation of the Paris Treaty has been under new and more vigorous management, but the results still continue to disappoint, we may perhaps conclude that the problem lies in the wording of Articles 65 and 66 rather than in a continuing tradition of lax application.

The success of EEC antitrust policy is evident in the fact that no major cartel has got by under Article 85 and the Commission has been wise in not *formally* opening the door to crisis cartels. The impact of the policy is all the more remarkable when we note that DG IV consists of only about 120 lawyers and economists. However the Commission has been criticized for the length of its procedures, although its retort is that it has to give defendants time to prepare their cases. The Commission has also been taken to task for focusing too much on multinationals, notably those of the US and Japan, but not surprisingly it denies that it has any such bias. *The Economist* (1981d) pointed out that the fines imposed have been too modest, being well below the 10 per cent of turnover ceiling. Recently however the Commission appears to have changed its posture on this issue and to have been disposed to fine up to the maximum. It has also been argued that appeals to the Court of Justice are too cheap – the interest on unpaid fines being sufficient to pay for court cases. There are also areas where the competition rules have not been applied – notably air fares. This is a great pity since a success on that front could provide much needed favourable publicity for the competition-creating activities of the Commission. That in turn would have strengthened the arm of the Commission in pressing governments to make progress on other issues of interest to the consumer. The regulation on mergers still remains unadopted but the Commission cannot be blamed for that. Mergers are a sensitive issue and not one over which member state governments are anxious to cede control. It is, for example, significant that while in the UK the Director General of Fair Trading can refer monopolies to the Monopolies and Mergers Commission, the referal of mergers remains a ministerial prerogative. Incidentally the merger power would be a necessary complement to a policy of encouraging cross-frontier collaboration – such get togethers may be beneficial but the preservation of competitive structures must also be a relevant consideration.

In the field of state aids the Commission has made notable progress in setting limits to regional aids. Although, notably since the onset of the post-oil-crisis recession, the Commission has expressed concern about the resurgence of general aids, the approach adopted in the *Philip Morris* case seems adequate to meet the problem. That case indicates that the fact that the Commission does not object to the taking of general aid powers does not imply that the exercise of those powers will therefore be automatically acceptable. Rather the Commission will wait and see how they are applied in specific cases and then test them against the requirements of Rome Treaty Article 92. Of more concern are recovery measures and sectoral aids. Here the Commission will have to be resolute in requiring them to be tied to rationalization measures and to be phased out within reasonable time limits. The problem here is similar to that in steel. The Commission has recently shown great boldness in seeking a way into the complex problem of the government financing of state enterprises. Despite strong objections from some member states the directive requiring member states to reveal the details of their financial relationships with such enterprises has been upheld by the Court of Justice. This is, of course, a very sensitive issue and just how the Commission will seek to prevent competitive distortions between public and private enterprises in the same Community industry is not clear. Requiring state enterprises to achieve a target rate of return is one possibility but all kinds of difficulties could arise in practice.

The EEC has made considerable progress on the issue of harmonization of technical standards although in 1980 the Commission had to admit that it had still issued only about 180 directives and that there was a need for about 300. Harmonization promises significant pay-offs in terms of economies of scale and increased competition and, contrary to popular opinion, does not present a prospect of dreary uniformity but rather of greater consumer choice. The harmonization burden could be significantly eased by the application of the possibilities opened up by *Cassis de Dijon* and related cases. Those cases also seem to eliminate the need for harmonization which appears to be trivial. It is important that member states should take the harmonization issue seriously. *The Economist* (1978) has, for example, pointed out that in the UK a certain amount of schizophrenia seems to exist on this point. Thus British lawnmower exports to Germany were adversely affected by new German noise standards but at the same time opinion in the UK was conspicuous by its facetious attitude towards the Commission's attempts to harmonize lawnmower rules. On the not unrelated point of the need for harmonization of product liability laws it has to be said that desirable as this might appear from the consumer's angle, the Commission has not produced evidence that legal differences produce significant competitive distortions or deter exports to markets where the strict liability principle applies. Considerable difficulties have been encountered in agreeing on a detailed directive and this has led the Director General for Fair Trading, Sir Gordon Borrie, to suggest that the quest for an immediate agreement on details should be abandoned in favour of a general agreement to move towards strict liability with the details being harmonized at some future date (*Financial Times* 1982a).

Progress still remains to be made on the indirect tax front. The present arrangements regarding VAT create a fiscal frontier and the Commission has been harshly critical of undue border formalities. Unfortunately a harmonization of rates and a shift to the origin principle seem a far prospect and the present unharmonized rates and the destination principle provide a half-way house wherein the Community is likely to shelter for a long time to come. Progress in the excise field has been painfully slow. As a result, competitive distortions do undoubtedly exist. On the other hand manipulations designed to shield home production from competing imports, as in the case of Danish schnapps, have been rooted out by the Commission.

The Commission has also made progress on the creation of a mechanism for eliminating discrimination in the matter of public works contracting and public procurement, areas where buy-national attitudes have in the past been rampant. However in both these fields a number of important areas were specifically excluded and as yet these have not been opened up to competition. It must also be admitted that this is an area of policy where public authorities are inclined to honour their obligations in the breach as well as the observance.

Success in the field of industrial and competition policy is very much dependent on political will. It is imperative that the Commission should show boldness in heavily fining firms which break the competition rules. Equally it must be relentless in its attack on state aids. Having said that it must be admitted that if there are villains in this piece they are to be found in the Council of Ministers and the member state governments. There is too much dragging of feet. We have been aware of inordinate delays in dealing with draft regulations and directives on matters relating to cross-frontier business arrangements and on topics such as the freedom to supply services in non-life insurance. When directives are adopted states take too long to write them into their national laws. A disposition to act in the spirit of those directives, and when breaches occur to accept the verdict of the Commission rather than to spin matters out by appealing to the Court of Justice, would facilitate progress. Equally a willingness to come sharply into line with Court of Justice judgements would inspire confidence. The propensity of states to find ingenious ways of avoiding their obligations under the treaties is well illustrated by the case of state monopolies. Only if the political will is there will the unity of economies, the closer union of peoples and the economic and social progress of countries, of which the Rome Treaty preamble so eloquently speaks, be achieved.

Appendix

Article 85 – Rome Treaty

1 The following shall be prohibited as incompatible with the common market: all agreements between undertakings, decisions by associations of undertakings and concerted practices which may affect trade between Member States and which have as their object or effect the prevention, restriction or distortion of competition within the common market, and in particular those which:
   (a) directly or indirectly fix purchase or selling prices or other trading conditions;
   (b) limit or control production, markets, technical development, or investment;
   (c) share markets or sources of supply;
   (d) apply dissimilar conditions to equivalent transactions with other trading parties, thereby placing them at a competitive disadvantage;
   (e) make the conclusion of contracts subject to acceptance by the other parties of supplementary obligations which, by their nature or according to commercial usage, have no connection with the subject of such contracts.
2 Any agreements or decisions prohibited pursuant to this Article shall be automatically void.
3 The provisions of paragraph 1 may, however, be declared inapplicable in the case of:
   – any agreement or category of agreements between undertakings;
   – any decision or category of decisions by associations of undertakings;
   – any concerted practice or category of concerted practices;
   which contributes to improving the production or distribution of goods or to promoting technical or economic progress, while

allowing consumers a fair share of the resulting benefit, and which does not:
(a) impose on the undertakings concerned restrictions which are not indispensable to the attainment of these objectives;
(b) afford such undertakings the possibility of eliminating competition in respect of a substantial part of the products in question.

Article 65 – Paris Treaty (extract)

1 All agreements between undertakings, decisions by associations of undertakings and concerted practices tending directly or indirectly to prevent, restrict or distort normal competition within the common market shall be prohibited, and in particular those tending:
(a) to fix or determine prices;
(b) to restrict or control production, technical development or investment;
(c) to share markets, products, customers or sources of supply.
2 However, the High Authority shall authorize specialization agreements or joint buying or joint selling agreements in respect of particular products, if it finds that:
(a) such specialization or such joint buying or selling will make for a substantial improvement in the production or distribution of those products;
(b) the agreement in question is essential in order to achieve these results and is not more restrictive than is necessary for that purpose; and
(c) the agreement is not liable to give the undertakings concerned the power to determine the prices, or to control or restrict the production or marketing, of a substantial part of the products in question within the common market, or to shield them against effective competition from other undertakings within the common market.

If the High Authority finds that certain agreements are strictly analogous in nature and effect to those referred to above, having particular regard to the fact that this paragraph applies to distributive undertakings, it shall authorize them also when satisfied that they meet the same requirements.

Article 86 - Rome Treaty

Any abuse by one or more undertakings of a dominant position within the common market or in a substantial part of it shall be prohibited as incompatible with the common market in so far as it may affect trade between Member States.

Such abuse may, in particular, consist in:
(a) directly or indirectly imposing unfair purchase or selling prices or other unfair trading conditions;
(b) limiting production, markets or technical development to the prejudice of consumers;
(c) applying dissimilar conditions to equivalent transactions with other trading parties, thereby placing them at a competitive disadvantage;
(d) making the conclusion of contracts subject to acceptance by the other parties of supplementary obligations which, by their nature or according to commercial usage, have no connection with the subject of such contracts.

Article 60 - Paris Treaty (extract)

1 Pricing practices contrary to Articles 2, 3 and 4 shall be prohibited, in particular:
   – unfair competitive practices, especially purely temporary or purely local price reductions tending towards the acquisition of a monopoly position within the common market;
   – discriminatory practices involving, within the common market, the application by a seller of dissimilar conditions to comparable transactions, especially on grounds of the nationality of the buyer.

The High Authority may define the practices covered by this prohibition by decision taken after consulting the Consultative Committee and the Council.

Article 66 - Paris Treaty (extract)

1 Any transaction shall require the prior authorization of the High Authority, subject to the provisions of paragraph 3 of this Article, if it has in itself the direct or indirect effect of bringing about within the territories referred to in the first paragraph of Article 79, as a result of action by any person or undertaking or group of persons or

undertakings, a concentration between undertakings at least one of which is covered by Article 80, whether the transaction concerns a single product or a number of different products, and whether it is effected by merger, acquisition of shares or parts of the undertaking or assets, loan, contracts or any other means of control. For the purpose of applying these provisions, the High Authority shall, by regulations made after consulting the Council, define what constitutes control of an undertaking.

2 The High Authority shall grant the authorization referred to in the preceding paragraph if it finds that the proposed transaction will not give to the persons or undertakings concerned the power, in respect of the product or products within its jurisdiction:
 - to determine prices, to control or restrict production or distribution or to hinder effective competition in a substantial part of the market for those products; or
 - to evade the rules of competition instituted under this Treaty, in particular by establishing an artificially privileged position involving a substantial advantage in access to supplies or markets.

In assessing whether this is so, the High Authority shall, in accordance with the principle of non-discrimination laid down in Article 4(b), take account of the size of like undertakings in the Community, to the extent it considers justified in order to avoid or correct disadvantages resulting from unequal competitive conditions.

The High Authority may make its authorization subject to any conditions which it considers appropriate for the purposes of this paragraph.

Before ruling on a transaction concerning undertakings at least one of which is not subject to Article 80, the High Authority shall obtain the comments of the Governments concerned.

3 If the High Authority finds that public or private undertakings which, in law or in fact, hold or acquire in the market for one of the products within its jurisdiction a dominant position shielding them against effective competition in a substantial part of the common market are using that position for purposes contrary to the objectives of this Treaty, it shall make to them such recommendations as may be appropriate to prevent the position from being so used. If these recommendations are not implemented satisfactorily within a reasonable time, the High Authority shall, by decisions taken in consultation with the Government concerned, determine the prices

and conditions of sale to be applied by the undertaking in question or draw up production or delivery programmes with which it must comply, subject to liability to the penalties provided for in Articles 58, 59 and 64.

Notes

1   Definitions and distinctions

1   These were covered by a separate Rome Treaty of 1957 which created the European Atomic Energy Community (Euratom). Although there is an industrial policy content in the Treaty, its practical relevance is very limited and for the most part Euratom will make only a minimal appearance in this book, primarily in connection with R & D activity.
2   Inhibit in this context means make more difficult, totally prevent or distort.
3   We should be under no illusion about the fact that these official processes are on occasions deliberately manipulated by governments in order to protect domestic producer interests.
4   These although usually governmental in origin may be defensively manipulated by the producer interests which help to establish and modify the standards.
5   For a general account of the meaning of industrial policy see OECD (1975). For a review of the types of policies which constitute industrial policy in the UK context see Fleming (1980).
6   For a discussion of adjustment policies see OECD (1979).
7   This is the European Council which has to be distinguished from the Council of Ministers.

2   Tariffs, quotas and equivalent measures

1   In the case of the Rome Treaty Articles 110 to 116, which come under the head of commercial policy, are relevant. Article 112 requires the member states to harmonize aid for exports to third

countries and Article 113 envisages a common commercial policy based on uniform principles which are to apply *inter alia* to exports to the rest of the world. The harmonization of export credit and export credit assurance have been singled out for special attention. Other policies which seek to eliminate competitive distortions in intra-Community trade also have the effect of eliminating them in the field of competition in third country markets – see the discussion on non-tariff barriers in Chapter 3.

2 It is of course true that a firm establishing a subsidiary in another state may wish to shift capital to it as well. To that extent the free movement of capital is relevant and Rome Treaty Articles 67 to 73 provide for that possibility. We shall not however analyse these provisions. For a discussion of them see Swann (1978, 148–57).

3 That is, indirect imports of goods already put into circulation in other member states which parallel direct imports from the producer country.

4 Article 223 of the Rome Treaty enables member states to control the trade in arms.

5 For an example of a case in which Article 36 was invoked against the import of pornography into the UK see *The Queen* v. *Henn and Darby*, [1980]1 *CMLR*, 246.

6 According to Article 222 of the Rome Treaty the creation of the common market must not prejudice the rules in member states relating to property ownership.

7 It also conflicts with the freedom to supply services.

8 The period designed to enable industry to adapt to the ECSC common market.

9 But in the case of Italy the relevant duties were those operating prior to the temporary 10 per cent reduction in force on 1 January 1957.

10 For a detailed analysis of Regulation 926/79 see Didier (1980). For a review of previous cases under the prior Regulation 459/68, *OJ* L93, 1968 see Bael (1979).

3 Non-tariff barriers – the state

1 For a discussion and cases concerning notification obligations in respect of state aids see Campbell (1980, 245–7).

2 Against which a state, or an individual if affected, may appeal. For

an instance of the latter see *Philip Morris* case discussed under the heading of general aids.
3   In 1979 the Conservative government withdrew RDG status for Intermediate Areas. Prior to that such grants were available for building expenditure only.
4   For the more general welfare argument see McLachlan and Swann (1967, 36–7).
5   The EC Commission points out that harmonization of standards can raise the quality of life in matters such as safety and the environment since the Community standard can be based on the best national practice available. Consumer choice is also increased. The notion that harmonization will lead to less variety is fallacious. Rather the existence of non-tariff barriers reduces national choice. Although products may be standardized in certain essential respects they can still exhibit wide variations of styling and performance. Thus the car in the EEC has been subject to considerable harmonization but the range of choice is still vast.
6   Recommendations for moving the UK towards strict liability have been made by the Law Commission and the Scottish Law Commission (1975) *Liability for Defective Products*, Cmnd 6831, and by the (1978) Royal Commission on Civil Liability and Compensation for Personal Injuries (Pearson Commission), Cmnd 7054.

4 Non-tariff barriers – cartels

1   For more details on the Community approach to the problem of double jeopardy see Harding (1979).
2   The Commission carried out a follow-up study to see what effect the decision had had on market behaviour. The Commission came to the conclusion that in 1972 there was still evidence of concerted behaviour. However the evidence available in respect of price increases in 1973 and 1974 seemed to suggest that some loosening up had occurred – see ECC (1975a, 80–1).
3   The decisions in respect of the fertilizer common selling syndicates gave rise to some controversy. Some doubted whether the firms were likely to behave independently in interstate trade given that they were free to co-ordinate sales policy in the domestic market and in exports to third countries. The Commission therefore carried out a follow-up study which seemed to indicate a satisfactory state of affairs – see ECC (1975a).

5 Non-tariff barriers – concentrations and other issues

1 Technically for such a merger to be truly horizontal the firms would not merely have to be steel producers but also produce the same steel products, e.g. sheet or beams of ordinary quality.
2 For a most thorough and illuminating account of the *GKN-Sachs* case see Tillotson (1980).
3 Undoubtedly the most readable account of industrial property case law is Campbell (1980).
4 Commentators are of the opinion that private undertakings such as banks and insurance companies, which often operate under licence, would not be included in this definition of Article 90(1).
5 Article 91 is also included. This relates to dumping but clearly this requirement becomes redundant in the post-transition period.
6 The *National Carbonizing* case, discussed above under ECSC dominant position policy, is a good example of a public corporation, the NCB, being caught up in a government price policy and, perhaps against its own better judgement, being charged with anti-competitive conduct.

6 Industrial policy – the EEC

1 The Paris summit was not the first occasion upon which the heads of state and of government addressed themselves to the need for co-ordinated and common initiatives in the field of scientific research and technological development – this endeavour was explicitly commended in the Hague summit communiqué of 1969.
2 This is the body representing industry in the Community – it parallels at Community level the work of bodies such as the CBI at national level.

7 Industrial policy – the ECSC

1 The basing point does not have to be the steel producer's factory.
2 During 1974 when there was a boom in the industry and prices were tending to rise the Commission, in order to slow the price rise down, extended the length of the waiting period from two days to a fortnight.
3 To try and prevent this the Commission carries out spot checks on Community producers. The fact that derelictions do occur is evident from the complaints made by UK steel producers about the

behaviour of other ECSC suppliers in the UK market in 1982 – see *Financial Times* (1982b).
4 From time to time the freedom to align down on offers from outside has been suspended – this was so in respect of state trading nations during the period 1964 to 1973.
5 On the competitive nature of the Community steel industry notably in recessions see Swann and McLachlan (1965); Stegemann (1977); Heusdens and de Horn (1980).
6 Eurofer, the European Association of Iron and Steel Producing Industries, was founded in December 1976. Its headquarters are in Luxembourg. The Commission no doubt welcomed the foundation of Eurofer because it was a useful vehicle in helping to organize the Simonet and Davignon measures.
7 Restraint efforts were not new. As early as 1965 the old High Authority had, in conjunction with the Japanese government, set up the ECSC–Japan Contact Group. In 1969 a three-year United States–Japanese–European restraint arrangement was entered into. It was extended in 1971 but lapsed in the 1974 boom. In October 1975 the Japan–Europe element was revived when the six largest Japanese producers agreed to restrict their steel exports to Europe. In the same year talks were held with Spain and Austria.
8 Some countries do however seem to have been more willing than others to slim down capacity. For example, in October 1982 it was apparent that while the UK had slashed steel employment by 52 per cent over the previous four years, France had managed only 26 per cent, Belgium 12 per cent and Italy 10 per cent. Not all the difference was due to the relatively acute nature of the UK inefficiency problem.
9 In 1982 the restructuring problem was complicated by the threat of the US to impose import duties on steel from the ECSC. It was alleged that subsidies received by ECSC producers gave rise to dumping. In the event the proposed duties were dropped in return for an undertaking negotiated by the EC Commission that ECSC exports to the US would be cut.

8 Concluding assessment

1 David Allen has pointed out that the EC Commission employs fewer people than Wandsworth Borough Council. This helps to put the Commission in perspective.

2 The Commission already receives notification and renders opinions on coal and nuclear investments – the latter under the Euratom Treaty. In 1972 the Council of Ministers also adopted measures which give the Commission information on planned investment in the oil, natural gas and electricity sectors. The Commission has indicated its intention, notably in the oil sector, to exercise a guiding influence – see EC Commission (1980c, 30).

References

Bael, I. V. (1979) 'Ten years of EEC anti-dumping enforcement', *Journal of World Trade Law*, 13, 395–408.

Bredimas, A. E. and Tzoannos, J. G. (1981) 'In search of a common shipping policy for the EC', *Journal of Common Market Studies*, 20(2), 93–114.

Campbell, A. (1980) *EC Competition Law*, Amsterdam, North-Holland.

Curzon Price, V. (1981) *Industrial Policies in the European Community*, London, Macmillan.

De La Torre, J. (1981) 'Public intervention strategies in the European clothing industries', *Journal of World Trade Law*, 15(2), 124–48.

Dennis, G. E. J. (1981) 'The harmonization of non-tariff barriers', in C. Cosgrove Twitchett (ed.), *Harmonization in the EEC*, London, Macmillan.

Didier, P. (1980) 'EEC anti-dumping rules and practices', *CML Rev.*, 17, 349–69.

ECC (European Communities Commission)

(1968) *First General Report on the Activities of the Communities*, Luxembourg.

(1970a) *Bulletin of the European Communities*, Supplement 4/70, Luxembourg.

(1970b) *Bulletin of the European Communities*, Supplement 8/70, Luxembourg.

(1971a) *Bulletin of the European Communities*, 11, Luxembourg.

(1971b) *Bulletin of the European Communities*, Supplement 1/71, Luxembourg.

(1972) *First Report on Competition Policy*, Luxembourg.

(1973a) *Bulletin of the European Communities*, Supplement 7/73, Luxembourg.

(1973b) *Bulletin of the European Communities*, Supplement 13/73, Luxembourg.

(1974) *Third Report on Competition Policy*, Luxembourg.
(1975a) *Fourth Report on Competition Policy*, Luxembourg.
(1975b) *Bulletin of the European Communities, Supplement 4/75*, Luxembourg.
(1976a) *Fifth Report on Competition Policy*, Luxembourg.
(1976b) SEC (76) 2813 def. 21 July.
(1977a) *Twenty-five years of the Common Market in Coal*, Luxembourg.
(1977b) *Sixth Report on Competition Policy*, Luxembourg.
(1977c) *Sixth Report on Competition Policy*, Luxembourg.
(1978a) *Safeguarding Freedom of Trade Within the Community: Communication from the Commission to the European Parliament, the Council and the Nine Member States*, 10 November.
(1978b) COM (78) 63 final 16 February.
(1978c) *Seventh Report on Competition Policy*, Luxembourg.
(1979a) *Eighth Report on Competition Policy*, Luxembourg.
(1979b) *Bulletin of the European Communities, Supplement 7/79*, Luxembourg.
(1979c) COM (79) 640 final 9 November.
(1980a) *Ninth Report on Competition Policy*, Luxembourg.
(1980b) *Bulletin of the European Communities, Supplement 1/80*, Report on the scope for convergence of tax systems in the community, Luxembourg.
(1980c) *The European Community and the Energy Problem*, Luxembourg.
(1981a) COM (81) 313 final 17 June.
(1981b) *Tenth Report on Competition Policy*, Luxembourg.
(1981c) COM (81) 67 final 20 February.
(1982a) *Eleventh Report on Competition Policy*, Luxembourg.
(1982b) COM (82) 160 final 10 June.

ECJ (European Court of Justice – case reference numbers may not take in all joined actions)

13/60 *Comptoirs de Vente du Charbon de la Ruhr Geitling, Mausegatt et Präsident* v. *Haute Autorité de la Communauté Européenne de Charbon et de L'Acier* (1962) 8 ECJR 165.

66/63 *Gouvernement du Royaume des Pays-Bas* v. *Haute Autorité de la Communauté Européenne du Charbon et de L'Acier* (1964) 10 ECJR 1047.

6/64 *Flaminio Costa* v. *ENEL* (1964) CMLR 425.

56 and 58/64 *Etablissements Consten SA and Grundig-Verkaufs-GmbH* v. *EEC Commission* (1966) CMLR 418.

24/67   Parke Davis and Co. v. Probel (1968) CMLR 47.
24/68   Commission of EC v. Italian Republic (1969) ECJR 193.
5/69   Volk v. Vervaecke (1969) CMLR 273.
48/69   ICI and others v. EC Commission (1972) CMLR 557.
40/70   Sirena SRL v. Eda SRL (1971) CMLR 260.
78/79   Deutsche Gramaphon v. Metro-SB Grossmarkte (1971) CMLR 631.
6/72   Europemballage Corpn and Continental Can Co. Inc. v. EC Commission (1973) CMLR 199.
8/72   Vereeniging van Cementhandalaren v. EC Commission (1973) CMLR 7.
6-7/73 Istituto Chemioterapico Italiano SpA and Commercial Solvents Corpn v. EC Commission (1974) CMLR 309.
40-8/73 Re the European Sugar Cartel: Coöperatieve Vereniging 'Suiker Unie' UA and others v. EC Commission (1976) 1 CMLR 295.
127/73 BRT v. SABAM (1974) 2 CMLR 238.
155/73 Italy v. Giussepi Sacchi (1974) 1 ECJR 409.
167/73 Commission of EC v. French Republic (1974) 1 ECJR 359.
2/74   Reyners v. Belgian State (1974) 2 CMLR 305.
8/74   Procureur du Roi v. Dassonville (1974) 2 CMLR 436.
15/74   Centrafarm BV v. Sterling Drug Inc. (1974) CMLR 480.
33/74   JHM Binsbergen v. Bestuur van de Bedrijfsvereniging voor de Metaalnijverheid (1975) 1 CMLR 298.
45/75   Rewe Zentrale des Lebensmittel - Grosshandels eGmbH v. Hauptzollamt Landau/Pfalz (1976) 2 CMLR 1.
59/75   Pubblico Ministero v. Manghera (1976) 1 CMLR 557.
91/75   HZA Göttingen v. Miritz GmbH (1976) 1 ECJR 217.
109 and 114/75 National Carbonising Company Limited v. EC Commission (1971) ECJR 382.
27/76   United Brands Continental BV v. EC Commission (1978) 1 CMLR 429.
87/76   Hoffman-La-Roche and Co. v. EC Commission (1979) 3 CMLR 211.
2/78   EC Commission v. Belgium the Import of Spirituous Drinks (1980) 1 CMLR 216.
91/78   Hansen GmbH v. Hauptzollamt Flensburg (1980) 1 CMLR 162.
120/78 Rewe-Zentrale A. G. v. Bundesmonopolverwaltung für Brantwein (1979) 3 CMLR 494.

154/78 *SpA Ferreira and Others* v. *EC Commission* (1980) 1 ECJR 907.
168/78 *EC Commission* v. *French Republic* (1980) 1 ECJR 347.
169/78 *EC Commission* v. *Italian Republic* (1980) 1 ECJR 385.
170/78 *Re Excise Duties on Wine: EC Commission* v. *The United Kingdom* (1980) 1 CMLR 716.
171/78 *EC Commission* v. *Kingdom of Denmark* (1980) 1 ECJR 447.
730/79 *Philip Morris Holland BV* v. *EC Commission* (1981) 2 CMLR 321.

Economist, The
  (1978) 28 October 1978, 59.
  (1981a) 24 October 1981, 46–7.
  (1981b) 19 September 1981, 68–71.
  (1981c) 10 October 1981, 69–70.
  (1981d) 25 April 1981, 60.

EECC (European Economic Community Commission)
  (1965a) *Eighth General Report on the Activities of the Community*, Brussels.
  (1965b) SEC (65) 3500, 1 December.
  (1966) *Ninth General Report on the Activities of the Community*, Brussels.

EPD (European Parliamentary Debates)
  (1961) 19 October.

Farrands, C. (1979) 'Textile diplomacy: the making and implementation of European textile policy', *Journal of Common Market Studies*, 18(1), 30.

Financial Times
  (1982a) 14 January, 10.
  (1982b) 28 October, 9.

Fleming, M. C. (1980) 'Industrial policy', in W.P.J. Maunder (ed.), *The British Economy in the 1970s*, London, Heinemann, 141–68.

Hallett, E. C. (1981) 'Economic convergence and divergence in the European Community: a survey of the evidence', in M. Hodges and W. Wallace (eds), *Economic Divergence in the European Community*, London, Allen & Unwin.

Harding, C. (1979) 'The use of fines as sanctions in EEC competition law', *CML Rev.*, 16, 591–614.

Heusdens, J. J. and de Horn, R. (1980) 'Crisis policy in the European

steel industry in the light of the ECSC treaty', *CML Rev.*, 17, 31–74.
Hough, J. R. (1979) 'Government intervention in the economy of France', in W.P.J. Maunder (ed.), *Government Intervention in the Developed Economy*, London, Croom Helm.
Howe, W. S. (1978) *Industrial Economics: an Applied Approach*, London, Macmillan.
Lasok, D. (1980) *The Law of the Economy of the European Communities*, London, Butterworths.
MacLennan, M. C. (1979) 'Regional policy in a European framework', in M. C. MacLennan and J. B. Parr (eds), *Regional Planning. Past Experience and New Directions*, Oxford, Martin Robertson.
McLachlan, D. L. and Swann, D. (1967) *Competition Policy in the European Community*, Oxford, Oxford University Press.
Menderhausen, H. (1953) 'First tests of the Schuman Plan', *Review of Economics and Statistics*, 25(4), 2–17.
Monnet, J. (1950) 'Memorandum sent by Jean Monnet to Robert Schuman and Georges Bidault 4 May 1950', in R. Vaughan (ed.) (1976), *Post-War Integration in Europe*, London, Arnold.
Motor, The
(1981) 15 August, 6.
OECD (Organization for Economic Co-operation and Development)
(1975) *The Aims and Instruments of Industrial Policy*, Paris.
(1979) *The Case for Positive Adjustment Policies*, Paris.
OJ (Official Journal of the European Communities – prior to 1958 this referred to the ECSC only.)

(1953)	21 July.	
(1956)	13 March.	
(1959)	1327/59	31 December.
(1962a)	36/62	15 January.
(1962b)	32/62	15 January.
(1962c)	204/62	21 February.
(1962d)	2751/62	28 November.
(1962e)	993/62	20 April.
(1964a)	915/64	9 April.
(1964b)	2545/64	20 October.
(1965a)	480/65	25 February.
(1965b)	533/65	6 March.
(1966)	37/66	6 January.
(1967a)	562/67	28 February.

REFERENCES 203

(1967b)	1301/67	14 April.
(1967c)	1303/67	14 April.
(1967d)	849/67	25 March.
(1968a)	L201/7	12 August.
(1968b)	L175/1	23 July.
(1968c)	L276/29	14 November.
(1968d)	L276/13	14 November.
(1968e)	L65/8	14 March.
(1969a)	L192/5	5 August.
(1969b)	L195/11	7 August.
(1969c)	L165/12	5 July.
(1969d)	L195/1	7 July.
(1969e)	L195/5	7 July.
(1969f)	L195/1	7 July.
(1969g)	L206/25	15 August.
(1970a)	L13/29	19 January.
(1970b)	C64/1	2 June.
(1971a)	L185/1	16 August.
(1971b)	L185/5	16 August.
(1971c)	L185/15	16 August.
(1971d)	L134/6	20 June.
(1971e)	L10/15	13 January.
(1971f)	L285/46	29 December.
(1971g)	L201/10	5 September.
(1971h)	L134/15	20 June.
(1972a)	L303/24	31 December.
(1972b)	L272/35	5 December.
(1972c)	L13/44	17 January.
(1972d)	L303/7	31 December.
(1972e)	L292/23	29 December.
(1973a)	L228/20	16 August.
(1973b)	L228/3	16 August.
(1974a)	L343/19	21 December.
(1974b)	L160/1	17 June.
(1974c)	L132/28	15 May.
(1974d)	C14/30	15 February.
(1975a)	L167/1	30 June.
(1975b)	L167/14	30 June.
(1975c)	L167/17	30 June.
(1975d)	L167/19	30 June.

(1975e)	L329/30	23 December.
(1975f)	L159/22	21 June.
(1975g)	L249/22	25 September.
(1975h)	L130/13	21 May.
(1975i)	L192/27	24 July.
(1976a)	C32/2	12 February.
(1976b)	C241/9	14 October.
(1976c)	L35/6	10 February.
(1976d)	C232/1	4 October.
(1977a)	L114/6	5 May.
(1977b)	L145/1	13 June.
(1977c)	L13/1	15 January.
(1977d)	C313/3	29 December.
(1977e)	L26/1	31 January.
(1977f)	C183/26	1 August.
(1978a)	L70/54	13 March.
(1978b)	L47/42	18 February.
(1978c)	L70/47	13 March.
(1978d)	L295/36	20 October.
(1978e)	L222/11	14 August.
(1978f)	L98/19	11 April.
(1979a)	L339/1	31 December.
(1979b)	L121/5	17 May.
(1979c)	L131/15	29 May.
(1979d)	L131/1	29 May.
(1979e)	L339/15	31 December.
(1979f)	C31/9	3 February.
(1979g)	L217/17	25 August.
(1980a)	L23/19	30 January.
(1980b)	L48/1	22 February.
(1980c)	L145/22	11 June.
(1980d)	C256/2	30 October.
(1980e)	L383/19	31 December.
(1980f)	L39/51	15 February.
(1980g)	L60/21	5 March.
(1980h)	L195/35	29 July.
(1981a)	C252/5	2 October.
(1981b)	C256/4	8 October.
(1981c)	L353/33	9 December.
(1981d)	L137/39	23 May.

Schuman, R. (1950) 'Statement by M. Robert Schuman, Minister of Foreign Affairs of France, on 9 May 1950', in S. Patijn (ed.) (1970), *Landmarks in European Unity*, Sijthoff, Leyden.

Servan-Schreiber, J.-J. (1967) *Le Défi Américain*, Paris, Denoel.

Spaak, H. (1956) Comité Intergouvernemental créé par la Conference de Messine, *Rapport des chefs de la délégation aux Ministres des Affaires Etrangères* (Spaak Report).

Statistical Office of the European Communities (1982) *Quarterly Iron and Steel Bulletin*, 2, Brussels.

Stegemann, K. (1977) *Price Competition and Output Adjustment in the European Steel Market*, Tübingen, JCB Mohr (Paul Siebeck).

Swann, D. (1979) *Competition and Consumer Protection*, Harmondsworth, Penguin.

Swann, D. (1981) *The Economics of the Common Market*, 4th edn, Harmondsworth, Penguin.

Swann, D. and McLachlan, D. L. (1965) 'Steel pricing in a recession: an analysis of United Kingdom and ECSC experience', *Scottish Journal of Political Economy*, 12, 81–104.

Tillotson, J. (1980) 'The GKN–Sachs affair: a case study in economic law', *Journal of World Trade Law*, 14(1), 39–67.

Select bibliography

Aislabie, C. J. (1980) 'Industrial policy in the European Economic Community', *Journal of Industrial Affairs*, 8(1), 1–6.

Allen, D. (1983) 'Managing the Common Market: the Community's Competition Policy', in H. Wallace, W. Wallace and C. Webb (eds), *Policy Making in the European Communities*, London, Wiley, 209–36.

Campbell, A. (1980) *EC Competition Law*, Amsterdam, North-Holland.

Chard, J. S. and Macmillan, M. J. (1979) 'Sectoral aids and community competition policy: the case of textiles', *Journal of World Trade Law*, 13(2), 132–57.

Cruickshank, A. and Walker, W. (1980) 'Energy research, development and demonstration in the European Communities', *Journal of Common Market Studies*, 20(1), 61–90.

Curzon Price, V. (1981) *Industrial Policies in the European Community*, London, Macmillan.

De Jong, H. W. (1975) 'EEC competition policy towards restrictive practices', in K. D. George and C. Joll (eds), *Competition Policy in the UK and EEC*, Cambridge, Cambridge University Press, 33–65.

De La Torre, J. (1981) 'Public intervention strategies in the European clothing industries', *Journal of World Trade Law*, 15(2), 124–48.

De La Torre, J. and Bacchetta, M. (1980) 'The uncommon market: European policies towards the clothing industry in the 1970s', *Journal of Common Market Studies*, 19(2), 95–122.

Dennis, G. E. J. (1981) 'The harmonization of non-tariff barriers', in C. Cosgrove Twitchett (ed.), *Harmonization in the EEC*, London, Macmillan, 18–25.

EC Commission (1980) *The European Community's Research Policy*, Luxembourg, Office for Official Publications of the European Communities.

Farrands, C. (1979) 'Textile diplomacy: the making and implementation of European textile policy', *Journal of Common Market Studies*, 18(1), 22-39.

Heusdens, J. J. and de Horn, R. (1980) 'Crisis policy in the European steel industry in the light of the ECSC treaty', *Common Market Law Review*, 17, 31-74.

Hodges, M. (1977) 'Industrial policy: a Directorate-General in search of a role', in H. Wallace, W. Wallace and C. Webb (eds), *Policy-Making in the European Communities*, London, Wiley, 113-34.

Joliet, R. (1980) 'Cartelization, dirigism and crisis in the European Community', *The World Economy*, 3, 403-45.

Korah, V. (1980) 'Concept of a dominant position within the meaning of Article 86', *Common Market Law Review*, 17(3), 395-414.

Korah, V. (1981) *An Introductory Guide to EEC Competition Law and Practice*, 2nd edn, Oxford, ESC Publishing.

Lasok, D. (1980) *The Law of the Economy of the European Communities*, London, Butterworths.

Lasok, D. and Bridge, J. W. (1982) *Introduction to the Law and Institutions of the European Communities*, 3rd edn, London, Butterworths.

McLachlan, D. L. and Swann, D. (1967) *Competition Policy in the European Community*, Oxford, Oxford University Press.

Martin, D. D. (1979) 'The Davignon Plan: whither competition policy in the ECSC', *The Antitrust Bulletin*, 14(4), 837-87.

Smith, P. and Swann, D. (1979) *Protecting the Consumer*, Oxford, Martin Robertson.

Stegemann, K. (1977) *Price Competition and Output Adjustment in the European Steel Market*, Tübingen, JCB Mohr (Paul Siebeck).

Swann, D. (1978) *Economics of the Common Market*, 4th edn, Harmondsworth, Penguin.

Index

administrative barriers to trade, 76
Allen, D., xii, 196, 206

Bael, I.V., 193, 198
Belgium: car prices, 44; coal import licences, 31; coal industry problems, 5, 31–2; coal industry sealed off, 31–2; liqueur imports, 23–4; pen prices, 44
Borrie, Sir Gordon, 185
Bredimas, A.E., 198
Bridge, J.W., 207
British Leyland, 46
Bureau Européen des Unions de Consommateurs, 43–4
BCO, 148

Campbell, A., 193, 195, 198, 206
CAP, 181, 182
capital, free movement of, 20
car prices, 43–4
cartels
  ECSC: information agreements, 107; joint buying, 107; joint selling, 102–7; Paris Treaty rules, 101–2; policy assessed, 183; price fixing agreements, 107; quota agreements, 107; Ruhr coal cases, 102–6; steel specialization agreements, 106–7
  EEC: *ACEC-Berliet* case, 88; aggregated rebates, 79, 87; *Aniline Dye* case, 83–5, 91, 93; Article 85 (3) exemption, 88–9; Article 85 (1) prohibition, 81–8; *Bomée Stichting* case, 97; capacity limitation, 94–6; *Cementregeling voor Nederland* case, 94; *CFA* case, 93; *Christiani and Nielsen* case, 86; *Cimbel* case, 87, 94; *Clima-Chappée-Buderus* case, 88, 100; *Cobelaz* case, 93; collective exclusive dealing, 79, 96–7; common sales syndicates, 78, 93–4; concerted practices, 83–4; *Convention Faience* case, 96–7; decisions of associations of enterprises, 82–3; *de minimis* rule, 86; *Dutch Sporting Cartridges* case, 97; enforcement of cartel rules, 89–91; extra-territorial jurisdiction, 85–6; *Floral* case, 93; *Franco-Japanese Ballbearings* case, 82; *FNCF* case, 88; *Genuine Vegetable Parchment* case, 86; *German Wall and Floor Tile* case, 97; *Glass Containers* case, 93; *Grossfilex* case, 86; *Grundig-Consten* case, 24, 98–9; industrial and commercial property rights, 26–7, 81, 128–31; information agreements, 80, 97–8; inter-state trade effect, 86–8; *Italian cast glass* case, 88; *Jallatte-Voss Vandeputte* case, 88; *Jaz-Peter* case, 100; joint R & D agreements, 80–1, 100–1; market sharing, 79, 96; *Paper Machine Wire* case, 97–8; Parent subsidiary relationship, 86; *Pioneer* case, 99; *Pittsburg Corning* case, 90; policy assessed, 183–4; Price fixing, 77–8, 92–4; *Quinine* case, 82, 91; quotas, 79, 94; *SAFCO* case, 94; *Savon Noir* case, 96; scope of Art. 85, 91–2; sole distribution agreements, 80, 98–9; specialization agreements, 80, 100; standardization agreements, 81; *Sugar* cases, 84; territorial protection, 80, 98–9; *VCH* case, 82, 87–8; *Vickers-Sopolem* case, 101; *Volk v. Vervaecke* case, 86
CERD, 139, 150
coal industry, 5, 23, 31–2, 36
common commercial policy: EEC, 21, 33–4; absence of in ECSC, 36
competition policy defined, 1–3
concentrations: phenomena, 108–11; policy towards, *see* dominant firms, mergers
COST, 137, 151
CREST, 150–1
Curzon Price, V., 155, 198, 206

customs unions: competition, 11-12; economies of scale, 10; trade creation, 10-11; trade diversion, 10-11

Dahrendorf, R., 41, 141
Davignon, E., 95, 171-6
Dennis, G.E.J., 66, 198, 207
Denmark: car prices, 44; electrical goods prices, 43; excise duties, 63, 186; pen prices, 44; transition period, 23, 33
discrimination: prohibition under Paris Treaty, 32, 121, 166-8; prohibition under Rome Treaty, 30, 70
dominant firms
 ECSC: Paris Treaty rules, 120-1; *National Carbonizing* case, 122-3; *OKU* case, 121-2
 EEC: abusive behaviour of, 108-11, 117-19; *BRT-SABAM* case, 117; *Commercial Solvents* case, 118, 124; *Continental Can* case, 115-16, 117; critical market shares, 116; dominance, meaning of, 112-15; *Eurofirma* case, 118; *GEMA* case, 116, 117; *Hoffman-La-Roche* case, 117; *NBIM* case, 117; relevant geographic market, 116-17; relevant product market, 115-16; Rome Treaty rules, 111-19; *Sugar* case, 116; *United Brands* case, 116, 117, 124
dumping
 ECSC: action against steel imports, 173; rules concerning, 37, 173
 EEC: cases, 35; rules concerning, 34-5

ECSC: cartel policy, 101-7; crisis pricing powers, 14, 168-9, 173-5, 180; crisis quota powers, 14, 169, 173-5; Davignon Plan, 171-6, 180; decision-making process, 16-18; discriminatory pricing rules, 32, 121, 166-7; dominant firm policy, 120-4; dumping rules, 37, 173; economic motivations, 9-12; General Objectives, 14, 163-5, 174, 180-1; integration process, 13-16; merger policy, 124-6; political motivations of, 12-13; protection from third countries, 36-7; quota elimination internally, 30-2; Simonet Plan, 171, 180; state aid policy, 55-8; state monopolies, 75-6; steel crisis 1975-, 169-71; steel pricing rules, 2-3, 14, 166-8; tariff elimination internally, 30-2; technical standards, 68; turnover tax policy, 64-5
EEC: BCO, 148; business integration, 136-7, 142-9, 181; cartel policy, 81-101; CERD, 139, 150; common commercial policy, 21, 33-4; common external tariff, 32-3; Common Market Patent Convention, 148-9; concerted (R & D) action, 154; Convention (draft) on mergers, 144-5; COST, 137, 151; cross-frontier mergers, 142-9, 181; decision making, 16-18; direct (R & D) action, 151-2; discrimination, 30, 70; dominant firm policy, 111-19; dumping, 34-5; economic motivations, 9-12; European Company Statute, 137, 138, 140, 145-7; European (draft) Co-operation Grouping, 138, 147; European Patent Convention, 148-9; excise duty policy, 62-6, 186; freedom to supply services, 32-42, 186; indirect (R & D) action, 152-4; industrial and commercial property rights, 26-7, 128-31; industrial policy, 134-61; integration process, 13-16; JNRC, 151-2; JRC, 151-2; merger policy, 119-20, 127; Multi-Fibre Arrangement, 5-6, 158-9; mutual recognition of companies, 142; political motivations, 12-13; PREST, 136-7; product liability proposal, 68-9, 185; protection (Art. 30), 26-7; protection (Art. 109), 25-6; protection from third countries, 35-6; public enterprise rules, 52-3, 71-3, 131-4; public purchasing policy, 69-71, 186; quotas, 21-34, 158-9; right of establishment, 37-42; science and technology policy, 136-9, 149-54; shipbuilding industry policy, 159-61; single industrial base, 138, 141-2; state aids, 45-55, 184-5; state monopolies, 71-5; tariff elimination internally, 21-30; technical standards harmonization, 27-8, 65-8, 185; textile industry policy, 155-9; turnover tax policy, 58-62, 186; VAT, 58-62, 186
EMS, 26, 125
Euratom: JET, 151, 180; JNRC, 151-2; JRC, 151-2; R & D, 8, 192
excise duties: distortions caused by, 62-3; *Commission v. Denmark*, 63, 186; *Commission v. France*, 63; *Commission v. Italy*, 63; *Commission v. UK*, 63-4; harmonization of, 64; Rome Treaty rules, 62-4

Farrands, C., 159, 201, 207
Fleming, M.C., xii, 192, 201
France: car prices, 42-3; coal industry,

57; discriminatory purchasing, 71; excise duties, 63; indicative planning, 7; Industrial Development Institute, 8; industrial policy, 6, 8; industrial policy attitudes, 140; insurance rules, 41; pen prices, 44; state monopolies, 72-6; steel import duties, 30, steel import quotas, 30; VAT, 58
freedom to supply services: in insurance, 40-1; in medicine, 41-2; Rome Treaty rules on, 37; *Van Binsbergen* case, 38

GATT, 23
Greece, 23
Groeben, H. von der., 2

Hallet, E.C., 13, 201
Harding, C., 194, 201
Heusdens, J.R., 196, 201, 207
de Horn, R., 196, 201, 207
Hough, J.R., 6, 8, 202
Howe, W.S., 8, 202

IMF, 23, 26
industrial and commercial property, 26-7, 81, 128-31
industrial policy: defined, 3-9
 ECSC: aids to steel industry, 55-6, 58, 172, 176; alignment pricing rules, 2-3, 14, 166-8; anti-dumping activity, 37, 173; basing point prices, 166-7; crisis price powers, 14, 168-9, 173-5, 180; crisis quota powers, 14, 169, 173-5; Davignon Plan Phase 1, 171-5, 180; Davignon Plan Phase 2, 175-6, 180; discrimination, prohibition of, 121, 166; Eurofer, 175, 181, 196; excess capacity in steel, 176; General Objectives, 14, 163-5, 174, 180-1; guidance steel prices, 173; loans to coal and steel industry, 164-6, 173-4; mandatory minimum steel prices, 173-5; mandatory quotas, 175; pricing experience, 168; price publicity, 166-7; pricing rules, 2-3, 14, 166-80; production programmes, 166, 171; steel crisis 1975-, 169-71; steel import licences, 173; Simonet Plan, 171, 180; voluntary restraint agreements, 173; voluntary steel sales quotas, 171, 175
 EEC: BCO, 148; business integration, 142-9; CERD, 139, 150; Colonna Report (1970), 138-40; Common Market Patent Convention, 148-9; Convention (draft) on mergers, 144-5; COST, 137, 151; CREST, 150-1; cross-frontier mergers – fiscal factors, 142-3; cross-frontier mergers – legal factors, 143-4; European (draft) Company Statute, 137, 138, 140, 145-7; European (draft) Co-operation Grouping, 138, 147; European Patent Convention, 148-9; industrial base, 138, 141-2; Industrial Base Memorandum (1973), 140-1; industrial concentration, need for, 135-7; JNRC, 151-2; JRC, 151-2; *Mitbestimmung*, 145-7; Multi-Fibre Arrangement, 5-6, 158-9; mutual recognition of companies, 142; PREST, 136-7; R & D (concerted action), 154; R & D (direct action), 151-2; R & D (indirect action), 152-4; science and technological collaboration, need for, 136-7, 141; Science and Technology Memorandum (1970), 139; Science and Technology Memorandum (1973), 141; shipbuilding industry policy, 159-61; textile industry policy, 155-9
insurance: freedom to supply services, 40-1, 186; right of establishment, 38-40
IRC, 8
Ireland: car prices, 43-4; discriminatory purchasing, 71; transition period, 22, 33
IRI, 157
Italy: administrative duty, 31; car prices, 43-4; coal industry, 23; coke import duties, 30; electrical goods prices, 43; excise duties, 63; man-made fibres, 157, 181; state monopolies, 71-3; statistical levy, 21; steel import duties, 30-1; steel industry, 30, 165, 174-5

JET, 151, 180
joint ventures, *see* mergers and cartels
JNRC, 151-2
JRC, 151-2

Lasok, D., 27, 202, 207
Luxembourg: car prices, 44; pen prices, 44; steel industry, 170

McLachlan, D.L., 5, 194, 196, 202, 205, 207
medicine: freedom to supply services, 41-2; right of establishment, 41-2
Menderhausen, H., 31
mergers
 ECSC: *GKN-Miles Druce* case, 124; *GKN-*

Sachs case, 127; joint ventures, 124-5; *Krupp-Stahlwerke Südwestfalen* case, 126; Paris Treaty rules, 124-5; steel merger waves, 125-6
EEC: Art. 86 in relation to, 119; *Continental Can* case, 115-16; cross-frontier, 142-9, 181; draft merger control regulation, 120, 184
Monnet, J., 14, 18, 163
Multi-Fibre Arrangement, 5-6, 158-9

NCB, 122-3
NEB, 4, 52, 133
Netherlands: car prices, 44; coal industry, 31; export aids, 47; *Philip Morris* case, 53-5, 184

OECD, 160, 192
OEEC, 23

PREST, 136-7
product liability: 68-9; Commission proposal concerning, 68, 185; development risk, 69: negligence approach, 69; strict liability, 69
public enterprises
ECSC: Paris Treaty rules, 131
EEC: state financial relations with, 52-7; 132-4, 145: Rome Treaty rules, 71, 73, 131-3
public purchasing: discriminations in, 69-70, 186; French and Irish transgressions, 71; public procurement rules, 70-1; public works contracting rules, 70; Rome Treaty discrimination rules, 70, 71

quotas
ECSC: cartels, 107; elimination internally, 30; mandatory in steel production, 175; sealing-off of Belgian coal, 31; voluntary in steel production, 171, 175
EEC: cartels, 79, 94; *Cassis de Dijon* case, 24-5; elimination internally, 21-2; equivalent measures, 23-5; Multi-Fibre Arrangement, 5-6; 158-9; protection (Art. 36), 26-30; third country trade, 5-6, 33-4

RDG, 50
REP, 49
right of establishment: insurance, 39-40; medicine, 41-2; *Reyners* case, 38; Rome Treaty rules on, 37

Sanders, P., 146
Schuman, R., 13, 18
Schuman Plan, 12-13
Servan-Schreiber, J.-J., 136, 205
shipbuilding, policy towards in EEC, 159-61
Simonet, H., 171
Simonet Plan, 171-2, 173, 180
Smith, Adam, 15
Spaak Report, 11
Spinelli, A., 138, 171
state aids
ECSC: coal subsidies, 56-7; coking coal subsidies, 57-8; Paris Treaty rules, 55-6
EEC: employment aids, 55; export aids, 47; general aids, 52-5; policy assessed, 184-5; RDG, 50; regional aids, 47-50; REP, 49; Rome Treaty rules, 45-6; sectoral aids, 50-2; state enterprise financing, 51-2, 185; TES, 55
state monopolies
ECSC: cases, 75-6
EEC: French 72-5; *Flaminio Costa* v. *ENEL* case, 71-2; *Hansen* v. *Hauptzollamt Flensburg* case, 75; Italian, 71-3; *Italy* v. *Giuseppi Sacchi* case, 71; *Miritz* case, 71; *Pubblico Ministero* v. *Manghera* case, 73; *Rewe* v. *Hauptzollamt Landau/Pfalz* case, 74-5; Rome Treaty rules, 71, 73
steel industry: aids to, 55-6; 112, 176; cartels, 101-7; crisis 1975-, 169-71; crisis pricing powers, 14, 168-9, 173-5, 180; crisis quota powers, 14, 169, 173-5; Davignon Plan, 171-6, 180; dumping, 37, 173; employment in, 171; excess capacity in, 176; General Objectives, 14, 163-5, 174, 180-1; guidance prices, 173; loans to, 164-6; mandatory quotas, 175; minimum prices, 173; pricing rules, 166-9; quota disarmament, 30-2; Schuman Plan, 12-13; Simonet Plan, 171, 180; tariff disarmament, 30-2; voluntary quotas, 171; voluntary restraint agreements, 173
Stegemann, K., 196, 205, 207
Swann, D., 5, 8, 194, 196, 205, 207

tariffs
ECSC: coal equalization levy, 31; elimination internally, 30-1; equivalent measures to, 31; levels in 1952, 30-1; third country trade, 36-7
EEC: common external tariff, 32-3;

Dillon Round, 33; elimination of internally, 21-6; equivalent measures to, 23-5; Kennedy Round, 33; protection (Art. 109), 25-6; Tokyo Round, 33
taxation, *see* turnover taxes *and* excise duties
technical standards
  ECSC: policy concerning, 68
  EEC: *Cassis de Dijon* case, 24-5, 28, 67-8, 185; effects of, 65-6; harmonization problems, 67; harmonization progress, 66-7; optional harmonization, 66; policy assessed, 185; reasons for, 65; Rome Treaty rules, 66; total harmonization, 66
TES, 55
textiles, Rome Treaty policy, 5-6, 94-6, 155-9, 181
Tillotson, J., 192, 205
de la Torre, J., 5, 198
turnover taxes
  ECSC: rules concerning, 64-5; turnover tax dispute, 64-5
  EEC: added value tax, 58-62; cascade tax, 58-9; common value added tax, 61-2; destination principle, 59-60; distortions in relation to, 60-1; origin principle, 59; rate harmonization, 62; Rome Treaty rules, 60-1
Tzoannos, J.G., 160, 198

UK: British Leyland, 46; British Steel Corporation, 170; car imports, 28-30; car prices, 43-4; Chrysler, 46; Department of Health and Social Security, 65; electrical goods prices, 43; excise duties, 63-4; export aids, 47; Fair Trading Act, 127; industrial policy, 8; insurance industry, 39-41; IRC, 8; JET, 151, 180; lawnmower harmonization, 185; Medicines Act 1968, 65; NCB, 122-3; NEB, 6, 52, 133; product related injury, 69, 185; regional aid, 48-50; RDG, 50; REP, 49; steel industry employment, 196; steel industry losses, 170; TES, 55; textile imports, 159; transition period, 23, 33
UNICE, 136

VAT, 58-62, 186
Vouell, R., 95

West Germany: Act against Restraints of Competition, 127; car prices, 44; coal imports from third countries, 36; coal industry, 5, 31, 36, 57-8; insurance industry, 40-1; liqueur imports, 24-5; *Mitbestimmung*, 145-7; state monopolies, 72-5; steel import duties, 30; steel industry, 170